History of Kylemore Castle & Abbey

Pax

*To Mary,
with all good wishes & blessings.
M. Magdalene FitzGibbon. OSB
25. 12. 2002.*

Kathleen Villiers-Tuthill

PAX

Kylemore Abbey Publications
Kylemore Abbey
Connemara
Co Galway

First published in 2002 by
Kylemore Abbey Publications
Kylemore Abbey
Connemara
Co. Galway
telephone: 00 353 (0) 95 41146
email: info@kylemoreabbey.ie
www.kylemoreabbey.com

ISBN 0-9542310-1-5
British Library Cataloguing
in Publication Data.
A catalogue record for this book
is available from the British Library.

By the same author
HISTORY OF CLIFDEN 1810-1860
BEYOND THE TWELVE BENS:
A History Of Clifden And District 1860-1923
PATIENT ENDURANCE:
The Great Famine In Connemara

Printed by ColourBooks Ltd.
Design, layout and cover by Bernard Kaye

Contents

Dedication

To the memory of the Kylemore Benedictine Nuns
who passed away while this work was in progress:
Mother Agnes Finnegan, Mother Mary O'Toole,
Sr Raphael Conroy, Sr Agatha Martin,
Sr M Jarlath O'Brien, Sr M Gregory Quaid.

List of Illustrations

Acknowledgments

My sincere thanks to Mother Abbess Magdalena FitzGibbon, O.S.B., for giving me the opportunity to write this book and for providing essential input on the final draft. My thanks to the entire Community at Kylemore Abbey for sharing with me their personal stories and their memories of past sisters and days gone by; for their patient co-operation and for their hospitality and friendship during my many visits to the Abbey. Particular thanks to Sister Benedict, Community Archivist, a constant source of knowledge and a tireless supporter of my work. She could not have been more generous in sharing with me her insights into community history or more patient in listening to my musings about the personality of Mitchell Henry and the early nuns.

I am deeply indebted to Professor Gearóid Ó Tuathaigh, for reading several drafts of the manuscript and for offering advice and guidance, his keen editorial judgment was of immense help. His encouragement and advice are a tremendous support to me in all my work.

To Paul Duffy, who, in addition to speaking with me on topics ranging from electricity to land reclamation, helped to keep up my enthusiasm as the days dragged into months and the months into years.

I am most grateful to the following descendants of Mitchell and Margaret Henry for their help with the genealogy of the Henry family and for providing family documents and photographs; Mark Mitchell-Henry, Scotland, Elizabeth Stone and her daughter Nancy Christensen, USA, Collette Mitchell-Henry, South Africa and Derek Mitchell-Henry, Canada. I take full responsibility for any errors that may yet become evident in the family tree produced in this work.

My thanks to the staff of the National Library for their friendliness, courtesy and assistance during my many visits to that wonderful building which, for almost three years, became my place of work. Thanks to David Taylor, for guiding me through the Local Studies Unit of the Manchester Central Library and for providing copies of articles relating to A & S Henry, Mitchell Henry's English political career and the Henry family.

I am also indebted to the staff of various libraries and archives; the National Archive, Valuations Office, Registry of Deeds, Architectural Archives, National Photographic Archives, Wexford Town Library, Church of Ireland Representative Church Body Library, Dublin, Genealogical Office, Dublin, Royal Agricultural Society of England, The Editor, *Manchester Evening News* and The Record Office, Parliamentary Archives, House of Lords, London, for allowing me use their photograph of Mitchell Henry. Thanks to Philip Temple, Royal Commission on the Historical Monuments of England, for material relating to Stratheden House; Lou Crawford for tracking down material relating to Zimmerman family of Cincinnati; Captain P.B. Sugrue, late of the Galway Fire Brigade; Garry Wynne, Castlebar, for use of the Wynne Photographic Collection; Eileen Hargrave, Margaret O'Connor and Nancy Hegarty for providing photographs of the Henry family; Iber Carthy, Enniscorthy, for use of the Crane Photographic Collection; Stephen and June Powell for the Samuel Usher Roberts photograph.

My thanks also to Ann Golden, Head Gardener at Kylemore; Eithne Kane, who interviewed ex-members of staff and past pupils; Ann Marie Mortimer, for typing the Nuns' interviews; Bridget Nee, Ann Guy and Mary Coyne, for sharing their knowledge of local geography and genealogy; Shirley Lead, for kindly providing census material from England; Wendy Dixon for material on the Blakes of Renvyle House; Prof. N P Wilkins, Dr Noel Kirby, Dom Paul McDonnell, Niall McGahan, Alan Wykeham Vaughan, Pete and Paula Vine, Bridgette Brew, John and Lena Gough, Julian C. Walton and Eddie Power.

Finally my love and gratitude to my husband, John, and to our two sons, William and Graham, without whose patience and support this book would not have been completed.

Foreword

Kylemore Abbey has been a Benedictine House for over eighty years. The Abbey, which was once a fairy-tale Castle, was built in the 19th Century by Mitchell Henry and stands today as a monument to a great Gentleman and kindly Landlord, who spent most of his fortune on the estate and for the good of the local people.

The Community of twenty-four nuns, who took up residence here in 1920, had fled their Abbey at Ypres, Belgium, at the outbreak of World War 1 in 1914. They were of mixed nationality and had displayed great courage and determination in the six years prior to settling at Kylemore.

The Community brought with them a strong devotion to the Benediction tradition and the Benedictine way of life. They also brought with them a history that stretches back much further than that of Kylemore. Founded in Ypres in 1662, our Community was made an Irish House in 1684. On the request of King James 11, and under the guidance of Lady Abbess Butler, the Community moved to Ireland in 1688. However, following James's defeat at the Battle of the Boyne two years later, the Nuns returned to Ypres, where they remained for the next 224 years.

Having gone through the vicissitudes of wars, extreme poverty and few vocations at times, the Community has reached this new Millennium. It is quite a tradition we carry with us, one which we cherish and shall always endeavour to keep fully alive.

Since its beginning, Kylemore has been a focal point in the West of Ireland. Previous generations of Benedictine Nuns, for whom Kylemore served as home, have left us with a legacy of love for the place, a sense of stewardship for its continuance and a recognition of its uniqueness in location and attraction.

Here, there is not only a natural beauty, there is an aura of peace and tranquillity and a sense of spiritualness. Peace is the Benedictine motto and at Kylemore Abbey it is a palpable presence. In the midst of a busy tourist area, Kylemore is an oasis of peace in a restless world and we, as a community, are glad to share this peace with all who visit. The Benedictine life is balanced with prayer and work (Ora et Labora) and at the Abbey we invite those who wish to do so, to join us in prayer.

Mitchell Henry was a deeply Spiritual person and it can only please him to know that a Community of Benedictines now has its home in his Castle, praying the Liturgical Hours, while maintaining the estate and undertaking the tremendous task of conserving and restoring its many natural and important heritage features.

© Kylemore Abbey

Mother Abbess Magdalena FitzGibbon, O.S.B.

Preface

The name Kylemore Abbey is a misnomer when one considers that the building to which it refers does not stand in Kylemore, but actually stands in the townland of Pollacappul: Kylemore townland lies a little to the east. Neither is the lake, visible from the tall front windows of the Abbey, Kylemore Lake, but is rather Lough Pollacappul. In fact at no time in the one hundred and forty year history of the Kylemore Estate was the townland of Kylemore included among its 15,000 acres.

Why then Kylemore Abbey, or Kylemore Castle as in former days, or Kylemore Lodge, the name given to the first building to occupy the site? The decision to use the name Kylemore was no doubt influenced by the fact that a portion of the grounds was covered by ancient forest, An Choill Mhór. But given that the name was already in use in the neighbouring townland it seems a strange choice. Could it be that Kylemore was easier on the English tongue than Pollacappul?

The building is however situated in Kylemore Pass, frequently referred to in Victorian writings as a place of great dramatic beauty. The deep valley and lakes that make up the Pass form a natural boundary between the Twelve Bens to the South and Duchruach mountain to the North. The lakes, Kylemore, Pollacappul and Maladrolaun, are fed by the many streams running off the mountains and drained by the Dawros River running West to the Atlantic.

Harriet Martineau, writing in 1852, tells us that there were no dwellings between Eastwood's estate at Addergoole and Kylemore Inn on the shore of Kylemore lake: 'The moorland is too wild for settlement and the misty mountains allow too little sunshine to encourage tillage.'[1] This was prior to Mitchell Henry. Ten years later the district had embarked on an era of intense development and improvement, the like of which had never been experienced in Connemara before.

Forty years under the guiding hand of Mitchell Henry turned thousands of acres of waste land into the productive Kylemore Estate. Mitchell Henry developed the Kylemore Estate as a commercial and political experiment. The result brought material and social benefits to the entire region and left a lasting impression on the landscape and on the memory of the local people.

In more recent times the name Kylemore is synonymous with Kylemore Abbey and the Irish Benedictine Nuns, for whom it is home. For many the Abbey is a place of pilgrimage, for others a tourist destination on the West coast of Connemara. But, for all, an ineluctable and rarefied atmosphere resides in this special place; a place of spiritual enhancement, a place of repose.

For the benefit of this study the history of Kylemore is dealt with in two parts; the History of Kylemore Castle and the History of Kylemore Abbey. The period covered is the one hundred and forty years from the time Mitchell Henry first took possession of, what was then, Kylemore Lodge, in 1862 right up to the present day. It is also the history of two communities; the community within and the community without.

From the earliest days of my research it became obvious to me that Kylemore was always a unique matrix of interdependent social networks. In the time of Kylemore Castle it was the occupier, his tenants and employees; for Kylemore Abbey it is the Benedictine Nuns, the students in their school, their employees and the many pilgrims and visitors who flock to their door.

When researching the history of Kylemore Castle, there seemed at times to be almost too much information coming to hand and, although it took several years to accumulate and evaluate, it was an exciting journey into life as lived in Connemara in the second half of the 19th century and of the social, religious and political divisions in place at the time. When working on Kylemore Abbey I was drawn into the rich history of the Irish Benedictine Nuns, spanning three hundred and thirty years, and introduced to the monastic life as practised by the Community, in keeping with the ancient tradition of the Order of St Benedict. All of which has greatly enriched my life and deepened my love for Connemara and its people.

Kylemore
Abbey

Westport

Clifden

Galway

Dublin

Limerick

Cork

Kylemore Castle

Part I

History of Kylemore Castle

1826-1910   Courtesy of the House of Lords Archive

1829-1874   © Kylemore Abbey

Mitchell and Margaret Henry

VINCIT VERITAS

2

Chapter 1
Establishing a Country Seat

Mitchell Henry was born in Manchester of Irish parents. His father, Alexander Henry, was a successful cotton merchant and one of a group of influential liberal reformers active in Manchester in the early years of the nineteenth century. His mother, Elizabeth Brush, was the daughter of George Brush of Willowbrook, Dromore, County Down.[1] Mitchell liked to boast that not a drop of blood flowed through his veins other than Irish, something which may have influenced his choice of wife, when, on 30 August 1849, he married Margaret Vaughan, daughter of George Vaughan, of Quilly House, Dromore, County Down. The couple were married at St Peter's Church in Dublin.[2] Margaret's father, a solicitor, had passed away some years before and she was then living with her mother at Rathmines in Dublin. Mitchell, a medical surgeon, was living in London, and had a practice in No 5 Harley Street, Cavendish Square.

Tradition has it that the couple visited Connemara while on their honeymoon. The region was renowned for its fishing and shooting and Mitchell, a keen fisherman, was drawn to it for that reason. The couple seem to have been enchanted by the beauty of the landscape in and around the Kylemore district and may even have stayed at Kylemore House where a Dublin man, Andrew Armstrong, ran a hotel.

However, in sharp contrast to the visual beauty of Connemara was the harsh reality of life lived by its inhabitants and from the beginning Mitchell seems to have been aware of their plight. Connemara was just then slowly recovering from a cholera epidemic which raged through the district during the first six months of the year 1849. And although the Great Famine was officially over, the effect of years of starvation and disease was still evident everywhere. The region, steeped in poverty, had already lost one third of its population through starvation, fever and emigration, and still more were desperately seeking a means of escape through emigration. Along the roadside could be seen the shallow graves of hastily interred famine victims, while many cottages in the hillsides still contained skeletons awaiting burial. The landlords too were bankrupt, two-thirds of the region was up for sale in the Encumbered Estates Court, set up to facilitate the sale of indebted estates. Day after day advertisements filled the newspapers giving details of the many estates and fisheries on offer. For a sportsman with capital the offers looked tempting, but the poor quality of the land and the high number of dependant tenants usually acted as a deterrent.

With the extension of the Midland Great Western Railway to Galway in 1851, Connemara, frequently referred to as the Highlands of Ireland, was offered to sportsmen as an alternative venue to Scotland for fishing and shooting. In the years that followed Mitchell became one of the growing number of Irish and English Gentlemen who visited Connemara during the fishing season and it became the couple's wish someday to own a home there. During these visits it may well be that the Henrys rented Kylemore Lodge, a fishing lodge built by Rev Robert Isaac Wilberforce sometime between 1853 and 1858, on property purchased from Henry Blake of Renvyle House in 1853. The Lodge was situated at the foot of Duchruach mountain (1,736 feet), on the edge of Pollacappul Lake, and sheltered to the East by ancient oak and birch trees. Between the Lodge and the lake shore ran the Westport to Clifden road, while on the opposite shore rose the gentle slopes of Diamond Hill (Binn Ghuaire 1,460 feet), Cnoc Breac (1,460 feet), Binn Bhán (1,577 feet) and Binn Bhreac (1,922 feet).

Time would show that Mitchell's frequent trips to Connemara, and his affinity with its people, gave him an insight into their circumstances and political aspirations which would prove invaluable in his future political career. However, just then Mitchell was rapidly gaining a reputation for himself in his chosen field of medicine. In 1854 he was elected a Fellow of the Royal College of Surgeons.[3] Henry is said to have written several valuable surgical works. In 1856 he translated from the French a treatise on *The Diseases Of The Breast And Mammary Region* by A. Velpeau. On the title page Mitchell is described as a Fellow, by examination, of the Royal College of Surgeons, Assistant-Surgeon and Lecturer on Morbid Anatomy at the Middlesex Hospital and Surgeon to the North London Infirmary for the Diseases of the Eye.[4]

Title page: A Treatise on the Diseases of the Breast and Mammary Region

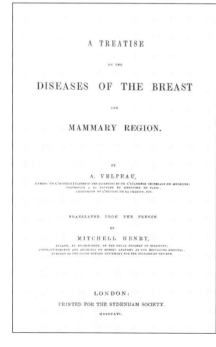

A TREATISE

ON THE

DISEASES OF THE BREAST

AND

MAMMARY REGION.

BY

A. VELPEAU,

TRANSLATED FROM THE FRENCH

BY

MITCHELL HENRY,

LONDON:
PRINTED FOR THE SYDENHAM SOCIETY.
MDCCCLVI.

In his capacity as Lecturer at the Middlesex Hospital Medical College, Mitchell delivered the opening address to the classes in 1859. In this speech we get an insight into the man and his philosophy on the requirements necessary in order to achieve success in life, advice perhaps similar to that preached to him as a boy in the Henry family home in Manchester. Self-discipline and perseverance were, in his opinion, essential tools for a successful life, along with 'earnestness of purpose' and a 'genuine love of truth': two qualities which he himself exhibited throughout his life and which would at times prove to be detrimental to his political career. Earnestness of purpose would, he told his audience, 'even overcome defects of early education', and a love of truth was 'amidst the rarest of human endowments, yet without it no man can be truly great, aye, even respectable'. He also cautioned them against failure to recognise the 'dignity of labour'. Without an adequate concept of such dignity, 'neither wealth nor station, nor an amply endowed intellect' could save them 'from self-contempt, or rescue your memories from deserved oblivion'. Earnestness was the 'talismanic key' that opened all locks, the passport to success in all things:

> If then you are engaged in study, study with earnestness; if attending a lecture, bring not your body only, but your mind also: and even if engaged in recreation, do it with your whole attention: above all, never fall into that dreamy state of almost imbecile fatuity, that state of half work, half play . . . Now is your day, perform your task here with diligence and earnestness, and show that you are men.[5]

Mitchell's obvious interest in and enthusiasm for medicine leaves one to assume that he was happy and fulfilled with his life in London. The couple had four children, two boys and two girls, and enjoyed a very full social life in London as well as making frequent trips abroad. However, on the death of his father on 4 October 1862, and on receipt of a sizable inheritance, Mitchell's life took on a whole new turn. He abandoned his medical career and instead turned his attention to politics and commerce.

Mitchell was greatly influenced by his father, Alexander Henry, a self-made man with strong religious, political and social beliefs. As a young boy, Alexander left the family farm at Loughbrickland, County Down to join his uncle in America. Alexander's uncle, also named Alexander, was a successful businessman in Philadelphia and a well known philanthropist with a special interest in education and the Christian missions in India. In America Alexander's skill as a businessman soon became apparent and within a short time he was made manager of his uncle's firm. He joined

Alexander Henry (1784–1862)

the Unitarian Church, much to the regret of his uncle, a staunch Presbyterian. This association with the Unitarian Church was to continue throughout his life and may well have influenced his decision to establish himself in Manchester, a town with a strong Unitarian community. In 1805, at the age of twenty-one, he left America and, with the encouragement of his uncle, he returned to Europe with the intention of setting up a business of his own.[6]

Alexander arrived in Manchester armed with a letter of introduction to Ashworth Clegg, a wealthy cotton merchant and prominent member of the Unitarian Church in Cross Street.[7] The congregation at Cross St had a tradition of public service and reform.[8] Many of its members were involved in local and national politics and campaigned vigorously for Parliamentary reform and for improvements in the education and living conditions of the working classes. Alexander was immediately accepted into the Unitarian community and went on to become one of its most active members.

Maintaining his links, both private and commercial, with his family in America, Alexander set up his business in Palace Street, importing raw cotton and exporting manufactured cotton prints. As the business began to expand he moved to Spear Street where he was joined by his brother Samuel and from then on the firm became known as A & S Henry. Together the brothers were a successful combination and A & S Henry grew rapidly, establishing branches all over America. In Manchester the company became known as the 'American House':[9] 'Messrs. A & S Henry were the leaders . . . in the English trade with America, and for many years were the chief exporters of manufactured goods to that country'.[10]

Cross Street Unitarian Chapel

6

A & S Henry company branches

Soon they expanded into woollens, worsteds, linens and jute, and established branch warehouses in Bradford, Huddersfield, Leeds, Glasgow and Belfast. Each branch had 'separate and distinct interests', with the parent house at Manchester retaining contro.[11] By the 1830s the company was also trading in Brazil, Australia and the South Seas Islands. In 1836 a large warehouse was opened in Portland Street, Manchester, and this was to remain company headquarters for the next one hundred and four years.[12]

The Henry company logo was a ship in full sail and over the years the brothers made frequent trips across the Atlantic. At the time the average journey took thirty days and Alexander liked to boast that he had made over twenty-five voyages to America in sailing ships. On one occasion he was left behind at Plymouth when he stepped ashore to assist an old gentleman whom he had met on the journey from London.[13]

A & S Henry company logo

Samuel Henry

Samuel Henry lost his life on one such trip in January 1840. He was travelling on the *Lexington* between New York and Providence, when the ship caught fire and almost all of the passengers and crew were lost. Alexander, now the sole owner of the firm, continued to trade under the name A & S Henry. In the years that followed, the Board of A & S Henry was expanded to include some branch managers and members of staff, a number of whom were rewarded with shares in the company; this move did much to contribute to the continued success of the firm in the years to come.

Despite an obvious heavy workload Alexander still found time to play his part in public service and politics. He was recognised as a generous supporter of the Anti-Corn Law League and an important member of the Liberal party in Manchester.[14] He represented South Lancashire in Parliament from December 1847 to July 1852,[15] at a time when Manchester Liberalism was synonymous with reform, and was for years President of the Lancashire Public Schools Association. One Manchester newspaper described him as 'a king among men. His patriotism and love of liberty could always be relied upon'.[16]

The Henry family home was a tall red-bricked Georgian house overlooking the Green in Ardwick, then a village on the outskirts of Manchester. In the centre of Ardwick Green was a large slightly serpentine lake surrounded by a grassy belt. In Winter, when the lake was frozen, it was used by skaters and the Green was a rendezvous for all public celebrations and the centre of village life. The road to London ran alongside the Green and a dozen coaches, making their way to and from the capital city, daily passed the Henry door.[17]

Out of the nine children born to Alexander and Elizabeth Henry, two sons died in infancy and there would appear to have been a threat to the lives of the twins, John Snowdon and Franklin. All of the children were christened at Cross St Unitarian Chapel, but the twins, perhaps in a moment of danger, were christened in the Presbyterian Church, Cross St, on 5 January 1825. However, twenty days later they were re-christened at Cross St Unitarian Chapel.[18] The Henry children enjoyed a privileged lifestyle, growing up in the affluence of middle-class industrial England. The family home was dominated by commerce and politics. Regular visitors would have included the renowned reformers, Richard Cobden, John Bright and Henry Ashworth, founder members of the Anti-Corn Law League. Conscious of their father's success, the Henry children would also have been aware of his work and political ideology in encouraging the lower classes to advance themselves, through education and self-discipline, as he had succeeded in doing before them.

Mitchell was the youngest member of the Henry family. He was born in 1826, and was named after a branch of his father's family in America; many of whom were medical doctors and one, Silas Weir Mitchell, M.D., was the author of *Hugh Wynne* and *The Red City*, recognised classics in American literature.[19] Born into this liberal background of reform and improvement, he carried his father's values with him all through his medical, political and private life. And although future political battles would bring him into conflict with the Manchester Liberals he was very much a product of their making.

On his death in 1862 Alexander Henry left almost £700,000 in assets. Generous bequests were granted to his grandchildren and household staff, but bequests to his brother, sister and their children in Co Down, made in the original will in 1860, were later revoked in a codicil added a year before his death. To his oldest son, Alexander, a convert to the Roman Catholic Church, who had become a Jesuit priest, he left five hundred pounds a year for life, and to one of the twins, Franklin, he left one thousand pounds a year for life. Two daughters, Elizabeth and Mary Ann, receive no mention, perhaps having preceded their father in death or having displeased him in some way. The residue of his estate was divided between his three remaining children, John Snowdon, Mitchell and their sister, Agnes Woods Wildes; the sons were each to receive two fifths and the daughter to receive one fifth. At a rough estimate the sons had inherited a quarter of a million pounds each, but the money could only be realised if all business and other assets were sold. This they did not do. Instead the company remained as before, a successful partnership of Henry family members and other Board members taken in by Alexander Henry, with John Snowdon, who was already employed in the business, and Mitchell becoming the principal partners. Mitchell was elected chairman and continued in that position until 1894:

> Although not engaging himself directly in the business of his firm, he [possessed] a thorough knowledge of all the affairs of the partnership, keeping himself daily posted in the firms transactions, and to a considerable extent directing its operations.[20]

Alexander Henry left £20,000 in trust for the four children of Mitchell and Margaret; John Lewis (born 1850), Margaret (b.1852), Maria (b.1855) and Alexander George (b.1857). However, between the years 1864 and 1872 the couple went on to have a further five children; Forward Howard (b.1864), Geraldine (b.1865), Lorenzo (b.1866), Florence (b.1870) and Violet (b.1872).

Within a year of his father's death Mitchell [hereafter referred to by his surname Henry] had made some dramatic life-changes. He soon left behind the life of a medical doctor and instead concentrated his attention on his new position as Chairman of A & S Henry. He simultaneously became involved in the remodelling of two properties; Stratheden House in London and Kylemore Lodge in Galway, converting them into magnificently luxurious homes for himself and his family. In November 1863 Henry, described in *The Builder* journal as 'the well-known wealthy and discriminating lover of fine arts', acquired two houses with extensive grounds overlooking Hyde Park in Knightsbridge: Kent House and Stratheden House. He later pulled down Kent House but retained Stratheden House for his own personal use. Under the direction of the architect, Thomas H Wyatt, and the architectural decorator, Frederick Sang, the interior of Stratheden House was 'fitted up and furnished very elaborately'. The house was built in the early 1770s by Sir William Chambers for a politician named John Calcraft, and the alterations were, according to the journal, quite splendid. The Henrys had travelled extensively over the years and the house became a showcase for the many treasures they had acquired and the influences they had experienced.

© Kylemore Abbey

Henry Family

Mitchell Henry with eight of his children. Taken by his second son, Alexander George, circa 1877.

Back row left to right: John Lewis, Mitchell, Forward Howard, Maria.

Front row: Margaret, Violet, Florance, Geraldine (seated) and Lorenzo.

> In the hall . . . the ceiling and frieze are appropriately embellished in encaustic colour, and a handsome tile pavement has been laid by Maw. A dual head, Diogenes and Socrates, a fine antique bust of Agrippa, and the Florentine Dogs, in Serpentine, are amongst the works of art it contains; while the walls of the staircase are hung with pictures, some of them originals and others copies of paintings by good masters. In the Dining-room the walls are covered with silk brocade; a lofty chimney piece, of carved oak, in the style of the sixteenth century, has been built up, including some beautiful carving of the period. The ceiling, modelled in the same style, is embellished with allegories, Raffaellesques, and gilding. The woodwork of the Library is ebonized, with gold mouldings and ornaments.

The ceiling, cornice and frieze, Venetian Oinque-cento in style, are partly on gold, partly on turquoise-blue ground. The panelled compartments contain arabesques in the borders and portraits of philosophers and poets. The walls are hung with heavy green silk from Lyons, as are those of the drawing-room. For the latter, the furniture, tables, chairs, consoles, and frames are modelled and finished in Rome and Florence after originals in the Pallazzo Pitti and in the Vatican. The walls of the Billiard-room are pale sea-green in colour, the woodwork being dark green with gilding. The ceiling, cove, and cornice are very elaborately embellished, Italian *Oinque-cento* in style. There is a remarkable carved settee in this room that once adorned a ducal mansion in Florence. The design of part of it is ascribed to Giulio Romano. A recess of this room, between marble columns, the back-ground of which is a positive Pompeian red, contains a statue of a flower-girl, by Wolf, of Rome. Other statues by the same sculptor, and a "Puck" by Lough, will be found elsewhere. And among the best things in the rooms we note a remarkable fine tea service of Sévres china, painted with portraits, and originally a present from Louis XIV to a member of the Visconti family. It is an exquisite result of the union of Art and Industry.

The principal addition to the house is in honour of sculpture, – a temple-like apartment or shrine, found to receive Melis noted group, "*The Pompeian Mother*" which was for some time one of the lions of modern Rome. The statue represents a woman who, unclothed, with the exception of some wind-pressed drapery behind, and holding her child in her arms, strives to escape the horror of the destruction of Pompeii by Vesuvius . . . Rumour gives 8,000 guineas as its cost.

This temple and its approaches have been painted in the Pompeian style. The greater part of the back-ground is red and black, with animals, birds, scrolls a rich frieze, a gilt dome, and a mosaic pavement by Minton. It is scarcely necessary for us to add that a very large sum has been expended on the works in Stratheden House.[21]

Stratheden House was to remain the family's London residence for the next forty years. The neighbouring property, Kent House, formerly the residence of the Duke of Kent, father of Queen Victoria, Henry pulled down in the summer of 1870.[22] He began redeveloping the site, making a new street, Rutland Gardens, but went no further. Three years later he sold the land to his architectural decorator, Frederick Sang.

© Kylemore Abbey

Kylemore Lodge in the 1860s

Described in 1864 as a handsome new house not entirely finished, partly furnished and expected to be occupied in the following summer.[23]

In September 1862, a month before his father's death, Henry leased Kylemore Lodge and two acres of garden from Patrick Macaulay, a Galway merchant. Macaulay held the property on a twelve year lease which he transferred to Henry at a yearly rent of £105. The Lodge was owned by two brothers, Rev. William and Edward Wilberforce, who had inherited it from their father the Rev. Robert Isaac Wilberforce. Rev. Robert Wilberforce, formerly a Protestant clergyman, had converted to the Roman Catholic faith and settled in Connemara with the intention of thwarting the work of the Irish Church Mission there. He purchased nine townlands, containing under 9,000 acres, from Henry Blake in 1853. The Great Famine had left Henry Blake in poor health and in serious financial debt and on 8 February 1853 he sold the nine townlands to Rev. Wilberforce for £10,500. Kylemore Lodge was constructed soon afterwards. Henry entered into negotiations with the Wilberforce brothers for the purchase of the Lodge and lands.

On lease of the Lodge he began carrying out improvements almost immediately: the building was enlarged and a glass house added to the east side. A steward, Archibald MacAlister, was installed to oversee the works and to undertake experiments in artificial propagation of salmon on the Dawros River.[24] It is worth noting that such experiments were already underway in Galway city where the Galway Fishery was purchased by two brothers, Edmund and Thomas Ashworth, in 1852. The Ashworths were cotton millers from Lancashire, a third brother, Henry, was one of the founders of the Anti-Corn Law League, and it is safe to assume that, given their shared interest in business, politics and fishing, the brothers were friends of the Henry family back in England and that the friendship continued after their arrival in the West of Ireland. The Ashworth brothers were at this time winning international renown for their piscicultural activities at the Galway Fishery, where, under the direction of their manager Ramsbottom, experiments in artificial propagation and rearing of salmon were proving successful and winning widespread publicity.[25] At Kylemore, hatching boxes had been laid down by MacAlister as early as December 1863.[26]

In the meantime the Wilberforce brothers began buying back leases granted by their father on various sections of the land and to fishing rights on the lakes and rivers. The process took almost four years and it was 31 December 1866 before Henry took possession of the nine townlands with extensive fishing and shooting rights, including Kylemore Lodge, from Rev. William and Edward Wilberforce for £9,480. The townlands; Lettergesh East, Lettergesh West, Mullaghglass, Lemnaheltia, Tooreena, Shanaveag, Pollacappul, Currywongaun and Dawros More, covered a little over 8,505 acres and ran from the main Westport to Clifden road, north over Duchruach mountain and down to the the Atlantic Ocean at Barnaderg Bay. The purchase gave Henry fishing rights to the northern bank of the Dawros river, as well as a number of lakes and smaller rivers; the Dawros River ran from Kylemore through Pollacappul and Maladrolaun Loughs and into the sea at Derryinver Bay. To complete his right to the southern bank Henry needed to purchase the townlands of Mweelin, Bunnaboghee and Addergoole.

He succeeded in purchasing Mweelin from Andrew Armstrong, on 21 October 1865. Armstrong, the renowned hotelier, was moving back to Dublin having leased Kylemore House Hotel to his land steward, Alexander Taylor.[27] Mweelin was without tenants but contained evidence of earlier occupation; the remains of a cairn, a penal graveyard and a holy well. It contained a little over 652 acres of poor quality land, rising to over one thousand five hundred feet, but, more importantly to Henry, included in the sale was the fishing rights to Lough Pollacappul which lay directly in front of Kylemore Lodge. A covenant added to the agreement granted Andrew Armstrong, his friends, his sons, servants and boatmen, permission to fish on the lake with a boat, 'tackling and all appliances used in single rod fishing or angling only'. Permission was restricted to one boat at any one time and was granted for the duration of the life of Andrew Armstrong and no further: Armstrong was not at liberty to sell or confer this right to any other person.[28]

Bunnaboghee was purchased from John Duggan for £400 and had a sitting tenant, John Walsh, who farmed the 195 acres of land.[29] Between Bunnaboghee and Mweelin stood Addergoole Farm, 900 acres of good land. The farm was previously held by Thomas Eastwood, but was just then in the hands of the Court of Bankruptcy. Eastwood had purchased the land from Francis J Graham and had built an attractive farmhouse, gate lodge and extensive farm buildings and reclaimed the surrounding lands. Henry purchased Addergoole Farm on 12 March 1868 for £1,590.

Almost immediately Henry ran into trouble with his neighbour Francis J Graham. Graham, under an old agreement with Duggan, was entitled to fish off the lands at Bunnaboghee but was now claiming more than that conceded by Henry and a lengthy legal battle ensued.[30] Graham was also claiming the right to shoot over 5,000 acres of mountain and scrub land, Adrigoole and Barnanang, which lay south of Addergoole. Henry leased these lands for a number of years before concluding a successful purchase with the trustees of the estate of Charles Richardson on 4 July 1878 for £6,500. For over two decades the case was argued out in several courts, until eventually a settlement was reached which, together with the sum total of the legal costs for both sides, came to over £8,000, considerably more that the cost of the fisheries themselves. 'No one', Henry told the House of Commons some years later, 'who had ever bought property in Ireland or made an investment there had failed to find that, by hook or by crook, he became involved in litigation'. There was, in his opinion, 'a great deal of speculative litigation in Ireland'.[31]

LETTERGESH EAST

MULLAGHGLASS

LETTERGESH WEST

TOOREENA

SHANAVEAG

CURRYWONGAUN

POLLACAPPUL

LEMNAHELTIA

DAWROSMORE

KYLEMORE CASTLE

ADDERGOOLE HOUSE

MWEELIN

ADDERGOOLE

BARNANANG

Plan
of the
FREEHOLD DOMAIN,
Known as the
KYLEMORE CASTLE ESTATE,
IN THE HEART OF
CONNEMARA,
COUNTY GALWAY, IRELAND.
For Sale by
MESSRS H. E. FOSTER & CRANFIELD,
IN CONJUNCTION WITH
MESSRS JAMES NORTH & Co.
1902

Scale of Miles.

Kylemore Book of Sale 1902

15

Other smaller sections of land were later purchased, bringing Henry's holding to roughly 15,615 (Irish) acres and costing a little over £18,000. From that time on the combined properties became known as the Kylemore Estate.

The primary reason for Henry's purchase of his 15,000 acre estate was for its fishing and shooting rights. The fact that much of the land was uneconomical and that it brought with it dependant tenants, thrusting upon him the unknown hazards of landlord responsibilities, was of secondary consideration. However, once in place Henry faced his responsibilities with a business-like efficiency tempered by a humane hand.

Drawing on his scientific and industrial background, Henry's approach to all aspects of his estate was both innovative and experimental. Every facet of its development, from the construction of the family residence, the ornamentation of the grounds, the development of the fishery, to the working of the farms, was evaluated and assessed. And every modern method and technique was used to enhance its appearance, its potential and its effectiveness. Such an approach was risky and in such a remote region necessitated huge expenditure. In every undertaking embarked upon expertise was employed in the planning and development and, when necessary, materials and skilled labour were brought in from the outside. Henry's ability to attract such highly qualified and able personnel gives testimony to his entrepreneurial skills and ability to sell a project 'off the drawing board'.

No expense was spared as Henry endeavoured to turn the entire estate into one giant laboratory in which estate management, landlord-tenant relationships and even Connemara itself, with its boggy soil, its incessant rain and salt-laden winds, was to be challenged. The experiment, begun so confidently in the 1860s, would continue throughout Henry's occupancy in Kylemore and, while it contributed greatly to the lives of his tenants and to the productivity of the land and scenic beauty of the region, it was perhaps the chief cause of his own financial ruin forty years later.

The lands purchased by Henry carried about 125 tenants, many of whom had lived on the land for the past twenty years or more. They would have viewed with trepidation the purchase of such a large tract of land by this businessman from England; would he, like so many of his neighbours, be an absentee landlord showing little interest in his estate, expending little on maintenance and yet demanding that it provide him with sufficient income to sustain it and afford him the pleasure of fishing its lakes and river and shooting the grouse on its hills?

The government on the other hand would have welcomed his arrival. He was precisely the sort of man they were trying to attract into the region; an industrious man with capital at his disposal. Recent years had seen a change in the ownership of many Connemara estates. New landlords, many of them absentee, had taken the place of old families who had for centuries been the proprietors of the land but had lost their estates in the aftermath of the famine. It was hoped by the government that these new owners would bring with them capital and expertise which would help to turn the region around, but this was not proving to be the case. The new owners were looking for a good return on very little investment and to that end had cleared off many of the tenants and replaced them with livestock. Time would show that Henry's liberal background coupled with a social conscience would give the tenants at Kylemore a landlord hard to be equalled not just in Connemara but throughout Ireland.

Pivotal to Henry's success as a landlord was his choice of steward, and to this position he appointed Archibald D. MacAlister, a Catholic from County Antrim. Under Henry's direction MacAlister began to develop the estate making it a model in estate management and landlord – tenant relations. Long before public pressure and eventual law reform would force Irish landlords to adopt the three F's – fair rent, fixture of tenure and free sale – Henry offered the equivalent to his tenants. Soon after taking over the estate he offered leases for forty years to all of his tenants, with the right to renewal on a revision of rent by arbitration, 'in which the tenant's improvements are not to be counted, and at the same time giving them the right to sell their interest, first offering it to their landlord'.[32] Instead of converting small farms into large grazing farms, hundreds of acres of land previously used for grazing was taken back and now became part of a reclamation experiment. In the townlands where the old 'rundale' system still prevailed the land was 'striped' and where necessary new houses erected by the tenants on their own holding. Henry 'assisted in putting them up and also in repairing and improving those already in existence'. Every assistance was given to help the tenants improve their holding. A new road to the shore was built, giving them access to seaweed, which they used in manuring the land. The principal crop was still the potato, but many tenants had a run of mountain on which to keep sheep and cattle and, 'as a matter of course, Connemara ponies'.[33] Those tenants who wished to work found employment on the many improvement works going on in the estate. Workers were paid weekly in cash and for their daily labour they received, in two months, the equivalent of their annual rent.[34]

All improvements and developments were advanced with great caution, so as not to upset the tenants, and MacAlister was later praised by the Royal Agricultural Society of England for 'combining prudence and caution with great intelligence in their execution . . . by gradually feeling his way, Mr. MacAlister [was] able to ascertain the best method of improving the condition of both of the land and of the peasantry'.[35] When it was discovered that almost none of the cottages on the estate possessed a window, instead of giving orders that 'windows should at once be put into all cabins' and thereby attract complaints from the tenants that their homes were 'ruthlessly destroyed', Henry put in a window for a single tenant and 'after a while, the improvement was thought to confer an air of greater gentility upon its possessor. When the neighbours complained that one had received greater advantages than the rest, their wishes were gratified at once, and now [1877] there is not a cottage on the property that has not a glazed window that can be opened to let in air as well as light'.[36] Lime was given to the most enterprising of the tenants and grass and turnip seeds distributed amongst those willing to vary their crop 'instead of confining themselves to growing potatoes, with the occasional crop of oats'.[37]

However, within two or three years of his first taking up his Connemara estate, Henry's generosity and fair-mindedness in his dealings with his tenants was misconstrued as softness by some and he was forced to have processes served on six of the tenants for non-payment of rent:

> some of the tenants, not, I believe of their own spontaneous notion, put it about that "Mr Henry was very rich and did not want the rent". I wrote to several and spoke to others, and at last directed that processes for the recovery of rent should be issued against six, for three half years and upwards in arrears. This was enough and the rents were paid, but the matter has given me much pain. I have considered it a duty to insist on some punctuality in the payment of rents, and have refused ever to allow them to be stopped out of the weekly wages, because, as I have often told the tenants, obligations are mutual, and they have their duty to do as well as I have mine. The men who did not pay their rents received their wages on Saturdays in the same way as any one else.[38]

To further enhance living conditions in the area Henry erected a village pump at Letterfrack[39] and a post and telegraph office close to the Castle. He set up a school at Lettergesh for the children of his tenants. This was done under the National Board and was apparently well attended, while another National Board school just a few miles away was lying empty. Henry's school was erected in 1868 and built of stone and slated, with separate classrooms for boys and girls. A four roomed schoolmaster's house, also of stone and slate, and a two roomed stone and corrugated iron roofed schoolmistress's bungalow were built close by.[40] Henry installed two Roman Catholic teachers at the school and this may have made it more acceptable to the parents. He offered the position of manager to the local Catholic priest, but he turned it down. Archbishop MacHale was against the state system of non-denominational education and would not have approved. The school was considered to be 'one of the best of Mr Henry's improvements' on his estate. [41] The children showed a great aptitude for learning and acquired 'habits of cleanliness and neatness' which contrasted 'most favourably' with their neighbours.[42]

The benefit of having such a man enter this poor, underdeveloped region did not stop with his tenants but was felt far beyond his estate boundaries. In the years since the Famine, conditions had improved for the people but still their total dependency on the land left them susceptible to crop failure, bad weather, blight and market influences: 'A bad crop of potatoes brings want and suffering always in its wake, and a single failure would even now bring back famine to the district'.[43] The majority of the tenants in Connemara tended to live from one harvest to the next, they were frequently in debt to the shopkeepers and regularly pawned their possession to see them through to the next harvest. In the winter of 1866–67, during the construction of Kylemore Castle, Connemara was once again in deep distress. It was an unusually cold winter with snow from January to April. Bad weather during harvest time left crops rotting in the fields, or going to market in bad condition and having to be sold at low prices. Despite the best efforts of the tenants and farmers, hundreds of cattle and calves died of starvation in the fields.

The shopkeepers were refusing to give credit and so the people were desperately in need of cash. In Clifden the pawnbroker's office was filled with beds, bedclothes and fishing gear, as the poor pawned their belongings and used the cash to purchase provisions. The men went in search of work for wages but there was little to be found. The only employment to be had was at Kylemore where the building contractor Thomas H Caroll of Dublin had begun the foundation work on Kylemore Castle. Large numbers were employed daily at a respectable wage and for the first time the government was made aware of the impact Henry's arrival was having on the district. Dr Terence Brodie, the Poor Law Inspector for the region, reported to Dublin Castle in May 1867:

> There is no large employer in this district except Mr Henry an English Gentleman . . . He and the contractor who is building a mansion for him at Kylemore-pass give daily employment to about 100 persons at wages ranging from 7/- to 10/- per week, and to earn this labourers come from Renvyle a distance of some miles.[44]

The works were extensive. Excavation, drainage and rock blasting went on around the Lodge, while at the same time work was underway on the Pleasure Grounds; two miles of 'cool and shady walks' along the margins of Loughs Kylemore, Pollacappul and Maladrolaun and the Dawros river. The Walled Garden, with its extensive range of glasshouses, was also under construction and many more were employed in reclaiming hundreds of acres of bog land throughout the estate. Over three hundred people were employed in the many works underway at this time and wages for labourers ranged from fifteen to sixteen pence a day. Skilled men such as masons, carpenters and plasterers were receiving six shillings and six pence per day, plumbers eleven shillings and two pence and smith (for sharpening tools) with helper, six shillings and two pence. Horse and cart were hired at five shillings per day.[45] A 'very different state of matters from what prevailed not long ago in that part of the country', the *Farmers Gazette* reported after visiting the estate in July 1870. The newspaper was full of praise for Henry's worthwhile endeavours:

> It is certainly a great matter to have a gentleman of Mr Henrys wealth and liberal spirit taking a fancy for the country and spending his money in beautifying and improving it, and thereby giving employment to the people, old and young, instead of wasting it on the turf or in some other way which would benefit nobody.[46]

Chapter 2
Building a Castle in the Wilderness

As the foundation works for the Castle were underway the Lodge remained occupied by the household staff. The plan, drawn up by Samuel Ussher Roberts, allowed the Lodge to be incorporated into the new building, leaving it at the very heart of the Castle. Roberts had designed Gurteen Castle in County Waterford for Edward Le Poer in 1863 and many of the external and internal features of Gurteen were carried over to Kylemore. The same builder, Thomas H Carroll, was used in the construction of both houses.

As well as being an architect Roberts was also a civil engineer, a qualification which would prove necessary given the constraints of the terrain surrounding Kylemore Lodge. He was also County Surveyor for the Western Division of County Galway. Prior to becoming County Surveyor, Roberts had a distinguished career as a Drainage Engineer with the Office of Public Works, and while with them was the chief engineer for the Corrib Drainage and Navigation Works. The Corrib Scheme, begun in 1848 and completed in 1854, linked Lough Corrib with Galway Bay via the Eglington Canal. He also designed the Galway City Waterworks, which opened in 1867. For over ten years he was involved in attempts to link Galway and Clifden by rail. Assisted by Robert Langrishe, he produced designs and costings for the proposed West Galway Railway at a public meeting at Oughterard Courthouse on 18 October 1861. However, despite Roberts's best efforts the railway failed to get off the drawing board. Again, during the Summer and Autumn of 1866 he, along with James Dillon of Dublin, led a new survey for the proposed line. And as late as November 1871 his proposals for a 'Galway, Oughterard and Clifden Railway' were put before a public meeting at Clifden Courthouse. On this occasion he was supported by Henry, who spoke in favour of his proposals and later subscribed £5,000 towards its construction. However, it was 1895 before Clifden and Galway were finally connected by a railway and the engineers were Ryan and Townsend.[1]

© Stephen Powell

Samuel Roberts.

Samuel U. Roberts

The Castle took four years to complete and construction costs came to a little over £29,000.[2] The first stone was laid on 4 September 1867 and a trowel to commemorate the event was presented to Mrs Henry by the builder Thomas H Carroll. Almost all of those involved in the design and construction of Kylemore Castle were Irish. The plaster work was by James Hogan & Sons of Dublin, well known for their highly decorative and detailed work, and the stonecutter was M. O'Brien of Ballinasloe. Henry held Irish architects and builders in high regard; the Georgian buildings in Dublin were, in his opinion, equal to anything in England, 'both in originality, construction, material, and in everything else'.[3] The surveyor was Benjamin Thomas Patterson and his detailed records, preserved in the Irish Architectural Archive, give us a valuable insight into the day to day work carried on at Kylemore between the years 1867 and 1871.

The site, although beautifully located, had many disadvantages. Squeezed between lake and mountain there was little room to develop the grand residence Henry had in mind. Roberts's engineering skills came into play in the construction of the Castle and where it proved impossible to remove the rock he simply built over it. This gave the Castle a snug appearance against the towering height of Duchruach mountain, an effect which produced perhaps one of the most picturesque castles in the country.

The Baronial style of the building, combined with Roberts's clever use of the natural attractions of the site, produced a stately structure with castellated walls crowned with turrets and towers. The Castle, covering roughly 40,000 square feet, dwarfed all other residences in Connemara at the time; nothing came near to it in size or grandeur. Inside there were over seventy rooms; the principal reception rooms were elaborately decorated in the style of the period, but the bedrooms and family rooms were kept small and comfortably furnished. Nothing was spared in the cost of its construction, all modern conveniences were added, such as indoor plumbing, gas lighting, service lifts to the upper floors and fire hydrants. The end result was a very beautiful, but modern, functional building, suitable for a large noble family and for lavish entertainment.

As was only to be expected, the construction of such a massive building in the wild barren landscape of Connemara drew many curious visitors and soon there were few in Ireland who had not read, heard of or seen for themselves Mitchell Henry's stately home on the shore of Lough Pollacappul. In July 1870 a reporter from the *Farmers Gazette* visited the site and found the Castle not yet finished but was immediately struck by its location:'Kylemore Castle is built on a platform or terrace, most of which

Kylemore Castle
with scaffolding to the rear.

has been quarried out of the face of the hill. The situation, however, is very commanding, and has been chosen with an eye to great effect'.[4] Alexander Innes Shand wrote in *the Times* of the difficulties overcome by Roberts in his design of the interior: 'You walk up a flight of stairs to the dining-room, each step being literally of rock, boarded over. You pass from block to block of the buildings by corridors and stairs that sorely task a stranger's bump of topography. And while the views from the three sides are magnificent, each window at the back looks into the cliffs'.[5]

Much of the exterior of the Castle has remained unaltered in the years since its construction. The principal wall, constructed of granite and lined with brick, is two to three feet thick and crowned with castellations. Five embattled towers rise from the East, West and Centre of the building and surmounting one tower is an octagonal flag staff turret. The roof also holds a bell turret which originally contained a massive swing bell.[6] The plinth, quoins, mullions and transoms to windows and the moulded cordons are all of limestone. The granite was brought from Dalkey, on the East coast of Ireland, by sea to Letterfrack and from there by cart to Kylemore.

The limestone was supplied by M. O'Brien of Ballinasloe and was transported by rail to Galway and from there by sea to Letterfrack. Local limestone was used for filling and foundation work. The final touches were put to the stone work on site and craftsmen brought into the area were housed in wooden huts.

The southern or principal frontage of the castle, which extends to about one hundred and forty two feet, has at its centre an oriel window. Immediately above the window a 'beautifully carved keystone representing the head and shoulders of a female figure with outstretched wings, the head surmounted by a coronet and the hands holding a shaped shield' still bears the Henry Coat of Arms. Under the oriel window is the Gothic arched entrance supported by three Peterhead granite columns with carved stone capitals of birds, animals and foliage.[7]

Sadly little of the original interior of the building has survived. However, photographs and detailed descriptions give us a glimpse of the luxurious accommodation enjoyed by the Henry family during their time at Kylemore. Inside the oak doors were four spacious halls, 'leading one into another through Gothic Arches' supported by Connemara marble pillars with Cain stone capitals. All four halls had polished oak parquet floors and the outer and inner entrance halls had oak panelled dado and panelled ceiling with deep mouldings.[8] In the halls there were a number of stuffed wild beasts, fishes and birds 'from the eel to the otter and fox'.[9] From the staircase hall rose, 'in three easy flights, the handsome grand oak staircase, about 6 feet wide, with oak panelled dado, massive newel posts' and ornamental balustrade supporting the mahogany handrail. The stairs was lit by a 'beautiful tracery window with rich stained glass panels in 16 divisions, the central portions with Coats of Arms etc., while above it a handsomely decorated ceiling of ornamental design in seven divisions with corbels, deeply moulded panels, centrepieces, bosses and openwork cornice of artistic design'.[10]

On the northern side of the staircase hall, up three steps passing under two Gothic Arches with Connemara marble columns and carved spandrels, was the gallery hall or saloon which was often used for dancing and games. Leading off the halls was a 'suite of magnificent reception rooms' suitably arranged for the purpose of entertainment and capable of dispensing hospitality on a 'lavish and extensive scale'. These included the drawing room, morning room, breakfast room, dining room, library, study, all with commanding views of Pollacappul Lake and Kylemore Pass. Stairs to the rear of the saloon lead to the billiard room, ballroom and access to the domestic quarters.[11]

Gallery Hall or Saloon

Measuring about 29 ft. 6 in. by 19 ft., having a handsomely carved stone chimney piece with Connemara marble pillar jambs curb fender and ornamental stove. The walls of this hall are lined with oak, the floor is of polished oak parquetry, and surrounding the upper portion is an ornamental gallery with panelled soffit in herring-bone pattern, shaped corner and central posts connected by openwork balustrade with shields supporting an oak handrail, the whole lighted from the roof by an appropriately designed lantern with panelled border of herring-bone pattern. [12]

© Kylemore Abbey

Drawing Room

This room has an Exquisitely Carved Statuary Marble Chimneypiece, a grand example of sculpture, the massive jambs with female figures and the scroll-shaped frieze with finely executed female head, surrounded by a wreathing of floral design, the whole in high relief; the hearth is of inlaid marble; the ormolu mounted front to fireplace is flanked by china panels, having figures of cupids and dolphins in medallions; the dog stove has an ornamental back panel, and the curb fender is of marble in keeping with the chinmeypiece. The scheme of decoration is in pure white; the walls are lined in tapestry, with handsome floral design in panels, having a light blue border surrounded by white and gilt moulding, and the ceiling has a heavily moulded cornice in openwork pattern and floral design. [13]

© Kylemore Abbey

Library

An enriched cornice surrounds the ceiling, which is divided by deep mouldings with floral ornamentations into a number of shaped panels and three centrepieces. The walls are lined with cretonne, the prevailing colours being of red and blue and the design embracing peacocks and other birds; while under the bay window is a marble enclosure with lattice work iron panels screening hot water pipes. [14]

Ballroom

This grand chamber forms a great acquisition for the purposes of entertainment, being of ample proportions for dancing purposes, private theatrical, concerts &c., on a lavish scale . . . the arched ceiling is supported upon carved stone corbels, has protruding rafters and central lantern light, on the southern side is a carved black marble chimneypiece and curb fender, open fireplace with ornamental iron back and side panels, tiled hearth and dog stove; the room is also heated by hot water; and at the western end is a large mullioned window. [15]

Twenty-four flagstaffs were erected on the walls of the ballroom, along with several very fine oil paintings: 'one of Christ driving the money changers out of the temple and another of St Catherine of Siena, healing the sick'.[16]

At the top of the staircase on the walls of 'a wide gallery landing' hung a very handsome portrait of Margaret Henry. Several more paintings were hanging in the painting gallery over the saloon hall, including one of the assembled members of the Irish House of Commons at College Green.[17]

Courtesy of National Library of Ireland, Kylemore Collection 1

Ladies Bedroom

From the landing access was gained to 'thirty-three bed and dressing rooms (two fitted with baths), two other bath rooms, gun room, smoking or school room, work room, linen room, and a number of lavatories. The whole replete in every detail for comfort and convenience and arranged to suit the occupation of a family of distinction'.[18] The bedrooms were conveniently arranged in different wings; the Eastern Wing, Western Wing and, up another flight of stairs, the Venetian Wing was added later.

The Eastern Wing held the principal bedroom or 'Boudoir', measuring twenty-three feet by twenty-one feet, dressing rooms, bathroom and other bedrooms. And on a slightly lower level was the gun room. The Western Wing housed more bedrooms, bathrooms, dressing rooms and by a separate staircase a work room, linen room and access to the domestic quarters; butler's, cook's and housekeeper's bedrooms, servant's bathroom and w.c. Another door led to the roof giving access to the bell turret which housed the swing bell.

Billiard Room

A flight of stairs at the western end of the first floor corridor led to the Venetian Wing, which comprised the school room (or smoking room) and eight bedrooms; the 'very complete bachelors' quarters'. At the end of the corridor was the coal and turf store and a door to an outside stone staircase for domestic use. There was also a luggage lift from the ground floor to the first and a lift for domestic use to the work and linen rooms above the Western Wing.[19]

© Kylemore Abbey

27

Courtesy of National Library of Ireland, Kylemore Collection 41

Staff on Castle Steps

© Kylemore Abbey

Domestic Offices
Kylemore Book of Sale 1902

In the rear of the central portion of the building, accessible from the staff quarters below stairs, 'without interference with the principal rooms of the Castle, and approached by a stone staircase', was the servants' wing, consisting of four large bedrooms.

Outside on the roof, 'between the Venetian and Servants' bedroom wings', on a stone terrace reached by an outside stone staircase, there was a fish larder, 'fitted with slate shelves and water spray', a vegetable larder and a boiler house, with furnace and boiler for heating the Venetian and servants bedrooms. Coal for the boiler was raised to this height by a hand-powered crane.[20]

Below stairs, 'well shut-off from the principal portions' of the Castle, was the housekeeper's room, store room, servants' hall, lofty kitchen, cook's larder, scullery and still room. Opening on to a stone paved court yard with a glass roof and tradesmen's entrance was the meat larder, large coal cellar, lamp room, second larder, beer cellar, store room with two wine cellars and lamp cupboards and a boiler room. On the upper floors were men servants' w.c., service room communicating with the dining room and a butler's pantry, a plate room, brushing room, china and glass room.[21]

Near to the eastern end of the Castle stood a 'fully-equipped Turkish Bath, comprising white glazed brick lined Hot and Intermediate Rooms, communicating with the Shampooing Room, fitted with a white marble shampoo table, zinc bath, with mahogany enclosure, lavatory basin, shower and douche (all with hot and cold supplies), and urinal; Cooling and Dressing Room, with fitted lavatory basin, hot and cold supplies; Furnace Room and furnace for heating'. Connecting to the Turkish Bath was a lean-to Orchard House and a small rose house.[22]

The Castle boasted an unlimited supply of water conveyed through a six inch cast-iron pipe from Lough Touther, situated over 400 feet above the level of the Castle.

The long and steep descent of the water main provided high pressure to all levels of the Castle and branches were taken off to the gardens, stables and other parts of the estate. A large water tank with a corrugated iron roof, capable of holding about 12,000 gallons, was positioned above and to the rear of the Castle. This tank was also supplied by a second and 'never-failing water supply' from a strong spring on Mweelin. The entire building was heated throughout with hot-water coils and pipes.

© Kylemore Abbey

The Castle had its own fire brigade and an elaborate system of fire hydrants was put in place. Hydrants were also fitted near the steward's house, the post office and farm homestead. The brigade was staffed by volunteers from the estate workers and supervised by Henry's second son, Alexander, who was himself trained by the London Fire Brigade. Drills took place regularly and Alexander was extremely proud of their quick response time. According to Henry family folklore 'the only real fire they ever had was in their station house when all their gear was destroyed as they could not get at it to put the fire out!'[23]

© Kylemore Abbey

The engine was made by Shond, Mason & Co, London. 'The force pump [was] worked by a very handsome vertical steam-engine, mounted on a four wheeled carriage, carrying a large board bearing the following inscription in large letters:- Kylemore Fire Brigade'.[24]

At first the Castle was lit by gas, candles and oil. The gas was made at a small gas-works situated at Addergoole Farm. It was however proving difficult to produce gas of 'very great purity' from such a small plant and the effects of impure gas on books, pictures, furnishings and humans was becoming unacceptable. Later, in 1893, it was found that the water pressure from Lough Touther was sufficient to produce electricity and the engineers J.G. Howell of London, were hired to design and install a system suitable for Kylemore. A 'Girard' high pressure turbine by H.J.H. King was coupled to a dynamo 'running at 800 revolutions per minute' and housed in a small power house erected one hundred and twenty yards west of

© Kylemore Abbey

Kylemore Voluntary Fire Brigade

the Castle. An automatic regulator was fitted to reduce the water pressure to meet the requirements of the number of lights in use and the 'current was conveyed to the castle by copper conductors thickly insulated with bitumen and placed in a wooden trough filled in with melted bitumen, which renders the conductor quite impervious to water or damp'.[25]

Turbine & Dynamo

Inside the castle all the most important fittings, which had previously been used for gas and candles, were adapted and fitted with two hundred and seventy 'incandescent' lamps. A hot closet was installed in the serving room for keeping plates hot during meals. At either end of the terrace in front of the castle were fitted two 'arc lamps of 500-candle-power each, mounted on wrought iron standards upon the stone balustrade. These lamps [lit] most effectively the various approaches to the castle, and at night produce a pretty effect, shining upon the waters of the lake in front'. Electricity was also taken underground to the stables, post office and a photographic dark room, 'where an arc lamp is fixed for enlarging purposes'[26] . The entire system was installed between April and July 1893 at a cost of £2,000.[27] The gas had cost roughly £400 per annum to produce while the electricity was considerably cheaper costing just £10 per annum.

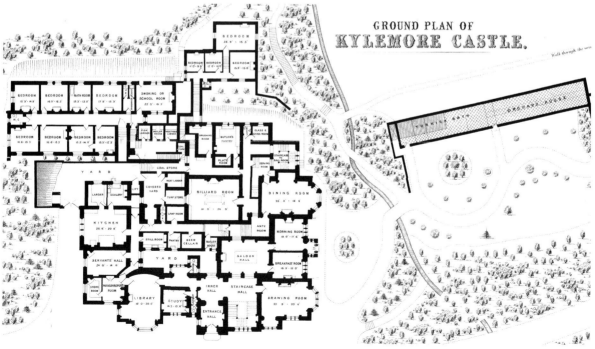

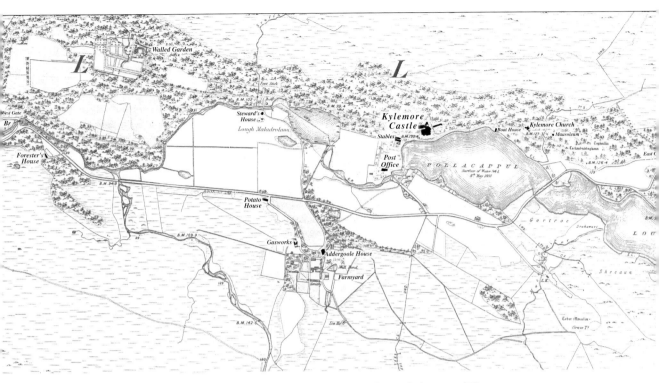

Ordnance Survey Map Sheet 23 1902

A short distance from the castle stood the stables and coach houses. The stables occupied two sides of a cobbled yard and could accommodate twelve horses. In 1878 there were twenty-nine horses on the estate, six of them were kept for farm work.[28] There were two coach houses, each capable of housing six full-sized carriages, as well as a two storey, three bed roomed, coachman's house. A little further south another two storey building housed a government post and telegraphs office and savings bank on the ground floor and a photographic dark room on the second floor, this could also be approached by a separate carriage drive from the public road. Letters and newspapers posted in London arrived at Kylemore at 9 o'clock on the following morning, seven days a week. MacAlister, as well as his usual duties as steward, also acted as postmaster for the district.

MacAlister's residence, the steward's house, was formerly the gate lodge for Addergoole House, situated on the west avenue close to Lough Maladrolaun and approached by a bridge over the Dawros river. The house contained four bedrooms, sitting room, kitchen and scullery with indoor plumbing. It had substantial outbuildings consisting of a fowl house, piggery and wash house, with two store rooms in the loft above. There was also a timber and corrugated iron turf shed and a w.c.

Courtesy of National Library of Ireland, NS 6697

Causeway dividing Lough Pollacappul in two.

Courtesy of National Library of Ireland, Kylemore Collection I

Italian Garden looking East

Courtesy of National Library of Ireland, NS 6701

Italian Garden looking West

At Henry's expense the road from Clifden to Westport, which ran right under the Castle, was re-routed in 1871 to the opposite side of Lough Pollacappul. The construction of a causeway and an iron bridge on stone piers and abutments, carried the new road over the lake to the townland of Addergoole, where it continued its journey west, rejoining the original road south of Tullywee Bridge. The construction of the causeway and bridge lead to the division of Lough Pollacappul, giving rise to the misapprehension that there were three lakes, with the 'new' lake commonly referred to as Middle Lake.

The old road then became the principal avenue through the estate, it was two miles long and had an entrance gate at each end. From the Eastern Gate on the shore of Kylemore Lough the avenue passed through 'the lower portion of a beautiful hanging wood', and along the northern shore of Lough Pollacappul where it divided in two, 'the upper road leading to a spacious terraced carriage sweep in front of the Castle, supported by a massive embayed stone wall with castellated parapet, at the foot of which is the lower road separated by a fine fuchsia hedge from the waters of Pollacappul Lough'. The upper portion continued its journey to the Western Gate close to Tullywee Bridge, passed along the shore of Lough Maladrolaun and 'crossing at intervals small mountain streams forming pretty water-falls in their precipitous descent to the Lough',[29] The lower portion ran south past the stables and Italian Gardens to the post office.

The entire avenue was bordered by an endless variety of native and imported trees and shrubs. Some planting had taken place earlier under the ownership of Wilberforce but this was as nothing when compared with that embarked on by Henry. In the immediate vicinity of the Castle, both on the lower ground and on the slope of the mountain, large scale planting was carried out converting the old oak and birch woods into 'extensive and richly adorned pleasure grounds'. The extent of the plantation was considerable, one source putting the figure at something like 300,000 trees a year, over several years.[30] The trees were planted for shelter and ornamentation. The plantation cost a substantial sum of money and would take many years to mature but would in time add greatly to the appearance of the Castle and to the pleasure of its occupants.

Among the trees planted for shelter were oak, ash and sycamore. Closer to the avenue, offering both shelter and ornamentation were macrocarpa, pine, beech, chestnut, elm, alder, lime, hawthorn and many others. Among the shrubs *Rhododendron ponticum*, pampas grass and New Zealand flax seemed to thrive the best. Close to the shore of Lough Maladrolaun, bog land was drained and planted with a variety of conifers offering an attractive approach to the walled garden one mile from the Castle. Exposure to the salt-laden breeze sweeping in from the Atlantic brought many a disappointment for the head gardener and his staff as they struggled to established the pinetum. *The Journal of the Royal Horticultural Society of England*, reporting on the conifer conference held in Chiswick in October 1891, published the following remarks by William Farmer, a gardener at Kylemore:

> The greatest evil which Conifers have to contend with in the west of Connemara is the strong salt-laden breeze which sweeps in from the Atlantic, and where it hits them with its full force, comparatively few of them thrive well under it. By far the best of all the species of Conifers growing here for withstanding the salt breeze are *Pinus insignis* and *Cupressus macrocarpa*, which seem to grow with increased vigour under its influence, and have far out-stripped all other Conifers in their growth. Both are perfectly hardy here, and the saline-laden gales which we so often experience have no injurious effect on these two valuable trees. *Abies polita* is among the best of the Spruces for standing the salt breeze. Where they are well sheltered from the maritime gales, most of the newer Conifers thrive well in Connemara.[31]

For the enjoyment of the family and visiting friends early footpaths, bridle paths and the old roads leading to Letterfrack and Currywongaun were adapted and new paths laid out so as to offer attractive walks through thick plantations and along the margins of Loughs Kylemore, Pollacappul and Maladrolaun. Local tradition has it that at one time Henry tried to have the village of Currywongaun re-located to allow for a more attractive approach

Currywongaun village   © Kylemore Abbey

At the western end of the Pleasure Grounds and approached by a road branching off the principal Carriage Drive to the
Castle are the

.. WALLED-IN ..

FLOWER & KITCHEN GARDENS

OF ABOUT

8½ Acres in Extent

Intersected by a Broad Gravelled Walk or Drive having at the eastern and western ends massive ornamental arched
Entrance Gates.

THE FLOWER GARDEN has been tastefully laid out and includes two lovely grass slopes, one either side of the
Central Broad Walk. These are arranged with **geometrically designed borders and beds**
interspersed with clumps of Pampas, Aralia Chinensis, Prunus Pissardii and other specimens. On
the higher ground on the South Side is an **embayed seat shelter** formed by well trimmed Escallonia
Macrantha, while on the opposite or northern side the higher ground is crowned by a

.. MAGNIFICENT RANGE ..

OF

Ornamental Glass Houses

So arranged as to secure the utmost amount of sunshine. The principal of these have shaped span roofs and
communicate one with another, forming a very handsome and complete set of show houses.

They comprise, starting at the western end—

VINERY, about 32ft. long, planted with young and thriving Muscat Vines;
FERNERY, about 31ft. long, prettily arranged with ornamental rock work;
CONSERVATORY or Entrance Corridor leading to
BANANA HOUSE, about 60ft. by 23ft., planted with fine specimen Banana Trees bearing excellent fruit;
CONSERVATORY or communicating Corridor leading to
TROPICAL HOUSE or Central Conservatory, about 61ft. by 18ft., planted with New Zealand Ferns, Palms,
Camellias, Roses, &c.;
CONSERVATORY or communicating Corridor leading to
FIG HOUSE, about 24ft. by 23ft., planted with some well-grown Fig Trees;
PALM HOUSE, about 34ft. 6in. by 23ft., opening to
CONSERVATORY or Entrance Corridor, leading to
FERNERY, about 31ft. long, arranged with ornamental rock work; and
VINERY, about 32ft. long, with well-grown Black Hamboro' and Madresfield Court Vines.

In the rear of the above range are

SOME FURTHER USEFUL GLASS HOUSES

CONSISTING OF

LEAN-TO VINERY, about 82ft. long and planted with Vines in variety;
LEAN-TO PEACH HOUSE, about 96ft. long, well stocked with thriving Peach Trees;
LEAN-TO VINERY, about 65ft. 6in. long, fully planted;
SPAN-ROOFED GREENHOUSE, about 26ft. long;
Ditto   **TOMATO HOUSE**, about 26ft. long;
Ditto   **NECTARINE HOUSE**, about 26ft. long and planted with thriving Trees; and
Ditto   **MELON HOUSE**, about 26ft. long.

Kylemore Book of Sale 1902   © Kylemore Abbey

---

to the beach at Mullaghglass, but the tenants created such opposition that he was forced to abandon the idea.

A mile to the west and approached by a road branching off the main avenue, the flower and kitchen garden was under construction at the same time as the Castle. Two houses, only one of which was occupied, and some out buildings were pulled down to make way for the gardens. The tenant, Anthony Coyne, was given financial compensation and a much better farm at Shanaveag. Horticulturists and garden enthusiasts watched with interest Henry's attempts at 'gardening on a gigantic scale' where innovative ideas were in practice and where 'every modern improvement [was] embraced' in its construction.[32]

The garden was built on a south slope at the foot of Duchruach mountain and was reputed to be 'a regular sun trap'. The site was carefully chosen. Like the Castle, its dramatic setting, backing into the mountain and facing the Diamond, was awe inspiring, but its principal advantages were horticultural. This was the hottest and brightest spot in the grounds. The natural fall of the land and the underlying esker gravel offered free drainage and a mountain stream from Lough Toucher brought water and decoration. The garden covered eight and a half acres, six of which were enclosed by a brick and stone wall, with two ornamental arched entrance gates in the eastern and western walls. Inside the garden the old road was converted into a broad gravelled walk or drive which ran from one gate to the other. The mountain stream divided the garden into two distinct areas; the flower garden and the kitchen garden. The flower garden consisted of two gentle grass slopes on either side of the walk with geometrically designed flower beds interspersed with pampas, *Gunnera manicata* and other specimens.

Courtesy of National Library of Ireland, Kylemore Collection

Walled Garden looking North,
circa 1910

Courtesy of National Library of Ireland, Kylemore Collection III

Walled Garden looking South,
circa 1880

Early views of the glasshouses.

Courtesy of Garry Wynne, Castlebar ©

Glasshouse interior.

© Kylemore Abbey

Crowning the northern slope was an extensive range of elaborate wooden-framed glasshouses, or hothouses, designed by Cranston's of Birmingham and laid out by the head gardener, James Garnier. The twenty-one glasshouses were arranged around a flower parterre, with a floral arch in the centre. The main range was built in the Gothic style and formed three sides of a rectangle. These were interconnecting and could be walked through from end to end: 'admitting their use as a Large Winter Garden'. There were additional houses on each side and immediately behind the main building. The glasshouses were filled with exotic fruits and plants, principally for domestic consumption, but were also used for experimental purposes: the tropical house contained a number of rare plants used chiefly for medical purposes and the banana house included plants of commerce. The houses were heated by hot-water circulation provided by three saddle boilers. Chambers to carry the hot-water pipes, five thousand feet in extent, were preconstructed under the houses. One of the boilers, situated outside the east wall, straddled a limekiln and was heated by burning limestone and coal: three-fourths of limestone to one-fourth of coal, this in turn produced lime for the gardens and the land reclamation works going on throughout the estate.[33] Seventy barrels of lime were produced each week and there was a saving of £200 per annum in the fuel bill.[34] The two other boilers were situated under the west vinery where there was also storage for about one hundred and fifty tons of coal.[35]

The garden contained a number of two storey stores and workshops, including a stable, coach house and accommodation for six garden boys:

> Mushroom house, with loft over; pot store, with fruit room over; tool house and store room; potting shed; work shop; paint store; young mens bothy, containing three bed rooms and kitchen, affording accommodation for six; stable and coach-house; lean-to shed.[36]

The kitchen garden provided all the culinary needs of the castle and was screened from the main drive by a double herbaceous border, backed by fuchsia and escallonia hedges. A variety of apple, pear, cherry, fig and plum trees were trained along the high walls, while standard apple, pear, damson and plum trees, and all kinds of bush fruits, stood in the garden itself. Beyond the southern and western walls was an outer vegetable garden, partly walled and sheltered by alder and sycamore screening hedges. This also acted as a nursery for young trees.[37]

The head gardener's house stood close to the glasshouses. It was an attractive building consisting of three bedrooms, two sitting rooms, hall, kitchen, pantry and a small yard with turf store and outside toilet. The first gardener to live here was James Garnier, who was responsible for the lay out and early development of the garden, and the last under Henry was William Comfort.[38]

© Kylemore Abbey

Head Gardner's House

Henry was proud of his gardens and used them to educate as well as entertain, to this end visitors were always welcome and encouraged to sign a visitors book. Even before work on the garden was complete intrepid travellers were calling and some were fortunate enough to be given a guided tour by the head gardener himself. The *Irish Builder* wrote in May 1872 that 'everyone who has witnessed Mr Mitchell Henry's gardening experiments at the Pass of Kylemore, both English visitors and native ones, are agreed that the arrangements are admirable; and the beauty of the flower beds, with the rich emerald green of the grass, invest the whole scene with an inexpressible charm'. However, on a more cautionary note it added, 'we trust that the wild gales of the Atlantic will not succeed in injuring the beauty of this oasis in the Wilds of Connemara'.[39] Garnier himself told the correspondent from the *Farmers Gezette* that he too dreaded the heavy gales which sometimes swept through the valley, and left so much damage in their wake.[40] To counteract their effect Henry was in the process of planting large numbers of trees on the high ground surrounding the garden.[41]

© Kylemore Abbey

Workman replacing glass

At Addergoole the farm buildings were improved and extended, new buildings were added and new innovative agricultural practices introduced. In time Addergoole Farm ceased to exist and it became known as Model Home Farm and it was hoped that here Henry would show 'the agriculturist in his neighbourhood the perfection of farming arrangements, with the latest and most economical improvements'.[42]

Addrigoole House, no longer needed as a private residence, was converted to a more functional building. The high ceilings were lowered and a second floor was added, providing eight bedrooms to accommodate the dairy and laundry maids. On the ground floor a laundry and dairy were installed. The laundry included a 'lofty Ironing and Mangling Room, with door communicating with adjoining Wash-house, fitted with a range of five wooden washing troughs, each with hot and cold water supplies'. Along a passage there was a second wash-house, 'with fitted wooden trough', with hot and cold water. There was also a 'fully-equipped hot air Drying Chamber, fitted with four sliding horses', as well as a store and larder.

The dairy consisted of a 'spacious Washing and Churning Room, having an open range, sink (hot and cold water supplies); and Cooling Room, with hot water pipes to keep an even temperature during winter'. There was also a large kitchen, with an open range, dresser and sink. Another large room was fitted with a mantel and stove and on the outside a furnace and turf shed.[43]

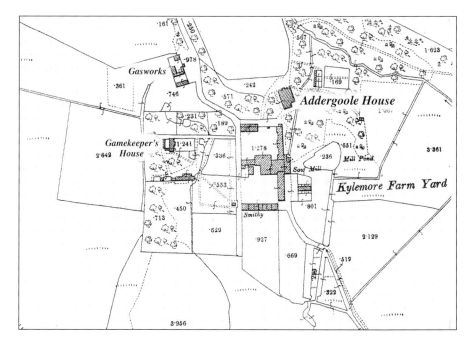

Map of Addergoole farm buildings.
Henry's Model Home Farm

Eastwood, the previous owner, had diverted a small river, *Shannon na Glaoch*, and reclaimed sixty acres of the old riverbed. Diverting the river gave a fall of from eleven to fourteen feet and, under Henry, this was secured by a mill dam and utilised by a turbine wheel of twenty-four horse power giving sufficient power to work a circular saw, a thrasher and other farm tools.[44] Two hours water-power was available at the turbine, after which the sluices were closed and the pond was allowed refill and the entire operation could then recommence.[45] Water storage was increased using the simple expedient of turf harvesting. Sections of the bog adjacent to the pond were cut providing large bog-hole which acted as supplementary water holding tanks improving the supply of water to the mill pond.[46] The turbine may well have been constructed to the design of Samuel U. Roberts who had already developed the use of turbines for pumping out sections of riverbeds prior to deepening. Roberts had also installed large diameter water-wheels to power the Galway City Waterworks and had designed, and installed, the most significant water-wheel constructed in Ireland during the 19th century.[47] The turbine at Addergoole was also used in experiments to compress peat for fuel, but these proved unsuccessful.[48]

Among the farm buildings already in place when Henry purchased Addergoole was a large barn built in the shape of a cross, sixty feet long in each direction. The stones used in its construction, and in the construction of other farm buildings erected by Eastwood, came from the ruins of a deserted village. The rest of the stones were used to fill up the bed of the river Eastwood diverted, 'and to form the bank of the new cut'.[49] Henry retained many of Eastwood's buildings and added new ones. The farm buildings were arranged 'so as to enclose two large yards, the principal entrance to which is through a pair of iron railed gates under a stone archway, surmounted by a bell' and comprised:

> stone built and slated Boiling House; Calf Shed with three boxes; Cow House for 23, paved throughout and having a feeding gangway with fitted water troughs and water supply to each; Fodder Store, with paved floor and loft over, and Two Rooms for Cowman over Calf House; Paved Machine House for root and corn mills with loft over and door opening to adjoining large Root and Fodder Storage; Corn Store, with range of three large iron grain rooms; Large stone built and corrugated iron roofed Barn, with concreted floor and four pairs of sliding doors; Second Four-bay Barn, with thrashing floor in one bay; Two Cattle Sheds, fitted with mangers; Lean-to Fitting Shed for 22 Bullocks, with troughs and water laid on to each; cobble paved Stable of 3 Stalls, Harness Room, stone paved, and Second Stable of 3 Stalls, with loft over the Whole; Turf Store, Two Loose Boxes and old boiler house; Eight-Bay Cart Shed, with iron column supports outside

the yard wall; and detached is a range of Eight Stone and Slated Piggeries, each with small yard opening to bigger yards adjoining and gangway down the centre of building.[50]

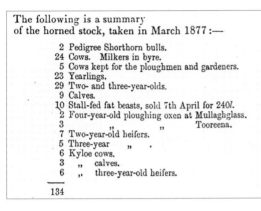

The following is a summary of the horned stock, taken in March 1877:—

2 Pedigree Shorthorn bulls.
24 Cows. Milkers in byre.
5 Cows kept for the ploughmen and gardeners.
23 Yearlings.
29 Two- and three-year-olds.
9 Calves.
10 Stall-fed fat beasts, sold 7th April for 240*l*.
2 Four-year-old ploughing oxen at Mullaghglass.
3   ,,   ,,   Tooreena.
7 Two-year-old heifers.
5 Three-year   ,, .
6 Kyloe cows.
3   ,,   calves.
6   ,,   three-year-old heifers.
———
134

Journal of the Royal Agricultural Society of England 1878

As well as the livestock shown here there was also twenty pigs, three breeding flocks of black-faced sheep and 'the total head of sheep was usually about 1,000'.[51]

The estate workshops were built of stone, with corrugated iron roofs and concreted floors and included the following: 'a Carpenter's shop, with fireplace and store loft over; Men's Mess Room, with fireplace; Store Room and Plumber's Shop, with fireplace and grain loft over the whole; Yardman's Bothy of Two Rooms and Kitchen; Large Cart Lodge, enclosed by pair of sliding doors; Smithy, with forge; Wheelwright's Shop, with lumber store adjoining; paint store'.[52]

Near to the farm buildings stood a detached, single story, gamekeeper's house with a yard and garden. Adjacent to the house was a 'pigeon house with turf sheds under, incubator house, boiler house, two fowl houses and enclosed yards, corn store, poultry house and large enclosed fowl run with small stream passing through same, plucking house, two duck houses and boys' bothy. Also a small duck pond supplied by a stream; and a detached stone-built game and meat larder'. A short distance from these was a 'modern cement-faced and corrugated iron-roofed dog kennels, in three divisions, with enclosed yards and water laid on in each, also another stone and felted poultry house'.[53]

A little to the south the building housing an Edmondson's gas works, which manufactured the gas for the Castle, was surrounded by a yard, two sheds and a man's bothy. Closer to the road three stone-built cottages were erected for the forester, ploughman and painter.

Chapter 3

Improvement and Advancement

The Kylemore Estate, like the rest of Connemara, was made up of mountain, lakes and bog. In keeping with his policy of improvement and advancement, Henry began reclaiming bogland almost immediately. At first it was land close to the Castle and Addergoole Farm and his tenants were encouraged to follow suit. Kylemore Pass was, according to Henry, 'favourably suited' for reclamation as there was very little deep bog and there was an abundance of limestone in the locality for burning into lime for use as fertilizer. There were two limestone quarries on the Kylemore Estate, one near the walled garden and the second at the foot of Mweelin. A kiln was erected close to both quarries. The deepest bog was to be found on either side of the Dawros river, on higher ground the moorland was covered with a thin layer of peat resting on metamorphic rocks of mica schist and hornblend. However, experience would show that a considerable difference exists between the reclamation of both.[1]

The first land to be reclaimed by Henry was at Mweelin on the opposite side of the lake from the Castle. Here sheep-drains, or surface drains, were dug to reduce rot among the flock. The system of sheep-draining was introduced into the district by an 'Ayrshire man' and was done with a 'Scotch' spade, cutting a small open trench across the face of the hill. For this three men were needed: two to cut and one to hook out the sods, the turf was then laid on the lower side. The trench, measuring twenty inches deep, twenty inches wide at the top and nine inches at the bottom, was left open and had to be cleaned out every seven years. The system proved very successful and benefited not just the sheep and cattle but also the grouse, who in wet weather showed a preference for drained land. Further early attempts to drain twenty acres below the lime kiln and closer to Lough Pollacappul were to prove expensive but instructive.[2] This was very deep bog 'so thick that cuttings nine or ten feet in depth had been made for the chief drainage'. Earlier drains, cut

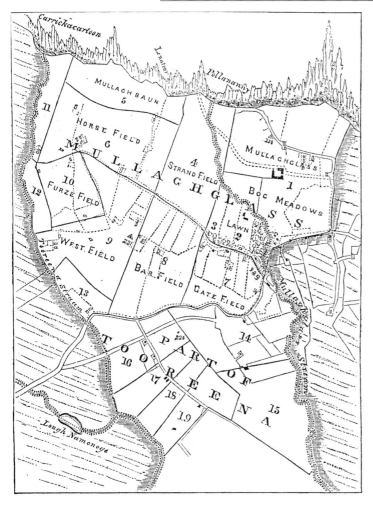

Plate 1 Map of Mullaghglass
*Journal of the Royal Agricultural Society
of England* 1878

in 1869, were set too far apart and had collapsed and new cutting was required. These minor drains were covered over but the principal drain was left open and used as a small canal for conveying peat and stones for the new road, or lime and other materials for the land.[3] The high cost here was deemed necessary for the completion of the Castle grounds but there was, in Henry's opinion, no profit to be had in the reclamation of bogs that were more than four feet in depth.

From the beginning Henry's reclamation works attracted a good deal of attention and praise in the press. For decades the possibility of draining Connemara's bogs and converting them into arable land had been discussed and debated. Henry took up the debate and, drawing on his scientific background, was anxious to investigate the matter further and test the commercial viability of large scale land reclamation in Connemara.

When, in 1874, the leases of two farms on his estate were given up Henry seized the opportunity and used the land for a more detailed study on land reclamation. As with all of Henry's endeavours at Kylemore the experiment in land reclamation would not only improve his estate but would be undertaken with the intention of benefiting society in general. The entire process of reclaiming the two farms was conducted on a scientific basis, detailed records and costings were kept and these were later examined by agricultural expert, Charles Gay Roberts, from the Royal Agricultural Society of England and by Professor Baldwin, Chief Inspector of the Government Agricultural Schools and Model Farms of Ireland. Professor Baldwin praised the Kylemore works in his evidence to the Royal Commission on Agricultural, set up by the Government in 1879 to enquire into agriculture and land usage in Ireland.

The two farms in question were situated in the townlands of Tooreena and Mullaghglass. Tooreena covered 736 acres, 103 acres of which carried nine cottages and was divided up among the tenants [numbers 11 to 19 on Plate No 1]. The remainder consisted of 633 acres of grazing land, 'one-half a nearly level flat of deepish bog running alongside the river, the other half moor heath, which with difficulty supported a few sheep and cattle. There [had] never been any buildings on this land, nor had a spade ever been put into it; and the tenant, being unable to pay his rent of £15 a year . . . was glad to give it up for a moderate consideration'. Henry divided this farm in two, 373 acres [number 28 on Plate No 2], consisting chiefly of deep bog, was sheep-drained and portions of this would be reclaimed later. The rest, 260 acres [numbers 20 to 27 on Plate No 2] was gradually reclaimed and was to become Greenmount Farm. In 1874 a cottage and stable, for a pair of horses and a pair of oxen, was built, but this in time was enlarged and more sheds for livestock were added. The work of fencing the farm and reclaiming the land began in 1874 and by 1877 a total of £1,619.10s.7d had been spent on wages alone.[4]

The farm at Mullaghglass, adjacent to Tooreena, covered 240 acres. In early times Mullaghglass was a village or *baile* with a cabin standing on every strip of land. But the village was depopulated by the Great Famine and 'twice afterwards it was repeopled, but the new comers were again driven away by failure of their crops'.[5] When Rev Wilberforce purchased the property in the 1850s 'he erected thirty cottages of stone and larch timber, at an average cost of £17 each', on what was the best land on the eastern portion of the

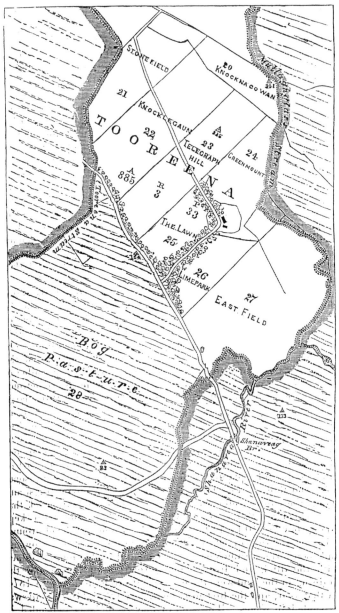

Plate No. 2 Map of Tooreena
Journal of the Royal Agricultural Society of England 1878

Mullaghglass House

© Kylemore Abbey

townland, and gave each tenant a strip of land. The remainder [Numbers 1 to 10 on Plate 1] was leased to a grazier. Wilberforce later erected a house and farm buildings on this land, Mullaghglass House, at a cost of £800. In 1874 there were still twenty-seven tenants in the houses erected by Wilberforce but the grazing farm had not been cultivated or improved.[6] Improvements on this townland were carried out jointly by Henry and the tenants and the benefits were felt by both.

Over the following three years as work was underway large numbers were employed daily on the various stages of reclaiming the land. According to Roberts, in May 1877 the average number of day labourers at Kylemore was two hundred and forty. Over a twenty-seven month period, between September 1875 and December 1877, the combined total for wages on both farms came to over £1,980. As soon as work was completed on their own holdings in early April the tenants of the estate, and others from the neighbourhood, came to work at the reclamations where boys were paid 5s and 6s per week, ordinary labourers earned 9s, and the 'gaffers' or foremen 12s to 15s. Girls earned 9d per day tending the turnip fields.[7]

An abstract of the amount spent in just two years on farm labour on both farms *Journal of the Royal Agricultural Society of England* 1878

ABSTRACT OF FARM LABOUR.					
Three Months ending	Mullaghglass, Nos. 1 to 10.			Tooreena, Nos. 20 to 28.	
	£	s.	d.	£	s.	d.
1875 31st December ..	55	19	4	97	12	1½
1876 1st April	73	6	7	72	16	4½
,, 1st July	76	7	5	159	13	5
,, 30th September ..	118	10	9½	171	15	4½
,, 30th December ..	81	5	10	121	3	10½
1877 31st March	82	13	6	79	3	9
,, 30th June	101	18	7	174	9	0½
,, 29th September ..	140	2	11	166	19	3½
,, 29th December ..	132	12	9	74	1	4
Total 27 months ..	862	17	8½	1117	14	7

The various stages of the procedure were explained in Robertson's paper to the Royal Agricultural Society. A principal drain was cut right through the bog to the gravel, next the secondary drains were cut, also down to the gravel, and these were supplemented by sheep-drains: about twenty inches deep and twenty inches wide on top,

	£	s.
2 ploughs (Gray's), at 3*l*. 10s. each	7	0
2 harrows	5	0
1 cart and harness	10	0
2 sets plough harness	3	0
4 sledges	2	0
American disc-harrow	4	0
Hay cutter, Richmond and Chandler's	2	0
Turnip pulper, Nicholson's	2	10

List of implements and utensils on Greenmount Farm on 1st February 1878

narrowing to six inches at the bottom. The bog then began to visibly shrink and became more solid. When the land was sufficiently dry the drains were cleared and deepened and a wedge-shaped sod, too wide to reach the bottom, rammed in 'so as to form a solid covering, with a water-channel of 6 inches deep below it'. The land was then dug by spade-labour or ploughed by oxen and given a dressing with lime. This not only broke up the soil but at the same time neutralised the acids and was referred to locally as 'boiling the bog'.[9]

By 1877 grass, oats, the finest potatoes, turnips and mangolds were grown on reclaimed land at Kylemore. Henry recommended farm-yard manure for potatoes and turnips and when this was not possible 'super phosphate and nitrate of soda' to be used. But he warned that the land would go back to bog if not kept under proper rotation; he recommended a five course rotation, 'namely, roots followed by oats, laid down with clover and grass seed, which remains for two years. After being broken up a second time, the land materially improves and becomes doubly valuable. I have no doubt that all bog-lands may be thus reclaimed, but it is up-hill work'.[10]

Henry himself admitted that there was nothing original in what he was doing at Kylemore, almost every existing acre of arable land to be found in Connemara had been previously reclaimed by some 'patient husband man who year by year with his spade reclaims a little bit from the mountain-side'. The significance of his reclamation works was that these were conducted on such a large scale and on a scientific bases. Part of the reclaimed land was then divided into two farms; Greenmount House Farm and Mullaghglass House Farm and these were retained by Henry himself.

Henry was pleased with the results of his experiment and referred to them frequently in the press and later in the House of Commons, holding them up as an example of what could be achieved when there was a willingness to expend a little capital with the hope of long term gain. Robertson however was slow to be convinced that the reclaimed land

There was also a three-horse thrashing-machine from the 'Reading Iron Works' this was moved from farm to farm as wanted.[8]

'would command such an increased rent as to insure a good return for the capital expended upon it'. Henry could, he argued, afford to finance further improvements on his home farm which would 'not be profitable for a mere tenant'. But he felt that the overall effect on the landscape should not be undervalued as 'anyone who has been long amongst dark peat-bogs and barren mountains, will understand how great an ornament in such a landscape is a patch of cultivated land'.[11]

Henry laid his success in land reclamation firmly at the feet of his steward, Archibald MacAlister, 'a county Antrim man, descended from one of the race of Highland Catholic Scotch settlers who have peopled the North of Ireland and added so much to its prosperity'. And what had been done 'economically and well would not have been done except for the prudence, patience, and thoughtful mind' of MacAlister.[12] The local men employed by MacAlister had gained their experience in similar work undertaken by Andrew Armstrong at Kylemore[13] and James Ellis at Letterfrack.[14] MacAlister told James H. Tuke during his inspection of the Estate in April 1880:

> To this day . . . I can tell Mr Ellliss boys; those he brought up are the best labourers I now have, and the best of the old men, too, all learned to work under him. He was the man for improving Ireland.[15]

Henry was later awarded the gold medal for drainage by the Royal Agricultural Society of Ireland and went on to drain and improve a further 4,000 acres,[16] all of which had been acquired without tenants. Henry felt it important that the fact be known that 'no tenant had been turned out to facilitate the reclamations, and care [had] been taken to leave the hearth-stones undisturbed, in accordance with local prejudices'.[17]

Kylemore estate was said to enjoy 'an indisputable reputation both for rod and gun' and since it was the fishing that first attracted Henry to Kylemore it seems only natural that this aspect of the estate should attract his attention as much, if not more, than any other. Fishing rights on the estate covered the Dawros and Culfin rivers and Loughs Anivan, Acreragh, Benchoona, Knappagh, Touther, Maladrolaun, Pollacappul and large portions of Loughs Fee, Muck and Kylemore. As previously mentioned Henry, no doubt influenced by developments taking place around him, began fish-farming at Kylemore almost as soon as he arrived. The 1850s and early 1860s were exciting innovative times for western fisheries. Experiments in artificial propagating of rivers with salmon, fish-farming and the cultivation of unproductive rivers were producing exciting results at the Galway Fishery, in Galway city, and Doohulla in Ballyconneely.[18] Henry's experiments too were proving successful. In a letter to the Commissioners of Irish Fisheries, dated 11 March 1899, he reported that in the year 1897–98, 42,000 eggs were laid down, just under ninety-eight percent of which hatched out and went into the lakes and river. Some years before he imported eggs from Rhine salmon and this had increased the weight of the salmon, but were in his opinion 'not very nice looking'. Eggs from Scotland were introduced over the years, but this was later discontinued for fear of introducing disease.[19] The fish hatcheries were situated on the southern side of Lough Pollacappul and was supplied by the high pressure water main from Lough Touther. And in 1902 it was described as consisting of a large enclosed pool, a second pool 'in six divisions and outlet to the Lough, stone and felted hatchery with special water spray and outlet to the open pools'. On the northern shores of Lough Pollacappul there was an ornamentally designed boat house with accommodation for several boats, along with water berths for two or three.[20]

The yield of salmon from the Dawros river could be as much as seven tons in a season. Salmon up to 20 lbs and white trout up to 5 lbs are not uncommon catches here. Lough Touther was very heavily stocked with brown trout and fish up to 5 lbs were regularly caught. Lough Fee and Lough Muck were famous for salmon and white trout fishing. Sea fishing, netting and trawling was also a source of revenue for the estate. According to the records, it was not uncommon for eighty to ninety large sole, hundreds of plaice, several turbot and numerous lobster to be caught in one single day's fishing. The estate also had its own oyster beds in Barnaderg Bay and at the mouth of the Dawros River.[21]

After initial failure in rearing pheasants, Henry eventually found success and the results were said to have been 'unusually large and brilliant in plumage', perhaps as a result of their feed which consisted of 'prickly comfrey, chopped and sprinkled with Indian meal'.[22] As well as pheasant the variety and extent of the estate offered a varied shoot and record bags of

Near to the Home Farm is a

Detached Gamekeeper's House

Cement faced and slated and having a good Piece of Garden Ground attached. It contains on one floor, Two Bed Rooms, Sitting Room, Kitchen and Pantry. Outside in Yard are tap for water supply, earth closet, &c.

Adjacent to this House are

SOME USEFUL OUTBUILDINGS

Comprising Pigeon House with Turf Sheds under, Incubator House, Boiler House, Two Fowl Houses and Enclosed Yards, Corn Store, Poultry House and large Enclosed Fowl Run with small stream passing through same, Plucking House, Two Duck Houses and Boys' Bothy. Also a small Duck Pond supplied by stream ; and a detached stone-built Game and Meat Larder.

At a short distance from the foregoing are

Modern Cement-faced and Corrugated Iron-roofed Dog Kennels

In three divisions, with Enclosed Yards and water laid on to each ; also another stone and felted Poultry House.

There are in addition

THREE STONE-BUILT COTTAGES

Suitably placed just off the main Letterfrack Road. These each have byre attached and Garden Ground and are occupied respectively by the Estate Forester, Ploughman and Painter.

At the foot of Mweelin Hill there is

A Lime Kiln and an unlimited supply of Limestone

Which is also used in connection with the heating of the glasshouses as previously described. Near this Kiln there is a Store Shed.

The whole of the foregoing Buildings and Lands, together with some few Plantations, &c., the entire Rights of Angling and Sporting over the Estate, form the necessary adjuncts for the full enjoyment and complete occupation of Kylemore Castle, and it is not too much to say that it would be difficult to surpass or even to equal such a replete and well-ordered Country Seat.

© Kylemore Abbey

Kylemore Book of Sale 1902

grouse, snipe, woodcock, wild duck, golden plover, hares, rabbits, partridge, wood pigeon, curlew and widgeon, were recorded by the Henry family and their many visitors to Kylemore Castle during forty years of occupancy.[23]

The Henrys did not lack for suitable social contact in their remote home in the West. Fishing was the great pull of the area and there were already renowned fisheries established at Ballynahinch, Doonloughan and Delphi. Just across Kylemore Lake Lord Ardilaun, great-grandson of Arthur Guinness, had a fishing lodge. One year after the completion of Kylemore Castle, Richard Berridge, a London brewer, purchased Ballynahinch Castle (1872). Around the corner at Lough Fee was Illaunroe (Oilean Rua) the lodge of Dr William Wilde, a surgeon, writer and antiquarian. Dr Wilde was the father of Oscar Wilde. Further north on the edge of Killary was Captain Thomson of Salruck and at Delphi Lodge, Captain Houston held over 50,000 acres of mountain pasture as well as a renowned fishery.[24] Ballynakill Harbour was a popular place for yachting and, in the Summer season, Andrew Armstrong's Kylemore House Hotel was a favourite among Irish and English anglers and Armstrong himself was a personal friend of the Henrys.

However, although living the life of a wealthy landowner and gentleman farmer, Henry was conscious that the life of privilege was enjoyed by only a few and the reality of life for his tenants and their neighbours was very different indeed. And in the years that followed the construction of Kylemore Castle he would do all that he could through example and public service to improve the lot of those less fortunate than himself.

Henry's early years at Kylemore brought him into contact with Connemara's recurring problems: religious conflict and starvation. Since the Great Famine the division between the people and the landlord class had widened and soon Henry would learn that one of the principal causes of this division was the activities of the Irish Church Mission To Roman Catholics. The presence of this Society in Connemara, and its aggressive proselytising activities, brought sectarianism and bigotry to the fore, causing conflict and division within the community and within many individual families.

The aim of the Irish Church Mission was to convert the Roman Catholics of Connemara to the Protestant faith. The Society had gone from strength to strength in the fifteen years since its foundation in 1847 and by the time Henry arrived in Connemara it boasted several schools and churches in the district: food and clothing were offered to the children who attended the schools and employment to their parents conditional on attendance at church on Sunday. Its principal mover in England was its founder Rev. Alexander Dallas, the Rector of Wanston in Hamshire, while in Connemara it was championed by Rev. Hyacinth D'Arcy, son of John D'Arcy the founder of Clifden, and former owner of Clifden Castle.

The local press at the time was full of the Society's campaign and its success in the mission fields of Connemara. It was a popular cause among the local landed gentry and an active social scene had grown up around the Society's activities. The Connemara Mission was regularly visited by influential churchmen from England and Ireland, many of whom assisted the mission with funds raised in their home parishes. The arrival and reception of such dignitaries was fully reported in the press of the day and listed among the organisers and supporters were almost all of the local landlords and chief employers of the locality. For many of the poor the inducements offered by the Society proved too tempting to reject, but acceptance also meant being ostracized by one's family and neighbours and being caught up in a bitter conflict which raged for many years between the clergy of both churches.

Henry was himself a practising member of the Church of England, however, his brother Alexander was a Roman Catholic Jesuit priest. It is said that it was to facilitate Alexander, during his visits to Kylemore Castle, and the tenants, that Henry built the Catholic Church at Creeragh. Henry never discriminated on the grounds of religion. In contrast to neighbouring landlords Henry respected and accommodated the religious traditions of his workers; all he asked in return was that they grant him the same courtesy. He was conscious of the lack of patronage offered by the landed families to local activities, other than those associated with the Society, and so he tried to redress this by participating himself whenever possible. The annual Ball and supper, hosted by the Henrys at Kylemore, did contribute, according to the press, to 'create good will and kind feeling amongst all classes in Connemara'. At one such Ball, held on the last day in February 1870, a group of about '200 of the tenants and workmen, mixing with the neighbouring landlords and gentry, enjoyed themselves through the hall and rooms of this noble mansion'. The *Galway Express* reported that the table was 'most tastefully ornamented with rare and matchless plants out of the renowned Kylemore

CRICKET IN CONNEMARA.

CLIFDEN v. KYLEMORE (12 A-SIDE).

This match came off on the 4th instant at Kylemore Castle, and resulted in a victory for the Clifden C. C., with five wickets to go down. The scoring on both sides was rather small, in consequence of the damp nature of the ground, and the excellent bowling of Mr St George Robinson for Clifden, and the Rev J. P. Mahaffy for Kylemore. Subjoined is the score:—

KYLEMORE.

	1st Inns.		2nd Inns.
T Carter l b w, b Concanon	2	hit w b Robinson	0
G Monfries b St Geo Robinson	5	b Robinson	3
L Garnier b St Geo Robinson	0	c Concanon b Robinson	0
Rev J P Mahaffy c Woole b Concanon	0	c Mecredy b Cotterill	8
J Garnier not out	2	not out	0
J T Maher b Concanon	3	b Cotterill	10
J Keogh run out	0	b Concanon	0
C Priest b Robinson	0	b Concanon	0
J Nevin, jun. b Robinson	0	b Robinson	0
A Corley b Robinson	0	b Robinson	0
J Nevin, sen. b Robinson	0	run out	1
J Graham run out	0	b Robinson	0
Byes	7	b, 4; w, 4;	8
Total	19	Total	30

CLIFDEN.

	1st Inns.		2nd Inns.
J Borris run out	0	run out	0
P C Gorham b Mahaffy	3	b Priest	2
J B Concanon b Monfries b Mahaffy	8	not out	11
E L Walker run out	1	c Maher b Priest	0
H Robinson b Priest	0	b Priest	0
R Mecredy l b w Mahaffy	5	c Maher b Mahaffy	2
St Geo. Robinson b Maher b Mahaffy	1	not out	8
F Cotterill b Mahaffy	0		
J J Gorham c Garnier b Mahaffy	0		
P J Prendergast c Garnier b Mahaffy	0		
J J D'Arcy run out	1		
M Toole not out	4	c Priest b Mahaffy	0
Byes, l; w, 4	5	b, 1; w, 4;	5
Total	24	Total for 6 wkts	28

Cricket Match at Kylemore
Galway Express, 9 September 1871

gardens'. Music was provided by the 'old Kylemore band' and Herr Ulla and his assistant from Galway. The party was still in full swing at sunrise the next morning:

> The visitors, guests, and youthful members of the Kylemore family enjoyed themselves thoroughly along with the people; and when the morning sun peeped over "Maam Turk", the early riser caught this gay throng engaging themselves with reels and jigs, while the early March Morning soon reminded them that there was other work to do. The company separated in the most orderly manner, giving three cheers for Mr and Mrs Henry, and praying God speed the work at Kylemore Castle.[25]

The differences between Henry and neighbouring landlords was not confined to religious tolerance and just treatment of his labourers and tenants; politically too they were divided. This would have become increasingly obvious when reports of his political campaigns in England reached the press and his views on denominational education and the disestablishment of the Church of Ireland became clear.

Chapter 4
English Political Career

Throughout his political career Henry espoused the Liberal creed but it was not until his 1885 campaign in Glasgow that he went forward as a Liberal candidate. His political career spanned twenty years, beginning in England in 1865 with an unsuccessful attempt in the general election of that year. This was followed by two further failures in 1867 and 1868. He eventually succeeded in the Galway by-election of 1871 and continued to represent that county for the next fourteen years. He represented Glasgow in 1885, but failed to win the Liberal nomination for that constituency in the general election of 1886.

At the outset it was his personal ambition to represent his hometown, Manchester, but somehow he never succeeded in winning the support and backing of the Manchester Liberals. He knew the leading members of the party intimately and was in correspondence with Richard Cobden M.P., and George Wilson, men with considerable influence among the Liberals in that town and friends and colleagues of his late father.

In July 1864, when it was expected that parliament would be dissolved any day, Henry wrote to Wilson, president of the newly formed National Reform Union:[1] 'it is time to be up and doing'. The call at the time was for extending the franchise, a secret ballot and a revision of the constituencies. Wilson was anxious to know Henry's mind on such matters. Henry wrote that he was in favour of extending the franchise while not in favour of the secret ballot; he was, however, prepared to accept that 'personal views must give way to great party interests'.[2]

Not receiving any words of encouragement in return, Henry wrote again in the same month: 'At present there is nothing for it but to wait, which I shall do with patience. As the time approaches I may perhaps hear of some constituency willing to make a trial of my services, and any hints or information you may favour me with in this direction will be very acceptable'.[3]

However, it would seem the Manchester Liberals were slow to be convinced and in his eagerness to be 'up and doing', Henry turned elsewhere. On the 1 November at a public meeting in the Town Hall of Woodstock, Oxfordshire, he declared himself for that Borough. His campaign literature described him as 'one who will ever act in accordance with the principles of the great Liberal party expressed in the words "The greatest happiness for the greatest number"'.[4] Seven months later in June 1865, he received an offer of support from Wilson to run for South Lancashire, his father's old seat. But by then Henry had been running a campaign and, being committed to Woodstock, felt honour bound to refuse. Painfully aware that he was walking away from what would seem to be sure victory and a safe seat for the future, he wrote to Wilson:

> It is, as you will well suppose, a sad disappointment to me not to be able to take my chance for South Lancashire, but I could not in honour and good faith desert this constituency. I am painfully aware that such an opportunity will probably never again be presented to me, but if I would hold up my head in future as an honest man, I must accept the sacrifice and cast my lot for the present with this small and oppressed Borough. With renewed thanks and kind regards to those who have thought me worthy of their consideration on this occasion.[5]

This was indicative of how Henry would behave in his future political career. Having taken the honourable stance he would stay true to his convictions even when it carried great personal loss.

The Liberals, under the direction of George Wilson, then offered their support to William Gladstone. Gladstone had been a member of parliament for over thirty years and was leader of the government in the House of Commons. He had declared himself in favour of extending the franchise and had lost his seat for Oxford University as a result of his criticism of the position of the Anglican Church in Ireland. In the election that followed Henry was unsuccessful in Woodstock and Gladstone was returned for South Lancashire.

Two years later Henry failed again, this time it was the Manchester by-election in November 1867, in which he attracted just 643 votes.[6] It was a year of heightened tensions between the people of England and Ireland. March 1867 saw a failed Rising by the Fenians which was followed in September by the arrest of two Fenian leaders in Manchester. The two men were later rescued by sympathisers. However, during the rescue a policeman was killed and five persons arrested; three of the five, although pleading their innocence, were later hanged. The execution of the "Manchester Martyrs" brought about a wave of anti-English feeling in Ireland. Likewise, the killing of a policeman and over twenty innocent people, when an attempt to rescue a Fenian from Clerkenwell prison in London went badly wrong, contributed to anti-Irish feelings in England. Nevertheless the events of that year caused Gladstone to look for ways of righting the injustices proclaimed by the Irish and he eventually brought down the government on the issue of the disestablishment of the Church in Ireland, resulting in a general election in 1868.

During the year a new Reform Bill had been passed and all urban house-holders were now entitled to vote. The number of registered voters in Manchester had grown from 21,878 to 48,246.[7] The constituencies too had been revised: Manchester was given an extra seat and South Lancashire was divided into South-Western Division and South-Eastern Division. Gladstone went forward in the South-Western Division. Henry's brother, John Snowdon Henry, went forward, surprisingly enough, as a Conservative in the South-Eastern Division.

Political parties in Britain had recently begun forming local committees to select candidates. When the Liberals named their three candidates for Manchester Henry was not among them. Henry refused to be dissuaded. He made public his objection to the selection of candidates by 'a small committee sitting round a green table'[8] and announced his intention to stand as an Independent Liberal to vindicate the freedom of election. An election committee was formed and within three weeks they had succeeded in obtaining the signatures of 11,000 electors 'pledging themselves to do all in their power to secure [Henry's] return'.[9] Henry was facing a field of three Liberals and two Conservatives, but with the increase in the electorate he felt confident of success.

The election was fought principally on Ireland's grievances. Throughout the campaign Henry displayed an intimate knowledge of Ireland, its history and its grievances. At a meeting held in Manchester, on the 17 August 1868, he set out his political principle; the disestablishment of the Church in Ireland, denominational education and, now that household suffrage had been granted, he was in favour of the ballot. Drawing on history - on the Norman conquest, the Reformation, the 1641 Rebellion, the Treaty of Limerick and the Act of Union - he attempted to explain to a packed hall the origins of Ireland's grievances. This was a long speech, but many among his audience would have been Irish, or of Irish extraction, and may perhaps have enjoyed the history lesson. His conclusion was that Ireland had never been fully conquered by England, neither had the English succeeded in spreading their religious beliefs there:

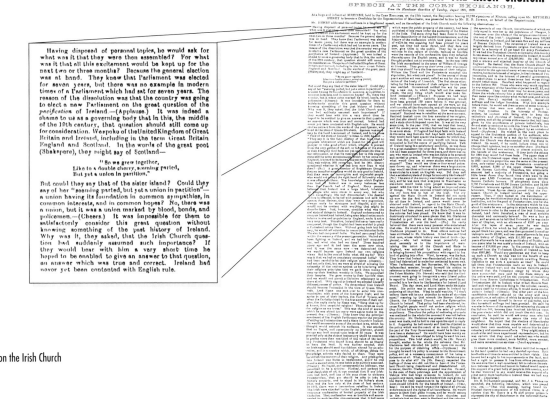

Henry on the Irish Church

Courtesy of Manchester Central Library

England [had] endeavoured to conquer Ireland, and Ireland, being as an island not so much inferior in size and population to England, made it not a very easy task. Therefore, Ireland had never been really conquered, though the English had been enabled to plant a Protestant colony there . . . The State Church in Ireland was entirely, or almost entirely, for the benefit of the aristocracy . . . The free exercise of their religion had been the cry from first to last of the Irish.[10]

In response to questions on the land question in Ireland Henry said that he had 'very decided opinions', opinions which he was putting into practice on his estate in Kylemore: 'Both landlord and tenants were entitled to their rights. The tenant had a right to his improvements and had a right to possess it free from odious persecution'. A 'well-considered bill' to reform the relations between the landlord and tenant in Ireland 'would receive the support of a great body of people' in England and, in his opinion, a great many landlords in Ireland.[11]

Opposition to Henry was strong, particularly among the Liberals who believed his appearance in the field would split the Liberal vote and benefit the Conservatives. Two of the three Liberal candidates, Thomas Bazley and Jacob Bright, were the sitting Members for Manchester. Jacob Bright was the younger brother of the previously mentioned John Bright M.P.,[12] and brother-in-law to Thomas Ashworth of the Galway Fishery. John Bright M.P., had sat in parliament with Henry's father and was a strong advocate of land reform and disestablishment of the Church in Ireland, and a man of influence within the Liberal party.[13] Henry was convinced that Manchester would not return a Conservative and so considered the competition for the third seat to be between himself and the third Liberal, Ernest Jones. A good deal of his campaign was concentrated on attacking Jones's political background. The Liberals responded, leaving Henry under attack from all sides, but still he persisted. Given the closeness that must surely have existed between the Bright and Henry families, this contest must have resembled a civil war among the Manchester Liberals.

At one point an influential Liberal member of the House of Commons offered Henry a 'safe' seat in another county, if he withdrew his candidature. He turned it down, preferring instead to run for Manchester, 'as honourable and responsible a seat as that of any country in the kingdom'.[14]

To the Irish Catholic Electors of Manchester, and there were many, Henry was introduced as 'a worthy son of a worthy Irishman . . . an extensive holder of land in Ireland, whose tenantry are happy and contented'.[15] To others he was recognized as a rich and generous candidate and attracted, what one newspaper called, 'clever and unscrupulous fellows' as advisors.[16] He was having difficulty obtaining favourable press coverage of his meetings and so, at his own expense, he published *The Manchester Evening News*. The first edition was published on 10 October and throughout the election it appeared daily to give the particulars of his campaign. After the election the newspaper was sold to the printer, William Evans, and is still in circulation today.

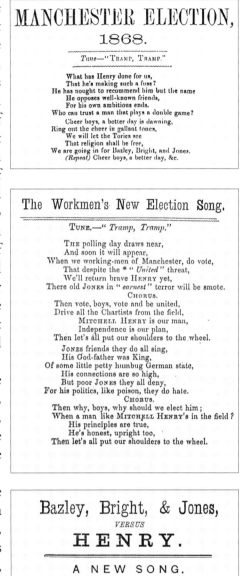

Courtesy of Manchester Central Library

Some street ballads popular in Manchester during the 1868 election

Courtesy of *Manchester Evening News*

The nominations for Manchester took place in Albert Square on the 16 November. The crowd was instructed by the Mayor to do their duty 'in the ancient mode, by a show of hands', and the following day 'to ratify that at the polling booth'.[17] On the following day Hugh Birley (Conservative) took the lead from the beginning and retained that position to the end. Bazley (Liberal) was coming in second and the battle for the third seat was not as Henry had anticipated; between himself and Jones, but between Bright (Liberal) and the other Conservative candidate, Joseph Hoare. When Henry realised that many of those who had pledged their votes to him had in fact gone over to the Conservatives and that the Liberals were in danger of losing the seat, he withdrew from the contest. His vote at the time was 5,236 but this would have increased had he remained in the race. Later, responding to Henry's critics, the *Manchester Guardian* argued that this selfless act by Henry had saved the day for the Liberals:

> It is to this action on the part of Mr Henry that Mr Jacob Bright is indebted to his seat . . . the release of Mr Henrys friends from their

pledges caused such an amount of support to be given to Mr Bright as placed him in that position of third member for Manchester.

However, Bright was anything but grateful and while addressing a meeting after the election, in response to a comment from the crowd, he remarked: 'I do not know how much money the 5,000 votes of Mr Henry have cost; but I know from this time forward there will be a conviction throughout this city that Manchester cannot be bought'.

Henry declared this to be 'a coarse and slanderous observation . . . and it came with ill grace from one who is indebted to my patriotism for his seat'. But the accusation stuck and over the years speculation continued as to how much money Henry spent on the 1868 election. One newspaper put the figure at £14,000 adding that he 'would not have begrudged another £14,000 if he had been successful'.[18]

Henry's actions in contesting the 1868 election would remain a contentious issue among the Liberals for some time and must have lost him many an old friend. However, the *Manchester Guardian* was quick to point out his eligibility as a candidate and praised his behaviour on the day:

> Mr Henry was in many aspects, in independent position, in abilities, in soundness of views, and in energy of character, exceedingly well qualified for the representation of Manchester in the House of Commons . . . In his disappointment we believe he may safely derive some consolation from the assurance that the number of electors who voted for him yesterday are but a small part of those who would gladly see him in Parliament. He proved his attachment to the political interest on behalf of which he took the field by retiring at a critical conjuncture in the contest. If he disturbed the operations of the United Liberal Committee by going to the poll at all, the Liberal party at large will not be slow to remember that he retrieved the error in time to save for them the second seat on which the Conservatives were pressing with so much vigour and appearance of success.[19]

Henry's brother was successfully elected as the Conservative Member for South-East Lancashire and remained in parliament until 1874. Gladstone lost his seat at South-West Lancashire and was instead returned for Greenwich. He succeeded in winning the election with a Liberal majority and the Church of Ireland was disestablished the following year.

In his speech, following the announcement of the final vote, Henry revealed his reluctance to try again for Manchester but he was not prepared to rule out politics altogether:

You need not be under any apprehension, after the labour I have gone through, that I shall be in a hurry again to represent a large constituency like this; but wherever I am, whether in the House of Commons or out of it, still I shall carry the conviction with me that I have acted no unworthy part but I have done my best to further Liberal principles.[20]

Three years later would find Henry fighting a by-election in Galway.

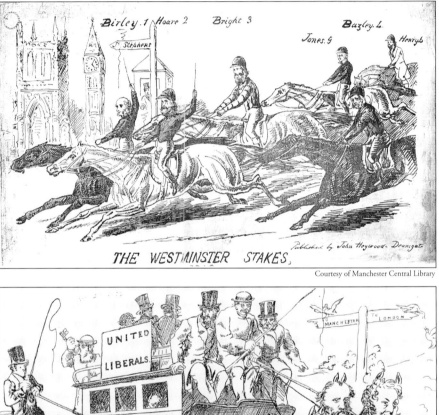

1868 Political Cartoons showing Henry bringing up the rear in the race for Westminster

Courtesy of Manchester Central Library

'A Winning Game' with Henry pulling his own load

Courtesy of Manchester Central Library

Chapter 5

Contesting the Galway Seat

The one absorbing passion of the Irish heart is for the preservation of its nationality; and if our fellow subjects in England and Scotland desire to find the key to explain the course of Irish politics from the earliest times, they must take it to their minds that this sentiment is undying and inextinguishable, and breaths, moreover, as strongly in those who have only a few hundred years of Irish descent as it does in the original Celtic population. [1]

Mitchell Henry, 7 March 1874

From the very beginning of his political career in Ireland, Henry spoke with authority on Irish history and on the Irish people. His deep understanding of the political and social needs of the country, already evident from his campaigns in England, left him with the view that the 'woes of Ireland were social and not political'. He endeavoured to bring this view to the English politicians at Westminster, and to the wider British public, but frequently despaired at their lack of knowledge of the country and empathy with those who were, after all, their fellow citizens. An able speaker in the House of Commons and on public platform, he was quick to use the press to reach a wider audience and took every opportunity to draw attention to the plight of the small tenant farmers of the West and the backward conditions under which they were forced to live. His ability, energy and sincerity soon won him the respect of his fellow Members. He became known for his outspokenness and tenacity, and yet, even his political opponents referred to him as being, 'mild and gentle-mannered'.

Henry's first Irish campaign was tame when compared with that fought in Manchester. It began on 9 February 1871, when, 'encouraged by assurance of support from a large number of influential Electors',[2] and from William Monsell, a leading Irish Catholic in the English Liberal party,[3] he offered himself as a candidate in the upcoming by-election for Galway County. Among the 'influential electors' were a number of Catholic clergy, merchants, large farmers and Catholic landlords; these were to form the core of Henry's political support for the duration of his term as representative for Galway County.

The election was the result of the unexpected resignation of the sitting Member, Viscount Burke, and was to be held later in February. In his election manifesto Henry declared himself of Liberal politics, holding similar views to that of all Irish Liberals; support for denominational education, a Catholic university and home rule:

In my opinion Ireland should be allowed to settle the Education Question in accordance with the views of the great majority of the inhabitants. It is their wish that the Education of the youth of Ireland should be accompanied with religious teaching . . . Centralisation shall cease, and Irish material interests be directed by Home Legislation.[4]

Henry received strong support from the local press. Recognised as an improving landlord, he received high praise as an employer and benefactor to Connemara. His record was undeniable and was referred to frequently at public meetings. One of the first public meetings held in support of his candidature was at Clifden on 13 February. The meeting was Chaired by Rev. Canon Patrick McManus P.P., and attended by the shopkeepers and Catholic farmers of the surrounding district. A resolution calling for home rule and the setting up a Repeal National Club in the town was passed. A further resolution pledging 'independent support' for Henry was 'unanimously and enthusiastically' adopted, declaring that as a long time resident in Connemara he was known to be

an indulgent and just landlord, dispensing comfort in a previously decaying populous district, and also knowing him in his judicial capacity, as an upright and patient magistrate, and as an extensive and liberal employer, and showing by every act of his, that he understood and discharged the duties of property. [5]

The only other candidate in the election was also a Liberal, Captain John Philip Nolan of Ballinderry, County Galway. A third candidate, Hyacinth D'Arcy of Newforest, withdrew early in the race. The *Galway Express* regretted that the absence of a Conservative candidate left the electorate

Galway Express 18 February 1871

60

with 'nothing to chose, on political grounds, between gentlemen who give' their full support to Mr Gladstone: 'They are all equally docile [holding] a monotonous uniformity of belief'. And so the people would have to select on the grounds of 'ability, position, influence, and the many other qualifications which are essential to a successful Parliamentary life'.

These qualities, the *Express* stated, Henry possesses 'in a high degree', being a man 'of considerable culture, possessed of debating power, sound business habits, and tact'. Politicians at this time did not receive a salary and so being independently wealthy he needed 'no place as a reward for services rendered', the writer adding that 'such a representative would be a valuable one, not only for the county but for the town'. If Henry was returned, the newspaper prophesied, 'we feel confident that he will prove a representative entirely devoted to the interests of his constituents; and that by his intelligence and ability he will soon make himself prominent in the councils of the nation'.[6]

Almost as soon as he had declared his intention to run, Henry's opponent, Captain Nolan, was in difficulty. Nolan, a Catholic landlord, had from the start attracted criticism from the Catholic clergy. He was accused of having cruelly evicted over ninety tenants from his land near Oughterard some years earlier, and was therefore unacceptable to the people. He was asked by Archbishop MacHale, at the time one of the most influential men in the West of Ireland, to retire from the contest for 'the peace of the country'. In doing so he received a promise that should he 'meet the charges brought against him in connection with the evictions by leaving the matter to three arbitrators', he would receive the support of the Archbishop at a future election.[7] The support of the Catholic clergy was of vital importance to a candidate because of the huge influence they exercised over the voting practices of their parishioners. Secure with this promise Captain Nolan retired on the day of the nominations.

Henry was then the only candidate and on Tuesday 22 February 1871 at 10 a.m., in the crowded Galway courthouse, he was returned unopposed. In his acceptance speech Henry expressed his pride in being elected to represent Galway: 'the most Irish of all other counties of Ireland'. In reply to those who referred to him during the campaigns as an Englishman, he proclaimed 'not a drop of blood flows through my veins other than Irish. My family have lived in Ireland and have worked for Ireland for centuries'.

The principal issues of the day had been solved, according to Henry, with the disestablishment of the Church of Ireland in 1869 and the passing of the Land Act in 1870. The only outstanding demands were denominational education and home government. He called for unity among Irish Parliamentary Members which would strengthen their demands on Irish issues:

> I am convinced that if the Irish people pursue an orderly course, continue to be loyal to our Sovereign, and work together for the common good of Ireland, then, have only their 103 representatives to speak with united voice to obtain all they seek.[8]

Courtesy of the House of Lords Archive

Mitchell Henry taken from House of Commons Album

After four election campaigns and untold expense, Henry's persistence had finally paid off and he had won his seat in parliament. He would continue to represent Galway County until 1884. However, the next fourteen years, during which Henry would continue to preach this steady, determined and unified approach, would prove to be some of the most turbulent in Irish political history. These were the years of Home Rule, Obstruction and the Land War. They were also years of hunger and agitation. Henry arrived in parliament six months ahead of Isaac Butt and four years before Charles Stewart Parnell, two men whose names are synonymous with this period in Irish history. He became a friend and supporter of Butt, although in time he, like many others, grew impatient with Butt's indecisiveness and lack of leadership in the late 1870s. For Parnell he had, to begin with, a grudging respect; and while not always supporting his tactics of obstruction, in the early years he openly recognised his courage and conviction. However, he later criticised Parnell for encouraging violence during the Land War, disrupting the parliamentary procedure and bringing parliament into disrepute. During the Land War the two clashed frequently on policy and tactics; this deteriorated to open warfare when Parnell sat with the Conservatives on the opposition benches after the 1880 election, rather than join the Liberals, with whom, Henry felt, rested Ireland's only hope of any resolution of their grievances.

Henry first spoke in the House of Commons on 2 March 1871, a little more than a week after his election, and he went on to contribute to almost every debate, particularly those which in some way touched on Ireland, for the remainder of his political career. Believing that 'the sole object of Parliament was not to pass laws, but to promote discussion and to ventilate public questions',[9] he professed he 'derived instruction from the speeches of hon. Members, who expressed themselves in intelligent and, generally, in dignified and business-like language'.[10] A very fine orator himself he sought, in return, to inform and instruct his fellow Members on the conditions and demands of the Irish people.

But he was soon to learn that not all Members of the House possessed this same open-minded approach and the hostility among fellow members towards the Irish representatives forced him to admit that he often 'felt it hard to struggle against the coldness, and even the disorder, which at times prevailed when Irish Members rose to speak'.[11] In the early years he confessed that he 'never spoke in that House without feeling as though he was undergoing a painful operation for he was sensible how much the views of Irish Members were out of harmony with the mind of the House; but he also felt very strongly the duty that was cast upon Irish representatives to be faithful to their convictions'.[12] Before long he formed the opinion that 'there was an attempt systematically to ignore Irish Members'.[13] However, despite this he told the House that 'as long as he had a seat in that House he would not lose the opportunity of protesting against the mode in which Irish legislation was carried on'.[14] And this he did repeatedly.

At a time when Irish Members were frequently criticised for their absence Henry could be relied upon to attend regularly and always to make the Irish presence felt. His first important speech was delivered on 25 July 1872, when he seconded Isaac Butt's motion calling for an inquiry into the address given by Mr Justice William Keogh, when delivering his judgment on the Trial of the Election Petition for the County of Galway.

The election in question was the 1872 Galway County by-election, which took place in February of that year. A vacancy had arisen when the second Member for Galway County, the Right Hon. W.H. Gregory, was appointed Governor of Ceylon. Captain Nolan again went forward, opposed on this occasion by Captain William le Poer Trench, a Conservative. As promised, Captain Nolan had the full support of the Catholic clergy, Captain le Poer Trench enjoyed the support of the gentry. The election was, by all accounts, hard fought, but in the end Captain Nolan polled nearly 2,000 votes and Captain le Poer Trench polled just 658. However, the return was petitioned against on the grounds of improper clerical influence and Judge Keogh was sent to Galway to try the case.[15]

Over several days large numbers of the public, clergy and laymen, were brought to testify before the court and at the end of May Judge Keogh delivered his verdict. After considering the evidence given at the trial the Judge found three bishops and several priests to be 'guilty of undue influence and intimidation at the Galway County election';[16] Captain Nolan was unseated and the seat given to Captain le Poer Trench.

Almost immediately there was uproar among the people because of the 'violent partizan speech',[17] uttered by the Judge in delivering his judgment. A public debate followed on the content of the judgment and on the Judge's language. A number of people called for the resignation of Judge Keogh, Isaac Butt put forward a motion to that effect in the House of Commons. Henry in his speech seconding the motion concentrated on the language used by the Judge rather than on the judgment itself. He declared that 'a person using such language is not fit to hold Her Majesty's Commission of the Peace; for, by the malice of his tongue, he has murdered peace'. For his criticism of the Catholic bishops and priests Henry charged Judge Keogh with 'deliberately outraging the religious feelings of a religious people'. After a lengthy impassioned speech, Henry proclaimed: 'The Judge seems to me to require retirement and repose – his temperament demands it'. He went on to warn the government that without justice there would be no peace in Ireland:

> You say that the great fault of Ireland is, that she has no respect for the law; be doubly careful therefore, who you make administrators of the law. The Judge, I say . . . who cannot command his passions, and lets loose his tongue among a Roman Catholic population, to speak of their religion and their character as this man has done, is a recruiting sergeant to increase the number of your troops in Ireland. Augment your Army you may, stretch your coercion laws you can; but there is one thing you cannot do – refuse justice and maintain your Empire in peace.[18]

Butt's motion was defeated but the following year all charges against the bishops and priests were dropped.[19]

Henry's speech was well received by his constituents and given extensive coverage in the press. On his journey to Kylemore that August at Westport station he was greeted by a large crowd accompanied by a band. Forty men 'with green ribbons on their hats' were ready to draw his carriage through the town but Henry declined; instead he received an address which congratulated him on the 'spirited and manly part' he took in supporting Butt's motion.[20]

In his early years in parliament denominational education was the principal issue for Henry, as it was for the influential Catholic clergy in his constituency. In 1872, during the debate on the Elementary Education Bill he called for tolerance and acceptance that individuals had the right to instruct their children 'according to their consciences': 'The foundation of all education must be lain in religious truth; and if we can only agree that no one body has the monopoly of religion in such a sense as that it has the right to impose its belief on the rest of the community we may speedily come to an agreement'.[21]

He entered the House strongly supporting Gladstone's Liberal government, but by 1873 had joined other Irish Liberals in criticising its proposals for education in Ireland. For the remainder of his political career he would continue to fight for denominational education and speak repeatedly on the subject during parliamentary debates.

However, for the Irish people the demand for Home Rule was rapidly winning support and would soon become the principal issue of the day. Henry was a committed Home Ruler; his election to parliament was recognised as one of Home Rule's first electoral successes. His support for the campaign soon brought him to the attention of the Irish and English press and within a very short time he was recognised as one of the principals among the Irish Members. He played a prominent role in the setting up of the Home Rule League in November 1873 and was considered 'next to Mr Butt, perhaps, the most vitally necessary member' of that organisation.[22] When an election was called in December he was one of those heavily involved in developing a campaign strategy for the League and canvassed for other Home Rule candidates before returning to Galway to begin his own campaign, an action he would later have cause to regret.

Polling was to take place on 13 February 1874 and the introduction of the secret ballot in 1872 was expected to reduce the influence of clergy and landlords in the voting choices of the people. But in Galway, however, clerical influence was still an important factor. Henry was standing on his parliamentary record:

> If you are satisfied that I have been an honest Member of Parliament; that
> I have said what I meant, and meant what I said; and that I have been
> faithful to the principles I professed on the Hustings when you elected me
> in 1871, I confidently look to a renewal of your trust, and ask you again
> to return me as one of your Representatives for this Great County.

This time, to his call for Home Rule and denominational education were added the demands for amnesty for the Fenian prisoners, amendments to the Land Act and the repeal of the Coercion Acts. He explained the form of Home Rule sought by the League:

> under the Federal arrangement proposed by the Home Rule League, the
> integrity of the Empire will be preserved, and Ireland will still possess
> her due weight in the settlement of Imperial matters . . . Let our

> watchwords be Home Rule and the restoration of an Irish Parliament;
> Religious Education . . . Repeal of the Coercion Acts, and Amnesty for
> all political offences; Amendment of the admitted defects of the Land
> Act, so as to raise up that safeguard of property in all countries - a
> prosperous race of freeholders.[23]

William le Poer Trench, now a Major, after just two years as an M.P., decided
not to contest the election. Galway County was a two seater constituency and
it was thought at first that the election would be a walkover for Mitchell
Henry and Captain Nolan, although three others were expected to go
forward; Capt. John Eyre, Eyrecourt Castle, Martin McDonnell, Dunmore,
and Hyacinth D'Arcy of Newforest. But the number of candidates was
irrelevant for the unanimous opinion of the people of Galway, echoed in the
Galway Vindicator editorial two weeks before the election, was that:

> whoever may be his colleague public opinion is undivided as to the
> claims of Mr Mitchell Henry. There is no second question on that. If
> there were a dozen candidates Mr Henry will deservedly occupy the
> place. His Parliamentary career has not alone reflected credit upon his
> county but upon the entire country . . . Mr Mitchell Henry is a man
> to be proud of, and it may with confidence be asserted that so long as
> he wished to represent this great county in Parliament, he shall always
> be able to command the voice and the vote of the constituency.[24]

In the end the two seats were contested by the same three candidates as in
1871; Mitchell Henry, Capt. Nolan and Hyacinth D'Arcy, only this time
D'Arcy stayed to the end. Everyone was confident that Henry would take the
first seat, for the second the press favoured D'Arcy, 'a Catholic gentleman of
splendid character and unblemished antecedents'.[25] Henry was late getting
started but once in Galway, with his usual energy, he immediately began to
cover as much territory as time would allow. At a meeting in Ballinasloe he
addressed the crowd from a window of Mrs Hayden's hotel, calling on them
to 'return none but Home Rulers to represent them'. With the ballot 'the
destinies of the Irish people were now in their own hands' If they did not
return faithful representatives it would be their own fault, and 'if it be their
own fault God help them for the future'.

No matter who formed the next government, he assured them, the Irish
representatives 'would work together and make their voice be heard in
London, until they got the liberty to which they were entitled'. It was his
hope that after the election 'there would be a meeting of the Irish members
in Dublin to determine on a course of action . . . and they would agree not
to give a vote for Mr Gladstone or Mr Disraeli or any other government

who would not give them what they wanted – a religious education for their children' and Home Rule. After explaining how to vote by ballot and giving an assurance of the secrecy of the system, Henry concluded by asking them 'on Friday next to place their cross opposite his name and to settle in their own consciences for whom the second vote should be recorded'.

At that the Chairman of the meeting, Rev. Thomas Mulkerrin C.C., came forward and proposed a vote of thanks to Henry for his address and told the crowd that they should adopt him and Capt. Nolan for their candidates for the county.[26] The clergy were once again in full support of Capt Nolan and, confident of Henry's success, were attempting to link the two men in the minds of the voters.

The press too was confident of Henry's success, but warned against complacency:

> Mitchell Henry has proved himself the most useful of Irish Members of Parliament . . . with his influence, position, power, eloquence and knowledge . . . His success must not be jeopardised. Neglect of him at the polling booths would be blackest of ingratitudes and blunder worse than crime. [27]

Galway elections had a history of violence and intimidation, but with the introduction of the ballot all that was now in the past. Instead of 500 voters converging on Galway to cast their vote, as was the norm in previous elections, there were now 5,220 registered voters, but only 67 of these were eligible to vote in Galway; the remainder voted at the forty-one polling stations scattered throughout the county. Polling day, Friday 13 February, found Galway polling station and indeed the entire city 'as still as death'. The correspondent for the *Galway Express,* lamenting the hustle and bustle of the past, reported:

> To judge from outward appearance, no one would know that an election for this important county was proceeding. The streets have all day been deserted – the voters are coming in so slowly that the poll clerks are literally lounging about, and the constabulary, who in former times had so much to do, with soldiers and dragoons assisting them, are pacing the hall of the court-house in thorough disgust, their arms piled in a corner, and not even a little boy near to chaff them . . . In the good old times, when elections lasted a month and the polling two days, a voter was a person of importance needful to be counted, and his vote, on a close poll, worth some consideration. Now, he is despised and neglected, and if courted at all, it is only for a few days before the election . . . [now] You may record your vote in peace and quietness, and no one will quarrel with you.[28]

The count took place on the Monday and was carried out by just one man, John Blakeney, the High Sheriff. Throughout the day it was still expected that Henry would be returned at the head of the poll, and so it was with some surprise that the result was learned at seven o'clock that evening: Captain Nolan 2,348, Mitchell Henry 2,270, Hyacinth D'Arcy 1,080.[29]

Nolan and Henry were elected. Captain Nolan's seventy-eight vote majority over Henry was explained by the *Galway Express* in apologetic tones:

> almost every voter in the county, without exception, believed Mr Henry to be secure, and unmistakably to head the poll, to ensure the election of Captain Nolan, some of them neglected to split with Mr Henry, and this, extended too far, gave Captain Nolan a majority. However, we presume it is an oversight which Mr Henry will readily forgive, and for which he will hold the people of Galway excused, as under different circumstances, they should be more than ungrateful not to testify their kindly feelings towards one so tried and true as Mr Henry, by placing him at the head of the poll.[30]

But Henry had his own explanation for the voting pattern of his constituents, as he told Butt: 'A few day before the polling a vast number of priests instigated I think by all three of the bishops went round and begged the voters to plump for Nolan – fearing he might be left out'.[31]

The election was a success for the Home Rule movement with fifty-nine Home Rule M.P.s elected. The ballot had, in Henry's opinion, 'given Ireland, if not a Representation more acceptable to the House of Commons, a Representation more true'.[32] However, Gladstone's Liberals were defeated and replaced by Disraeli's Conservatives.

After the election the promised meeting of Home Rule M.P.s was called for by Butt, Henry and four others. The group resolved 'to form a separate and distinct party in the house of commons, united on the principle of obtaining self-government for Ireland'.[33] The Irish Home Rule party elected Isaac Butt as its leader and Henry was among the nine Members elected to form the first parliamentary committee. Party Members were united on the principal of Home Rule but free to act individually on all other issues. In the coming years the party would meet strong opposition in its attempt to have some form of Home Rule adopted by the House of Commons and frustration would lead to disillusionment with Butt's leadership and eventually to a lack of unity among its members.

However, the campaign got off to an early start when parliament resumed in March and almost immediately Butt called for a parliamentary inquiry into the 'dissatisfaction of the Irish people with their system of government'.[34] In the debate that followed Henry told the House that those advocating Home Rule sought unity not separation:

> The subject of Home Rule had been calmly and deliberately considered in Ireland, and by the voice of the great body of her representatives that integral part of the United Kingdom had declared her firm conviction . . . that the whole system of the government of Ireland must be changed if we were really in the future to stand shoulder to shoulder as a united, consolidated power.[35]

The motion was defeated but re-introduced into the House by Butt on 30 June. On this occasion it fell to Henry to put forward the financial and economic argument. Touching on the subjects of emigration, agriculture, the manufacturing and fishing industries, absentee landlords (for whom he had a particular disdain), taxation, banking and railway construction, he supported his argument with facts and statistics. He asked his audience to 'take a practical view', as he set out to show that English management of Irish affairs had failed and all that was asking for now was to let the people of Ireland manage these for themselves:

> neither Ireland could do without England, nor England without Ireland. As against the world, they must be a united Empire, having one Sovereign, one Army, one Navy, one foreign policy; whilst, in their internal affairs, admitting of those rational diversities of thought and action which must exist in the case of people whose race and religion were as different as the resources and capabilities of the countries were different.[36]

He elaborated further on the fiscal argument in a speech delivered at the Rotunda in Dublin on 26 October 1875, which was later published. Here he argued that Ireland was determined to have a rearrangement in the terms of the partnership set out under the Act of Union, which would give to the Irish People the management of Irish affairs, the disposal of Ireland's surplus revenue and the lighter imposition of Irish taxation.[37]

He returned again to the subject in the House, during the third reading of the Customs and Inland Revenue Bill on 29 May 1876, when he called on the government to relieve Ireland 'from a burden of Taxation beyond her ability to pay':

THE FINANCIAL AND ECONOMICAL

CONDITION OF IRELAND :

A SPEECH

DELIVERED AT THE ROTUNDA, DUBLIN,

OCTOBER 26, 1875.

Revised and Annotated.

BY

MITCHELL HENRY,

M.P. FOR THE COUNTY OF GALWAY.

DUBLIN:
THE IRISH HOME RULE LEAGUE.

1875.

Henry's Speech at the Rotunda

This money which you take from Ireland you spend in England on your manufacturing and other establishments for purposes of State. You return little or nothing of it to Ireland. You take capital from a poor and struggling country and add it to the capital of Great Britain. I ask you to look in a wise and statesmanlike manner and see if some portion of that amount which you raise in Ireland every year might not be laid out for the benefit of that country as you lay it out now for the benefit of England?[38]

© Kylemore Abbey

Mrs Margaret Henry

In November 1874 Henry took a well earned holiday in Egypt. The couple frequently travelled abroad and on this occasion were accompanied by some friends and by some of their children. The two youngest, Florence and Violet, were aged under four and two and would have been under the care of a nanny and nurse. The four middle children, Alexander, Forward, Geraldine and Lorenzo were accompanied by their tutor Charles Larbalestier. Larbalestier, a keen student of lichenology, had only just taken up the position and would remain with the family until 1878. During his time with the Henrys Larbalestier collected many rare specimens of lichen in Connemara, details of which were later published in the 3rd edition of Rev. W. A. Leighton's *Lichen-flora of Great Britain, Ireland and the Channel Islands*.[39]

While in Egypt Margaret Henry became ill with dysentery and, after sixteen days of illness, she died on 4 December at the age of forty-five. On the 12 December 1874 the *Galway Express* carried the following announcement:

We deeply regret to announce the death of Mrs Mitchell Henry, which melancholy event took place recently in Egypt, while with her husband and family on a tour through the East. In all the relations of life, as a wife, a mother, or member of society, she was admired, respected, and beloved. Although at the head of the princely mansion of Kylemore, and surrounded by everything calculated to minister to the most cultivated taste, she spent much of her time in endeavouring to ameliorate the condition of the surrounding peasantry. The domestic affliction caused by her premature decease is largely sympathised with by relatives, friends, and the public generally.[40]

Henry was greatly affected by the death of his wife and it would take him many years to recover, if indeed he ever did. He had her body embalmed and may even have kept her with the family in Egypt, where they are believed to have remained for the rest of the Winter and into the Spring. When Margaret's body was brought to Kylemore tradition has it that Henry was reluctant to place it below ground and so it lay for some time in the staircase hall, perhaps awaiting the construction of the mausoleum in the grounds.

Once back in Kylemore Henry was slow to leave and did not return to the House of Commons until summoned by the whip to participate in the debate on the Peace Preservation (Ireland) Bill on 30 April 1875. A short time later while visiting Dublin Henry suffered another blow with the passing of his good friend Andrew Armstrong. Armstrong had retired from Kylemore House Hotel and was living in Rathmines in Dublin. At the time of his death, early on Sunday morning 6 June 1875, he was travelling to take breakfast with his good friends, Henry and Dr Nedley, at the latter's home in Cavendish Row. When the cab arrived Henry and Dr Nedley went out to greet him and on opening the door of the cab were shocked to find Armstrong dead inside.

© Kylemore Abbey

The Mausoleum

Henry had been a friend of Armstrong's since his earliest visits to Connemara and would have learned from the older man's experience in their shared interests in land reclamation, agriculture and fishing. Armstrong had lost his wife some eighteen months previously and was survived by six children. Renowned for his years spent as a hotelier in Connemara, where he counted among his guests the rich, famous and powerful, he was widely known and respected throughout England and Ireland. For Henry his death, coming so close on that of his own wife, was a severe blow and seemed to compound his recent loss. Writing immediately to Butt to inform him of Andrew's death, he is clearly greatly shaken by the experience: 'to think of my friend, in whose house and who's chair I now am – dead now but living somewhere else at this moment (for I do not credit <u>the long rest</u> in the grave which people speak of), is <u>very woundful, very acheful</u>'.[41]

Henry returned to Kylemore and there, surrounded by his family, he busied himself with agricultural matters. He telegraphed Butt giving a date for his return to London, but then changed his mind. In a letter of apology he tried to explain his lack of enthusiasm for political matters:

> Truth to say poor Armstrongs death has quite upset me – and I find it hard to rally my spirits as to take an interest in politics . . . I am just in this state of mind that I might run off any day, or remain a day or two longer. I find a satisfaction in being with my family here – and they are all I would wish them to be.

71

MacAlister, the steward, was on holidays in Scotland and Henry felt his presence was needed at home 'amongst the great number of people employed' on the estate. And as if to emphasise a point, he ended the letter like a true farmer: 'the weather is bad – but the crops look well – We want dry weather for the Hay. You will see from this note that I am dull as ditch water'.[42]

His family were again a great comfort to him when he experienced the loss of yet another friend from the West, Dr Robert John Morgan.[43] Dr Morgan had worked in Connemara during the time of the Great Famine and may again have been one of Henry's friends from those early days. Once again Henry remained on at Kylemore informing Butt that he was too ill with bronchitis to travel and 'fretting at the death of my dear friend Dr Morgan and except that I feel so happy with my children, who are all that a person can desire, I don't know exactly what I should do'.[44]

Margaret's remains were, in time, laid to rest in a mausoleum next to the main avenue. A very beautiful Gothic Church was later erected as a memorial chapel to her memory. The Church was built to the east of the

Venetian Wing under construction

© Kylemore Abbey

Castle, just off the main avenue. It was designed by James Franklin Fuller, a well known ecclesiastical architect who was considered an authority on the Hiberno-Romanesque style. Fuller also designed Ashford Castle in County Mayo for Lord Ardilaun. Work began on the Church in 1877 but it was not fully completed until 1881.

Courtesy of National Library of Ireland Kylemore Collection 55

While on site Fuller also did some work on the Castle and would later, in his memoirs published in 1916, try and take credit for the entire building, giving just passing recognition to Samuel Ussher Roberts: 'In the early stages of this building the County Surveyor of Galway was associated with me'.[45]

The Church was designed to be a 'cathedral in miniature'. The exterior was of limestone, with projecting corner buttresses, carved angelic gargoyles and a copper roof. A square tower, surmounted by pinnacles, stood at the eastern end and a Gothic porch entrance, with red Peterhead granite pillars, dominated the western end. The interior was said to have been 'suggested by the beautiful Chapel of St. Stephen's at Westminster', and was highly decorative, using yellow Caen stone and Irish marbles. Connemara green, Cork red and Kilkenny black marble pillars with carved Bath stone capitals supported the gothic arches of the ground Bath stone ceiling, which was arranged in four sections 'with protruding mouldings and finely carved bosses'.[46] The stone work was executed by Henry Sharpe of Kells, County Meath, and the foreman stone-cutter on site was H. Bampton. Bampton was assisted by his two sons and H. Tomlin, all of Dublin, all four worked at Kylemore between August 1879 and April 1880. The external carvings were by William Bryant.

Courtesy of National Library of Ireland Kylemore Collection 53

In keeping with the main aisle six Gothic windows flanked the sides of the Chancery and behind the alter there was a plain glass tracery window. Incorporated in the south transept was a beautiful stained glass tracery window with images depicting Fortitude, Faith, Charity, Hope and Chastity. A door to the right of the Chancery lead to the Vestry which was fitted with a fireplace and staircase, giving access to the Tower. In front of the Altar there was a trap door through which coffins could be lowered to the vaults below. The vault was believed to be inspired by the mediaeval vault of Bristol

Courtesy of National Library of Ireland, Kylemore Collection 72

Gothic Church Under Construction

Cathedral and contained 'seven deep bays fitted with stone and slate shelves available for a large number of interments'. It was reached by outside steps and accessed through iron doors. A second set of steps at the tower end lead down to the boiler house. For whatever reason, Margaret's remains were never removed to the Church vault but remained in the mausoleum; neither would any other member of the Henry family be buried there.

Although still a relatively young man of forty-eight and left with nine children ranging in age from twenty-four to just two years old, Henry never again married. His oldest daughter, Margaret, then eighteen, took over the running of the house and the responsibility of the younger children. On 6 August 1878, Margaret married Edward Lovett Henn, son of Thomas Rice Henn, Q.C., J.P., and Deputy Lieutenant for Co Clare and Recorder of Galway, of Paradise Hall, Kildysart, Co Clare and 48 Upper Mount St, Dublin. The ceremony took place at St James' in Piccadilly, London and was performed by Rev Henry Latham, Vice-Master of Trinity Hall Cambridge where Edward was a Fellow.[47] The young couple lived at the Henry family home in London, Stratheden House, and Margaret continued her role as mistress of the house for many years.

J.F. Fuller

Chapter 6

Moderation in the Face of Obstruction

In time, Henry returned to his work with the same enthusiasm and energy previously exhibited. The Irish Party was making little headway against the Conservative government's opposition to their proposals, but this did not diminish his determination to participate in the day to day procedures of the House.

Henry had a great respect for the freedom and dignity of the House of Commons and was quick to point out any erosion of standards or infringement, as he saw it, by any Member or government. He was of the opinion that any individual entering the House, no matter what prejudice he held against it, would 'in the course of a very short time conform himself to the manners and customs of the House'. Because within the House 'a spirit of fair play governed their proceedings'. And it was 'that circumstance which had enabled them to preserve the liberties they enjoyed'.[2]

He was similarly vigilant as to the treatment awarded to the House and its Members in the press. He deplored recent changes in the system of reporting the proceedings of the House by many of the national newspapers. A practice of 'sensational reporting' had taken the place of full reports. 'Sketches of what occurred, or of what was supposed to have occurred', were given to the public in a trivial manner which displayed a lack of respect for the House. At one time he suggested that seats in the press gallery be allocated only to those newspapers inclined to give full and frank report of proceedings.

It was his regret that very little attention was given anymore to the entire question, just brief paragraphs to one side or the other of any argument. He laid the blame for this method of reporting on the pace of modern day life:

> Owing to the great extension of telegraphic enterprise; to the rapidity
> with which everything was done now-a-days; to the short time people
> had at their disposal; and to the appetite which of late years had been
> created for sensational writing, the reports of the debates in

The battle of the dissolution of the Empire was begun in the House of Commons itself by an organised system of obstruction.[1]

Mitchell Henry

> Parliament were . . . more farcical . . . The newspapers, which were multiplying everywhere, and doing so much good, gave condensed reports of what took place in Parliament; not in the shape of reports, however, but as sensational sketches . . . the consequence was, that they never . . . read the other side of the question, and thus their views were altogether warped on great public questions.[3]

He called for the setting up of an official record of the proceedings of the House, other than the privately owned Parliamentary Debates, published by Hansard.

The appearance and manners of Members also came under attack and this he held as unfair: 'God knows! Gentlemen who worked till 2 or 3 o'clock in the morning might be excused if sometimes they were a little ungainly in their manners'.[4] The whole thing was indicative 'of a decline in public taste'. He had in the past complained that he and other Irish Members were ill-treated in the press: on more than one occasion he himself had been depicted as 'addressing the House with my hat on, and looking like a street ballad singer coming out of a public-house'. He recalled, 'one publication stated that my favourite attitude was to seize my hat and advance in the manner of a "French lover" on the stage'. Such attacks had little effect on him personally, he told the House of Commons, but he did worry that the public would have their 'minds debauched by being taught to believe that this sort of thing is Parliamentary history'.[5]

Another issue which occupied his attention at this time was the plight of the forty Fenians still held in prison. The question of the amnesty for these men was raised time and again by members of the party. Butt was himself president of the Amnesty Association which had for years conducted a nationwide campaign for their release. In August 1875 Henry put forward a motion in the House calling for their release. It was time, he said, for those in authority to say 'Justice is satisfied – go in peace – sin no more'.[6] After a short debate the motion was withdrawn. A year later he spoke again on the subject, on 1 August 1876, when he described the prisoners as 'misguided men'.[7]

By the close of the 1875 session Butt was already losing his grip on the leadership of the party. The necessity for earning a living kept him frequently absent from parliament as he attended to his law practice in Dublin. Henry and other members of the party tried to find ways of alleviating Butt's financial burden and scheme after scheme was attempted, but without success. At one time Henry recommended that Butt resign from politics and return to his law practice:

My advice to you is to retire from political life altogether and to return to your profession. This state of things cannot go on – and if the Irish will not make any sacrifices to retain your services – you are not justified in continuing to sacrifice yourself.[8]

In the absence of strong leadership the 1875 session saw the emergence of a new faction in the party: the obstructionists. Lead by J.G. Bigger, these men attempted to delay the passage of English business through parliament by a series of long speeches, forcing the House to sit well into the night. Commenting on Bigger at this time, Henry told the House that as a North of Ireland man 'he belonged to that body of Protestants who were rightly considered to have a share of the virtue of persistency amounting, perhaps, sometimes to a suspicion of a shade of obstinacy'.[9]

The two years that followed, 1876 and 1877, saw the Irish Party introduce a number of Bills into the House in an attempt to try and have some Home Rule measures adopted; including Henry's Registration of Voters (Ireland) Bill in May 1876 and Irish Taxation Resolution in July 1877. All, but one, were voted down. Anger and frustration with their failure to have Irish issues more fully debated was causing division among party members. Butt's tactics were proving too moderate and conciliatory for many party members and for the public in general. The more militant wing, the obstructionists, including among their number Charles Stewart Parnell, increased their actions to such an extent that new rules were introduced into the House to try and check them. Henry, recognised as an 'active moderate', called for the retention of Butt as leader but pressed for more vigorous action in parliament.

While not altogether approving of the actions of the obstructionists he was willing to explain and defend them in parliament:'it had merely been the expression of a determination on their part that certain questions should be sufficiently debated'. To some extent their actions had, he felt, produced excellent results, as in the case of the Prisons Bill. He disapproved however of their obstruction of the South Africa Bill. His chief complaint was that they acted as a faction, without first consulting other members of the party: 'Had they taken the step of consulting those who sat near them upon the subject, their conduct would at all events have assumed a respectability by which it was not now distinguished'.

Courtesy of National Library of Ireland R27,446

Charles Stewart Parnell

However, he also recognised that their actions were winning popularity in Ireland and warned the House that the obstruction of Irish business by the government 'would have the effect of producing obstruction of a different character in future'.

> He [Henry] and the other hon. Members who advocated Home Rule had come to that parliament pledged to carry out, under the leadership of [Butt], a policy of wise conciliation . . . [But now] The Irish people were tired of useless conciliation, and, if the House did not arouse itself, means would be found to enforce such debates on Irish questions as would induce the House to consider Irish matters in a different spirit. He did not mean this in any way as a threat, for he honoured the House, and considered it a privilege to belong to it; but it must not be supposed that the Irish people were as anxious as the House to put down Irish Members . . . the House would be greatly mistaken if it supposed that there was not the most intense sympathy in Ireland with the course of conduct pursued by the hon. Members for Meath [Parnell] and Cavan [Bigger].[10]

A public meeting was held in the Rotunda on 22 August 1877 in support of Bigger and Parnell. Henry did not attend, but sent a letter calling for unity among party members, support for Butt as leader and a new departure for the future:

> This opinion I can express with the more freedom because it is well known that I have always been an advocate of a sterner policy than that which had been hitherto adopted. The energy and determination of all members of the party ought to be utilised for the general good . . . there must be discipline and accord in parliamentary matters.

What was needed was:

> a new departure in our line of politics. We have been mocked and derided in all our efforts. With one trumpery exception, not one Home Rule bill has become law, and the ignominious rejection of the Irish University Bill has crowned the tale of our discomfiture. Let us carefully avoid any slight to our parliamentary leader, whose services and experience are unrivalled; but let us, *later on,* when excitement and heart-burning have subsided, hold another conference in Dublin, and determine on a regular and systematic campaign, calculated not to please our enemies, but to advance the Irish cause.[11]

In a further effort to try and unite the party in a more vigorous campaign in the House and to have Butt adopt 'a policy of selective obstruction',[12] Henry wrote to the *Freeman's Journal* on the 8 September criticising absenteeism, lack of organisation and earnestness among party members:

> Is it no wonder that in the House of Commons we are not supposed to be sincere. We do not look like a party that intends to win; we never cheer each others efforts, but some one or other is too often found ready to "repudiate" the sentiments of a brother Home Ruler, which he has probably caught up wrongly during a flying visit to the House between a convivial dinner and a noisy adjournment to the smoking room.

Criticising Butt's frequent absences from the House and lack of leadership, he continues: 'If battles are to be won a general must always be with his army, directing its movements, encouraging his soldiers by his presence, adapting his tactics to the exigencies of the hour, and above all, having a fixed plan of the campaign in his head'. More frequent meetings of the Parliamentary party were called for and 'patient consultation' between party members and their leader.

On the issue of Obstruction he wrote:

> I, for one, believe that we shall not be called upon to practise obstruction for the sake of obstruction, but solely for the purpose of passing good laws or for defeating bad ones. Experience has taught me to place no confidence whatever in expectations of English support for Home Rule bills. We are too apt to be deluded by the smiles, the hints, and the honeyed words of members who think that the proper way to get round an Irishman is to flatter his vanity and love of approbation at the expense of the majority of his countrymen . . . take the three great Irish test questions-Home Rule, the Land Bill, and religious education – I say we have made no way whatever . . . and unless we can manage to impress the house and the country with the conviction that we believe in our own measures and intend to carry them, we may go on as we are until what Shakespeare calls "the crack of doom".

He was not in favour of 'a pig-headed course of obstruction'. He was in favour of vigour and reality in their proceedings. And while not condoning the actions of the obstructionists he did recognise that what made 'Mr Parnell and some others so hateful to the English Press and to some of the English members is that they think them formidable, because [they were] not likely to be bought by office, or by what is quite as fatal, by personal flattery'.[13]

A party conference was held in October and resolutions calling for a 'united and energetic action under the leadership of Butt'[14] were proposed and passed. However, with Butt's bad health and financial difficulties continuing to keep him from the House, the struggle for power within the party did not end there.

The split in the parliamentary party was causing dissent among supporters back home and, despite his very active and well publicised attempts to encourage a more vigorous parliamentary campaign, an attempt was made by some Catholic priests, supporters of Parnell, to discredit Henry before his constituents at a public meeting held in Clifden on New Year's Day 1878. Henry had come to Clifden to address his constituents 'on the political situation and on his own political conduct'.[15] The meeting was announced from every Catholic pulpit in the parish the Sunday before and 'the people were called upon to gather in thousands to give Mr Henry, M.P., . . . a real Irish welcome'. The large platform erected opposite Mullarkey's Hotel was occupied by local dignitaries and almost every priest in the locality. At about two o'clock Henry arrived and the meeting got underway. The chair was taken by Edwin Eyre, of Clifden Castle, proposed by Dean McManus P.P., of Clifden. Henry stepped forward and delivered his speech.

There was nothing new in what he had to say, he first addressed the failure of the Home Rule Party to have any of its measures adopted, Bills put forward by party members were 'ignominiously and contemptuously kicked out of Parliament'. He went on to criticise the Land Act and called for fixity of tenure, free sale and, where disagreements over rent arose, settlement by arbitration. He concurred with the policy of obstruction, he told his audience, 'until it interfered with the South African Bill', which he believed to be 'an excellent and praiseworthy bill', but the energy 'thrown away in that policy of obstruction' ought to be used more effectively for Irish interests.

As the speech went on it became evident from the number of interruptions by hecklers that 'the reception was not so cordial as one might expect'. On its conclusion a vote of confidence was called for by Dean McManus and seconded by Joseph Gorham. Press reports differ as to what occurred next; some say that the motion was carried, but others report that before it was put to the vote 'great uproar followed', with almost everyone on the platform speaking at once, and 'the crowd called loudly for Father Conway'. Henry was about to leave the platform when Father Walter Conway, the curate from Ballyconneely, announced that he had a few questions to put to him in the presence of his constituents. Conway then proceeded to accuse Henry of absenteeism in the House and failure to attend party meetings: to which Henry replied that one should not assume that 'because I do not vote I am not present'. And went on to explain that there were times when he refrained from voting on amendments put forward by other members of the party rather than voting against them. With regard to the party meetings, he had missed two due to illness and refused to attend two others 'because I refused to be a party of passing a vote of censure on those so called Obstructionists – Mr Parnell, Mr O'Connor Power, and the rest'. Conway then accused Henry of evicting tenants of his Kylemore estate and proceeded to give the names and circumstances of individual cases. Henry replied that Conway's statement was 'absolutely without foundation': 'I must say that it is absolutely untrue that I evicted or drove off a single human being from the Kylemore estate, I have spent ten or fifteen times the rent of my estate on improvement'.

Father Conway then called on the people not to vote for a Protestant: 'Remember . . . he is a Protestant. Will you return him at the next election whenever that may be? Let those who are prepared to vote for him at the next election put up their hands'. No hands were raised, but instead a cry went out: 'we will not vote for him'. With that Henry was led from the platform and into Mularkey's Hotel by Dean McManus and Edwin Eyre. They were followed by others from the platform, but there were some who stayed and, under the leadership of Father Conway and Father William Rhatigan, further speeches were made and a vote of no confidence in Henry was proposed and seconded. The meeting eventually dispersed with Father Conway and his supporters retiring to another hotel on the opposite side of the street, leaving the *Galway Express* to comment: 'And thus the advocates of Home Rule in Connemara, forming themselves into two hostile camps'.[16]

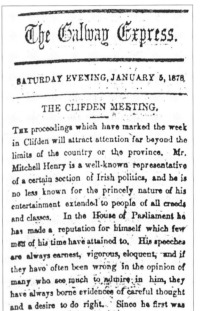

Galway Express
5 January 1878

The criticism of such a high profile party member by his constituents would, according to the *Galway Express,* 'attract attention far beyond the limits of the county or the province'.[17] And this proved to be the case. Reports of the proceedings at Clifden and a debate on their effect on the Party and the Home Rule cause filled the pages of the national press in the weeks that followed. The press unanimously condemned those who opposed the vote of confidence in Henry and all went on to refer to his 'patriotism and earnestness' in the national cause. They lamented any damage that may have been done to his reputation; the great worry was that the story would be picked up by the English press and used against the Party and thereby damage the cause.

The *Freeman's Journal* deplored the 'scene which discredited New Year's Day, insulted one of the best members of the National Party, and . . . outraged public opinion in the western archdiocese'. They warned that 'harm of a very serious nature had been done' to the Home Rule cause and the story that the 'Irish people have repudiated one of the ablest and most sincere representatives of Home Rule' would be used by the English press against them. They criticised those who carried out such 'a violent, a personal, and an ungrateful attack made on a gentleman whose sacrifices have been constant and weighty'. Father Conway's 'methods of argument' were 'too violent . . . too vulgar, for thinking men to stoop to answer . . . Mr Henry's success in Parliament has been remarkable amongst successes which twenty years ago, even ten years ago, would have amazed the Irish people'.[18]

The *Nation* wrote that Henry was not listed among those politicians which the paper regularly censured by name for frequent absenteeism or neglectful of the interests of the country. There was, in their opinion, nothing in Henry's speech which could have provoked such an attack. The speech was 'outspoken and patriotic', critical of the 'contemptuous treatment which Irish demands' received in the House and calling for more vigorous action by the Irish party. If anything, Henry had been a little too modest in regard to his own activities and this the paper was happy to redress:

> Mr Mitchell Henry, with characteristic modesty, did not dwell much, or at all, on his own service to the national cause, but this is not because he had no services to which to point. Since his accession to the Home Rule ranks, he has given freely of his time and money in furthering the Home Rule agitation; he has ever maintained a manly and straight forward attitude in Parliament; he has shown a lively interest in every question of importance to Ireland; and on a particular question – that of the financial grievance of Ireland – he is *facile princips* in his advocacy of the Irish demand.

Taking into account that in Connemara he was seen as a public benefactor, it continued,

> We feel not only amazed but ashamed of the treatment meted out to Mr Mitchell Henry by some persons in Clifden. It is unjust, it is marked by dire ingratitude, and it must be condemned by the general body of Mr Henrys constituents if it is not to react injuriously on the

country. It tends to weaken Mr Henrys hands in his endeavours for the public good, and the country cannot afford to have the moral position of one like him destroyed . . . there is no man of honour and intelligence within the four seas of Ireland, no matter to what party he may belong, who will not laugh to scorn the idea of Mitchell Henry being censured for his behaviour as a member of Parliament, and others who are notorious delinquents escaping scot free.[19]

The people and clergy of Connemara immediately distanced themselves from the language and claims made by Fathers Conway and Rhatigan. Father Conway was a curate in Ballyconneely some distance from Kylemore and admitted that a Father Freeley, former curate at Ballynakill, was the source for his accusations. Father Rhatigan was new to the area, he was appointed curate at Clifden just two months before and was accused of not being fully informed on the district. Archbishop MacHale, a guest at Kylemore Castle in the past, in a letter to the *Freeman's Journal*, wrote that it was with 'surprise and regret' that he read of the disturbance in Clifden. He severely censured the priests involved, describing them as 'raw recruits in the field of politics', who did not consider the disastrous consequences of their actions. Praising Henry for his devotion to Home Rule he called for tolerance on all sides: 'There has not appeared among us a more earnest, efficient, and persevering advocate of Home Rule than Mitchell Henry'.[20]

Dean McManus in a telegraph to the editor, which appeared on the same day, condemned and denounced the actions of, what he referred to as, 'a few rowdies'.[21] Father M. Holland, Prior of the Carmelites, wrote directly to Henry to express his condemnation. Describing himself as one who took a keen interest in public questions and public representatives:

> my sympathies are intensely on the side of Irish Nationality and of every reasonable and sincere effort in that direction, I approve of your public career. I cannot be unmindful of your high position, your early adoption of the national programme, your public enlightened pronouncements of most Irish questions, your speeches, votes, and recent letters, your generous aid, and manly defence of the national demand; and last, though emphatically not least, your trenchant, and I trust effectual, castigation of hypocrisy and insolence devoid of patriotism. Therefore, sir, do I look on the conduct of the Clifden curates as disreputable and disgraceful to the priesthood of Ireland calculated to be injurious to the national cause, an argument in the mouths of our enemies against our just demand, and discouraging to those who labour patriotically for the welfare of our country.[22]

However, despite the condemnations, Father Conway continued his accusations of eviction and ill-treatment of tenants, this time through the press. Henry challenged him to state the particulars of any single case, declaring that:

> since I purchased this estate not a hearthstone or a roof-tree has been removed, and that I have added twenty families to the rental . . . during the fourteen years I have lived here I have never had a disagreeable word with a single tenant, or heard anything but exclamations of gratitude and blessing.[23]

Father McAndrew P.P., at Ballynakill, the parish in which Kylemore Estate stood, wrote to the *Freeman's Journal* to refute the accusation made at the meeting by Father Rhatigan that tenants' houses had been removed to make way for 'beautiful lawns and beautiful pastures' at Kylemore:

> In the interest of truth and justice I write to contradict . . . this statement . . . or the homes of no tenants ever occupied "the beautiful lawns and beautiful pastures" on the estate of Kylemore. These lawns and these pastures have been rescued for the most part from nature, "stern and wild". They have been made beautiful by labour and reclamation. And the immense sums of money expended on their transformation have made many homes happy, not only on Mr Henrys estate, but also on adjoining properties.

The only tenant to be discommoded was Anthony Coyne, whose cottage lay close to the gardens, an agreement was reached between himself and Henry and

> He removed with pleasure, for his condition was much improved by the change. An excellent slated house was built for him which very favourably contrasted with the thatched cabin that he had left. He got more and better land than he previously occupied. He is to-day a prosperous contented man. A married son and his young family live with him, and they enjoy the advantage of having within fifty yards of their fine house by the public roadside the magnificent schools erected by Mr Henry for the children of his tenantry. Surely this case could not supply the shadow of a pretext for the charges that have been put forward.[24]

The following day, 8 January, the *Freeman's Journal* carried a letter from Dean McManus, co-signed by the 'clergy, freeholders and people of Connemara' (over 160 signatures), stating their wish:

> to record that Mr Henry never did evict or ill-treat a tenant, but, on the contrary, treated them with the most paternal solicitude; that he has been a benefactor not only to his own tenants, but to persons

residing on other estates as well as his own, by giving them employment when hard pressed by destitution; that when destitution was prevalent he and his family did everything in their power to mitigate the distress, to feed the hungry, and to alleviate the sorrows and miseries of the sick poor.

Tenants' Letter
Freeman's Journal 10 January 1878

In the same paper Father Conway repeated his allegations that Henry was guilty of taking up 'at least four farms, comprising over a thousand acres, and adding them to his demesne', and went on to name the tenants removed; Pat O'Neill and his son, Watts and John Walsh of Letterfrack. He also accused Henry of raising rents above the value of the land, of prosecuting tenants for non-payment of rent and of preventing the tenants from taking the seaweed and sand from the shore. He describes Henry's tenants as','the poorest and most wretched in that part of Connemara . . . Mr Henry is eye-witness to this misery every time he passes on the new road made through the tenants' holdings, for which they were promised but never got compensation, to visit said farm'.[25]

Two days later the same newspaper carried a letter signed by the 127 tenants of the Kylemore Estate declaring the charges against Henry to be 'unfounded' and testifying that 'Mr Henry has done more for them than any landlord ever did'.[26]

Henry answered Conway's accusations with detailed explanations in every case. In the case of Paddy O'Neill and his son; O'Neill was well-known grazier in Connemara, who leased several thousand acres 'in various parts of the district, on which he grazed cattle, driving them from one tract to another as they eat the pasture bare. He, of course, gave no employment, and never ploughed or manured an acre of land'. He held 240 acres at Mullaghglass, leased from the previous owner of the land. He resided some miles away but his son moved on to the farm and shared the house with the herd. When the lease expired Henry declined to renew it. The Watt's case was 'a mistake for Joyce'. Joyce held a farm at Tooreena. There were never any houses or dwellings on this 633 acres of land which was also used

MR. M. HENRY, M.P., AND HIS TENANTS

TO THE EDITOR OF THE FREEMAN.

Currywongane, Kylemore, Galway,
January 8th.

SIR—Presuming on your love of justice, we trust you will kindly publish the accompanying protest from the entire tenantry of the Kylemore estate, every one of whom have gratefully testified that Mr, Henry has done more for them than any landlord ever did.—Signed on behalf of the tenantry,

JOHN COYNE, Tenant.
THOMAS SULLIVAN, do.
STEPHEN WALLACE, do.

The following is the document referred to :—

We, the entire tenantry of the Kylemore estate of Mitchell Henry, Esq., M.P., having heard with deep regret of the base calumny against our generous and liberal landlord, Mr. Henry, M.P, think it our duty to give publicity to our feelings of indignation, and to contradict the totally unfounded charge made against his character at the Clifden meeting.

We always believed Mr. Henry to be a kind and considerate landlord, and feel bound to say in justice to Mr. Henry that to our knowledge there never was a single tenant evicted off the Kylemore estate since Mr. Henry became proprietor of it.

We have ever known him to be generous and charitable, and we feel deeply grateful for all his goodness to us.   (Signed)

Martin Coyne, John Coyne, David Gavin, Peter Hallinane, Andrew Coriey, Michael Thornton, Pat Murray, Stephen Duffy, Widow Diamond, Anthony Coyne, Wm W Casson, Michael Connelly, Mary Coyne, P M'Donogh, Martin Walsh, John Nee, Charles Moxham, Thomas Kelly, John Fitzpatrick, James Varley, Hugh Burke, Mary M'Donnell, John Mullin, Michael Garvey, Widow Conneelly, Peter Joyce, Valentine Conway, Pat Joyce, Stephen Wallace, Ambrose Burke, John Lyden, Pat Keely, Pat Morgan, John Joyce, Martin King, Anthony Conry, Pat Conneely, William Wallace. Tom Coyne, Tom Coneely, Tom Coyne, Thos Joce, Pat Wallace, John Lyden, Michael Butler, Tom Sullivan, sen; Tom Sullivan, jun; Michael Laffey, Stephen Wallace, Pat Heanue, Widow Moran, Martin Flaherty, Widow Coyne, Daniel Nee, Tom Donnelly, Peter Joyce, Michl. Joyce, Pat Flaherty, Pat Kane, Gregory Conneely, Pat Lyden, Michael Coyne, John Coyne, John Coyne, Michael Mulkerins, John Keane, Martin Harwood, Wm Heanue, Frank Kearney, Tom Falerty, Tom Joyce, James Donnellan, John Gibbons, Bart Faherty, Widow Gibbons, Myles Joyce, Michael Coyne, Michael Faherty, Martin Coyne, Widow Foland, Pat O'Flaherty, Pat Gibbons, Andrew Malley, Edward Conneely, Michael Joyce, John Kance Thomas Conry, John Walsh, Michael Kerrigan, Tom Kerrigan, James Kerrigan, Martin Delany, Thomas King, John Thornton, Harry Walsh, Anthony Conry, Widow Mulkerrins, Stephen Wallace, Michael Nee, M Flaherty, J Flaherty, Martin Kane, John Conry, Martin Conry, Darby Heanue, Roger Conry, John Burke, John Kearney, M Kane, Tom Freehill, P Kane, T Kane, John M'Donnell, Pat Coyne, Darby Nee, Michael Conry, John Lyden, Michael Conry, Martin Thornton, Michael Gollehar, B Coyne, Pat Coyne, Anthony King, Pat King, Owen King, Michael King, Darby Nee.—127 tenants.

for grazing. Joyce gave up his lease before it expired and Henry began reclaiming the land and that of O'Neill's. This was the reclamation work which had given so much employment in the locality and had attracted the attention of agriculturalists and the press. In the case of John Walsh, believed to be the tenant at Bunnaboghee, described by Henry as 'a most respected man'. Henry had reduced his rent when Walsh informed him that he was in financial debt and unable to pay. Henry went on to spend £50 doing up Walsh's house so that he could take in a lodger to assist with the rent. Later, when he fell two years in arrears, Walsh went to Henry with the intention of giving up the farm, but was persuaded to try again for another year. But in the end Walsh felt he was unable to continue and he gave up the farm. Henry gave him £70 'to set up a shop' which his wife ran, while Walsh and his son were employed in the Castle garden.

Henry denied that he had forbidden the taking of sand or seaweed from the shore:

> It is an absolute falsehood to say that I deprived any tenants of seaweed and sand. On the contrary, I made a new road, the better to enable them to obtain it, and I charge nobody for seaweed or for turbery, as is the case elsewhere. Doubtless there is still much misery on parts of my estate, but I cannot make people provident all at once, nor can I control the seasons, or build and improve houses faster than I am doing.

Henry explained how Anthony Coyne, the tenant who occupied the land on which the walled garden now stands, had given up that farm in exchange for a much better one closer to the main road. And in response to the accusation of having raised rents, he wrote that he had indeed raised the rents at Currywongaun from £20 to £25 a year, after having improved the dwellings and built roads:

> the townland, which is very extensive and on which the four tenants live, and are extremely prosperous,was formerly held by one man, with the others as under-tenants. These tenants now grow turnips, mangolds, and sow artificial grasses, all of which were unknown in the country until I gave them the seed and set them the example, and there are not in Ireland more prosperous or more contented men, nor could they be men more angry with my calumniators.

Henry explained the generous terms under which his tenants held their leases and the extent of the employment offered to them on the estate and recounted the incident in which he had processes served on six tenants for non-payment of rent. He was angry at being forced by 'those three hot-headed young men' to bring such details out into the open. Neither did he appreciate their attempts at stirring up trouble between himself and his tenants:

> To be accused of ill-treating tenants sounds to my ears as strangely as it would to be accused of habitual drunkenness or of habitual theft. For some time at any rate, I shall continue to give employment, and shall endeavour not to feel faint and weary.

The depth of sorrow such accusations had caused him was revealed when, for the first time in public, he recalls his wife's brief time at Kylemore:

> Few, indeed, were the words of sympathy that ever fell on the ears of the peasantry around my dwelling until my family became resident among them, and never certainly before that time had they felt the soft touch of a ladys hand when sickness had laid them low, I know that they are grateful, and I know, too, that if these three curates have calumniated me, they have much more calumniated them. One phrase common amongst them when the great sorrow fell upon my house, will never fade from my memory, and has often brought tears to my eyes – for when she who was their benefactress and their friend, but not their landlord, was taken away, these "ill-used" tenants said – "It is not our mistress we have lost, but our mother." [27]

Any pain felt by Henry at the personal attacks made on him in Clifden and in the press were pushed aside six days later when parliament opened on 17 January 1878. Butt was too ill to attend and Henry, acting as leader, put forward the Irish amendment to the address in reply to the queen's speech. Giving a brief outline of the party's history to date, the number of Bills introduced by Irish Members and their lack of success, he repeated their demand for a 'reasonable University education for the great masses of the Irish people' and Home Rule similar to that enjoyed by Canada, Jersey and Guernsey. However, it would seem he did not anticipate a favourable response to this repeated request as there was, he went on to point out, 'a lamentable ignorance of Irish affairs' among Members of the House of Commons: 'Nobody ever thought of going to Ireland to study its conditions, yet everyone thought they knew how to deal with it . . . It seemed almost incredible that the responsible Ministers of the Crown had never cared to go to the country which had given them so much trouble . . . If the House of Commons could understand the fervour of the patriotism of the Irish people they would do justice to them and to their religion'.[28] The amendment was voted down by 301 votes to 48.[29]

As the year advanced the party continued to disintegrate and was losing the support of the press and public alike. Although still refusing to criticise Parnell in public, in private Henry wrote to his friend W. J. O'Neill Daunt

> [Parnell] is clever and courageous – but utterly without judgment and holds anyone who differs from him in the slightest degree in contempt . . . [and] although very calm in manner he gets intensely excited in speaking and will say some terrible things of something or somebody. When challenged, as he often is, he <u>utterly denies having said it</u>.

Repeating his opinion that 'a certain amount of action and obstruction [was] essential', but obstruction as practised by Parnell was, in Henry's opinion, suicidal:

> Parnell acts like a child – really I should not be surprised to see him someday trip up the Speaker as he enters the House, in order to upset and make a sensation . . . The truth is that where there is a time of insanity you can calculate nothing. Sudden uncontrollable impulses arise and upset all calculations.[30]

Butt's health continued to decline until his death on 5 May 1879. The election for his replacement as Chairman of the party was between William Shaw and Henry. Timothy Healy, in his book *Letters And Leaders Of My Day*, tells us how Bigger and Parnell voted and why:

> Bigger voted for Mitchell Henry, whose tenure to the Chair was likely to be effective. Parnell voted for Shaw, whom he knew he could oust. So Shaw was chosen.[31]

The split in the party was now deeper than ever, Shaw was recognised at the leader of the official Home Rule Party with the more advanced members of the party looking towards Parnell. A general election was anticipated in the near future and Parnell set about increasing his popularity and support. The lack of progress with Home Rule and the decline in the party's popularity left a political void which would soon be filled by events taking place on the ground. Agricultural depression, bad weather and crop failure would bring the West to near famine in 1879 and would contribute to the spread of a vigorous land campaign with far reaching consequences.

Chapter 7

Tenant Rights

Throughout the unusually wet summer of 1879 Michael Davitt, one of the Fenians released from jail in January 1878, and local leaders organised meetings in every town in Mayo and many of the surrounding counties. The demand at such meetings was for rent reduction and relief. As the movement gathered momentum it developed into a campaign for Tenant Rights and, given its potential, it was quickly picked up by Parnell and given a nationwide appeal.

Henry had always kept rents low, but that September as rent day approached, on seeing the conditions around him and the very real threat of famine, he gave a remission to his tenants of half a year's rent:

> I consider it is the duty of a landlord to share in the unavoidable losses arising from bad years, for which none of us are to blame, and I will therefore allow to each of my agricultural tenants the remission of the whole of the present half years rent . . . I trust that this arrangement will tide us over our difficulties, and I confidently rely on your preventing the accumulation of arrears, which are simply destructive to the happiness and well-being of all concerned.[1]

However, not all Connemara tenants were so fortunate. In the thirty years since the Great Famine many of the Connemara Estates had increased their rents and as conditions deteriorated the tenants were feeling the effect. A meeting calling on Connemara landlords to reduce their rents was held in Clifden on 6 September 1879, at which Henry was the principal speaker. The meeting was unusual in that it

Courtesy of National Library of Ireland

Vanity Fair Album 19 April 1879

was organised by the local Catholic clergy and had on the platform almost every priest in the district (excluding Conway and Rhatigan). Archbishop MacHale strongly objected to such meetings, fearing they would encourage the spread of secret agrarian societies. Such societies were condemned by the church because of their secret oaths and violent nature and feared by the authorities because of their rapid spread through a district.

Henry, with his usual eloquence and passion, called for an immediate and permanent reduction in rents to the levels of twenty years before. He spoke at length on the conditions that had brought them to this point, the causes of the present distress and the need to address them. Conscious of the presence of members of the press, he asked the crowd to remember that he was speaking to a much wider audience than that present and requested their patience as he laid out a few facts to acquaint the general public in England with the true state of conditions in Ireland, on the needs of the ordinary people and on the wrongs done to them by over taxation, absenteeism and an indifferent government. His speech was moderate in tone and content when compared with speeches delivered at similar meetings in Mayo under Davitt. Henry, retaining the line of the official Home Rule Party, was calling for Home Rule, while Davitt at a meeting held in Westport in June had called for 'total separation'.

Members of the clergy, who spoke after Henry, were more forceful in their message. Father McAndrew called on the government to rectify present conditions and help prevent 'poverty, crime, and ultimately revolution'. Land agitation was the ruling question of the day, he told the crowd and 'so long as unjust laws were valid, so long would deeds of blood follow – deeds against which humanity revolted, and which religion deplored'. Father Joseph Maloney P.P., at Roundstone, told them not to choose men of the landlord class to represent them in the next session of Parliament, 'but there were some good and benevolent landlords there, and amongst them such men as Mr Mitchell Henry, who should be kept there'. A resolution calling for the three F's: Fair Rent, Fixity of Tenure and Free Sale, as well as a system of 'tenant proprietary', was put forward by Father Fahy C.C., and carried.[2] Later this meeting was marked as the beginning of land agitation in Connemara.

Henry turned down an invitation to speak at the Tuam meeting which took place on the following Sunday, stating that it was his policy not to attend political meetings on Sundays. The same explanation kept him from other meetings in his constituency in the months that followed. His letter of apology, advocating the three F's and a reduction of rents, was read to the Tuam meeting:

Where rents have been raised in late years they will have to come down, for the tenants cannot continue to pay them, and all the tenants, whether low-rented or not, must be given security of tenure with fair rents, ascertained, if necessary, by arbitration, and the right of freely selling their interest . . . I have no doubt whatever that out of the present evils which have fallen so hardly on us great and permanent good will come to all. A famished and starving people cannot be neglected and our self-complacent rulers in England, will find nature herself is fighting on our side.[3]

Davitt, speaking at the same meeting, called for 'peasant proprietorship' and criticised Henry and the other Member for Galway, Major Nolan, for not supporting the more active policies of Parnell. Fixity of tenure did not go far enough 'in the opinion of the people of Ireland', Davitt told his audience. Major Nolan's obstruction activities 'had, no doubt, rendered good services in the House of Commons, but both he and Mr Mitchell Henry would have to support the platforms of Mr Parnell'.[4]

Courtesy of National Library of Ireland R12,820

Michael Davitt

Such speeches and demonstrations were usually backed up with action. The tenants went to their landlords and with one voice demanded a reduction in rents and if this was not met intimidation began: cattle and sheep were pushed off cliffs, houses were burned, ricks of turf, stacks of hay, straw and barns were set alight. An atmosphere of intimidation and violence was spreading through the West, accompanied by warnings of pending famine.

The torrential rain of the summer continued unabated into the autumn. Henry, as the representative for the area, made a personal inspection of hundreds of Connemara farms and found that two thirds of the potato crop was inedible and almost no turf had been saved, leaving the people without food or fuel for the coming winter. Fears grew of yet another famine hitting the West. With memories of the Great Famine still fresh in the mind of many every effort was made to impress on the government the seriousness of the situation. Local committees were formed and letters issued to the press requesting charitable donations. The priests and people of Connemara sent a Memorial to the Lord Lieutenant, acquainting him with conditions and requesting assistance:

an unprecedented universal calamity has befallen the industrious tenant and labour class all over this vast district, such as has not been witnessed for many years, caused by a series of inclement seasons and bad harvests.

They asked that public works such as the construction of a railway between Galway and Clifden, the finishing of old roads and the erection of fishing piers and quays, be sanctioned for a region where a vast population were 'able and willing to earn their bread with the sweat of their brow'.[5]

Henry urged that 'small useful works should be undertaken, which would be of permanent value to the people'. He offered to take out 'a considerable loan', to be used in the district and on his own estate, under the direction of the Board of Works. The Board of Works supported the proposal, but it was rejected by the government 'in favour of a distribution of charity'.[6] Charitable funds were set up by the Duchess of Marlborough, wife of the Lord Lieutenant, and the Lord Mayor of Dublin, and the funds raised were used to purchase food for distribution to the poor.

Henry strongly objected to the government's preference for relieving distress with charity rather than employment, seeing it as demoralising for the recipients: 'the very worst method of assisting people who are anxious to give a return for what they receive'.[7] With his usual benevolence he did all he could to alleviate conditions in his own area and was praised in the press for giving employment to 'not only his tenants but the entire area'.[8] Many rents fell due in November but without a crop to sell and no possibility of obtaining employment few tenants were in a position to pay and many were under threat of eviction.

As Tenant Rights meetings continued to be held Sunday after Sunday throughout the constituency, Henry's persistent absence worried his supporters. It was feared that Parnell might take advantage of the situation and put forward an alternative Home Rule candidate at the next election. Pressure mounted on Henry to set aside his 'conscientious convictions' and join the people in their demands. A meeting was planned for Galway city on Sunday, 2 November 1879, and Parnell was expected to speak. The meeting was called to urge the government to begin public works immediately and help save the lives of a starving people. Henry, on learning of the 'charitable character' of the meeting, agreed to attend and the *Galway Vindicator* cheered his decision: 'We are very glad to be in a position to state that our popular and able County Representative, Mr Mitchell Henry, will attend our public meeting tomorrow in Galway and will give the people of Galway the advantage of his eloquent advocacy'.[9]

Henry received 'quite an ovation from the meeting', but the crowd had come to see, and to hear, Parnell. Parnell, now president of Davitt's recently formed Irish National Land League, told them that as the tenant farmers could no longer pay the rents demanded of them, they must make a stand somewhere and the line had been drawn at a fair rent. In the fight that would follow they must stand fast to their homesteads or be branded cowards by future generations:

> If when Providence places at your hand an opportunity of securing for yourselves and for your children, and the future of all Irishmen, justice, happiness and prosperity. If you are too cowardly, too disunited to pluck the chance, to take advantage of the opportunity – then I say there is no hope for Ireland.[10]

He put forward a resolution, which was passed, calling for the Surplus Church Fund to be used to create a peasant proprietary and that support be given at the coming election only to those Parliamentary candidates 'who will endeavour as far as possible to create a peasant proprietary for the tenant-farmers of Ireland'.

It was the adoption of the concept of 'peasant proprietorship' that was giving Henry difficulty, although on this occasion he told the crowd that it was a measure he had advocated for years and gave examples of how it might be achieved. Turning to the main purpose of the meeting he warned that 'the angel of death' was hanging over the country at the present time and called on the government to begin public works and bring employment to the people in their own districts.

The previous day, on a platform in Athenry shared with John Dillon and Matthew Harris, close associates of Parnell and Davitt, he told the crowd that, in time, a considerable stride would be made in the direction of peasant proprietorship, but this could not be done in a day and would not be preferred by all. A large portion of the population 'may in the course of time become proprietors of their own farms', however, it might suit a great many others 'to pay moderate, fair and fixed rents rather than part with their money to buy the land when they want it to stock their farms'.[11]

Eight days later, on 10 November, at the 'Great Irish Demonstration' in Manchester, Henry again shared the platform with Parnell. On this occasion they were joined by John O'Connor Power, M.P., and N. J. Finigan, M.P. The purpose of this meeting was to 'unite all sections of the Irish party in view of the approaching election'. Parnell praised the unity displayed by the tenant farmers; the land agitation had taught them the strength that lay in organisation. Henry praised the unity of the Irish party. Irish members could no longer be bought by honours, rewards and titles, he told the audience, they were now a voice to be listened too. Finigan called on all to unite 'on the broad platform – call it whatever they like – of Home Rule or the active policy'.[12]

However, Henry's declaration that 'he belonged to the Liberal Party. He detested and abhorred Toryism in all its aspects',[13] would prove to be the greatest of the differences between the two men. Time would show that Parnell was prepared to side with either party in order to win whatever advantage he could for Ireland, while Henry's support for the Liberals would eventually separate him from the majority of Irish Members.

On 23 November Henry was back again in Galway attending yet another Sunday meeting, this time in Ballinasloe. Again the meeting was held to draw attention to 'the distress which presently weighed so heavily on the tenant-farmers' and to 'determine how famine could be kept from the doors of the people'.[14]

Throughout January and February of 1880 the newspapers carried details of terrible poverty and starvation in the West. Henry brought the plight of the people to the House of Commons, reading excerpts from newspapers, among them a letter from Father Conway, now in Screeb, South Connemara, and letters sent to him from community leaders in Galway. Henry warned the House that 'it would be worse before it became better'. Public works and seed potatoes were needed: 'Unless hundreds of thousands of pounds were expended, there would be no harvest at all next year'.[15]

In the absence of public works he favoured the distribution of 'a little relief in money' so that the people could continue to cultivate their farms:

> Thousands of people in the West of Ireland were now kept from death by the distribution of yellow Indian meal, which, with a little water, and some seaweed, if they could get it, mixed with periwinkles, formed the food of thousands of Her Majestys subjects.[16]

Over the next few months food, clothing, blanket and seed potatoes were issued by the charitable funds and delivered by ship to the islands along the Connemara coast. Donations of cash from individuals and organisations, including the Land League, were immediately put to the purchase of seed potatoes, to replace those consumed by the people.[17]

When the election came around in April support for the Home Rule party was divided. Throughout the country Parnell was making every effort to have men of his choosing elected in place of the official Home Rule Members. It was rumoured that a Parnellite candidate would stand in Galway, but this was rejected by the *Galway Express* which felt that the two sitting Members for the County 'had too firm a hold on the Constituency to be disturbed, even at the instigation of Mr Parnell'.[18] In his election manifesto, printed in the local press, Henry criticised the government's handling of the present crisis. The lack of public works had created the necessity for charity which brought shame on the people: 'sending the hat round the world when all the while we have ample wealth in our own country, if we were allowed to utilise and retain it, they are insulting to our self respect'. Where differences in definition on policy arose he was careful to choose words which would appeal to the broadest possible electorate. What the country required, he told his constituents, was 'the right of Self-Government, or, in other words, Home Rule; a complete reform of the Land Laws, so as to make the Cultivator as far as possible the Owner of the Soil; and, where that is not possible, to give the tenant the security of fixity of tenure, valued rents, and free sale'.[19] This was coming close to the demands made by Parnell but still falling short of those made by Davitt. However, it was sufficient to stave off any threat of an opponent from the more advanced section of the party and on 2 April 1880 Mitchell Henry and Major Nolan were returned unopposed.[20]

The Liberals won the election and Gladstone was back in power. Parnell had greatly increased his support among the newly elected Home Rule representatives and was elected Chairman of the parliamentary party, with Shaw staying on as its leader. When Parliament reopened Parnell and his supporters sat with the Conservatives in the opposition benches, William Shaw and his supporters, Henry included, sat on the government side. Henry attracted criticism for his decision but he replied stating his conviction that Gladstone's government was determined to deal with the Land Question 'in a thorough and complete manner'[21] and that they would, in time, get a good Land Bill based on the three F's. As Henry saw it, the differences between the Irish Members sitting on the government benches and the Irishmen sitting on the opposition side, could be explained by a brief history of the Irish Party after the arrival of Parnell in Parliament in 1875:

> For about one Season afterwards things went on tolerably quietly; then . . . the system of Obstruction sprang up. That system of Obstruction was carried on with the avowed object of bringing Parliament into contempt, and preventing that Representative Institution, the House of Commons, from legislating . . . Obstruction grew from day to day. Now, the great difference between Obstruction which was legitimate and the Obstruction which was resorted to by certain of the Irish Party was easily seen. Occasional Obstruction to great measures was a permissible thing in the House; but Obstruction on every occasion upon measures great and small, carried on for the purpose of Obstruction and delay, was unconstitutional, and rebellious against that House.[22]

Before the 1880 election, he had spoken frequently against the policy of Obstruction, and had, he believed, been returned 'as an opponent of Obstruction, and as a supporter of Mr. Butt's policy of conciliation. As such, he had always spoken in the House, and as such he would continue to speak so long as he held his seat'.[23]

The next three years would prove a bumpy ride for Henry. Not only refusing to sit with the Parnellites, he would persist in criticizing their every action and argument, displaying scant regard for his personal political career and popularity, not to mention safety, back home. And although seated with the Liberals he never fully allied himself to them, but instead considered it his duty to instruct the government on the causes of Ireland's misery, which he claimed were 'chiefly physical and only of a small extent political'.[24]

Evictions for non-payment of rent increased in the summer of 1880; in some instances the tenants were simply unable to pay, in others there was an organised withholding of rents. James Hack Tuke, a Member of the Society of Friends, familiar with Connemara through his visits there during the Great Famine, was again visiting the district in April and found that tenants on Henry's estate who had paid their rents had their houses 'slightly injured as a mark of displeasure from those who had combined not to pay theirs':

> It is deeply disappointing that tenants who are so liberally treated by their landlord, and to whom so much work is given, should be found combining together to refuse their rents. Whilst it may be hoped that the number is small who are acting in this way, no more striking proof can be given of the injury resulting from the extreme doctrines which have of late been so widely taught in some quarters.[25]

A Bill intended to compensate evicted tenants was passed in the House of Commons but failed in the House of Lords. In response agitation on the ground was intensified and the influence of the Land League increased. As the Land League grew in strength and popularity its demand for 'the land of Ireland for the people of Ireland', became the catch phrase of the day and although its leaders urged peaceful persuasion it was not long before agrarian outrages became common place.

Agrarian combinations intent on enforcing their will on a variety of aspects of land occupancy and use frequently resorted to acts of intimidation and violence. Such combinations were a feature of life in Connemara at the time, particularly in and around the neighbourhood of Kylemore. Through the mutilation of animals, intimidation of landlord employees and setting fire to stores and buildings, they sought to intimidate the landlords and their agents and settle old scores, usually with very particular and local origins.

However, the violence and intimidation did not end with the landlords, tenants too were targeted. Tenants who paid rent had threatening notes stuck on their doors in the middle of the night and those who took over land where the previous occupant had been evicted were dragged out of their beds and beaten, or in some cases shot. Sometimes the motive for the shootings was unclear, as in the case of the 'Letterfrack Murders' which took place in Baunoges in April 1881 and the 'Maamtrasna Murders', in August 1882.

As this violent atmosphere intensified back home, Henry became more outspoken against Parnell, the Land League and its leaders at Westminster. He criticised Parnell and his supporters for their clever use of language 'liable to be interpreted in an ambiguous manner', which encouraged the tenants to violence, while at the same time taking care that they themselves did nothing that would bring them 'into the meshes of the law'. To those leaders of the Land League who advocated the withholding of arrears of rents he called for 'fair play'. Landlords who had 'held their hand and not pressed their tenants in time of distress might expect, if the harvest was good', to receive some portion of that which was due. There were, he reminded the House, good landlords as well as bad, and while the income from his own rents was small and because of his mercantile interests 'it personally made less difference to him than to many others whether they were paid or not. But it would wound him to the quick if his tenants did not manifest an appreciation of the forbearance that had been shown to them'. 26

He was convinced that the acts of violence, so common at the time, were foreign to the Irish nature and would not have come about if they were not driven to it by the provocative speeches of Land League leaders and intimidation by secret societies. He felt the League was misleading the people with false promises:

> I have never yet conversed with any man who, in his heart of hearts, believed that landlords can be got rid of, or the hiring of land be prevented any more than the letting and hiring of cabs and horses; and as I hold all shams and impostors in abhorrence, I cannot connect myself with those who are deluding our fellow countrymen by promising them impossibilities, and leading them into serious danger to their lives and liberties.27

However, he was of the opinion that even if the tenant was given a free gift of his holding he would find it impossible to make a living out of it. For a more permanent solution to Ireland's economic and social problems a 'spirited system of developing the resources of the country', was needed. Ireland was, in his view, a vast underdeveloped estate which could easily be made productive with government investment. There was little likelihood of the industrial resources of Ireland being developed by private enterprise, he told the House, and therefore it fell to government to invest in the construction of roads and railways, as they had done in India, and in reclaiming waste land. Added to this 'taxation and absentee drain' must be addressed. He would continue to support the Liberal government until the promised Land Bill would appear, but if the government failed 'to keep their word, or bring forward crude and half-hearted measures of reform, no one will attack them with a clearer conscience, or with more outspokenness' than himself.[28]

But Henry's policy of 'wait and see' was out of tune with the majority of his constituents back in Galway. His refusal to join Parnell in opposition and his continued verbal attacks were seen by many as betrayal. When, after the Christmas holiday, he returned early to London in January 1881, a rumour went about that he had to leave Kylemore because of threats. He wrote to the press denouncing the rumour and stating that he was forced to return to his work as Commissioner with the Royal Commission on Agriculture, and that his family had remained on at Kylemore.[29] In a letter to the English Radical League, formed to support the government in their policy towards Ireland, Henry again affirmed his belief that the Liberal government would do 'full justice to Irish tenants' and criticised the Land League for inciting the people to violence. What he had learned during his visit to Kylemore had clearly shaken him:

> Unfortunately this present agitation has unhinged society completely and I doubt whither since the French Revolution there was ever such a reign of terror as now exists in Ireland. The leaders of the movement do not want the Land Question settled in a just manner, because they know that if the bulk of the people have a secure hold on their farms, and can feel sure that their improvements will belong to themselves, they will become orderly and contented. This would not suit the extreme men who are fattening on the agitation and secretly urging on the poor ignorant people to dangers which they themselves do not share . . . Let us work together for justice to all, and especially to the poor man, but let us sternly set our faces against the outrages on men and beast, and the reign of terror, which is a disgrace to civilisation.[30]

Taking such an unpopular stance left Henry isolated politically and would eventually lose him his seat. But there were still some among the press who recognised that Henry would never shirk from voicing his opinion, no matter how unpopular it made him. The *Galway Vindicator,* when publishing the above letter, commented:

There are very few among the Irish Representative Body who have the courage of their convictions as Mr Mitchell Henry. He gives his opinion fearlessly and independently on every subject and there is no man among the Irish Representative Body more zealously and honestly patriotically devoted to the true interest of Ireland.[31]

When Parliament resumed on 6 January the government announced its intention to introduce additional powers to deal with the increase in agrarian crime in Ireland. Parnell, who was now Party leader, and his supporters, responded with obstruction. Henry, Shaw and the other Irish Members seated with the government seceded from the Parnellites and now considered themselves 'a separate and moderate party'. Declaring that they would oppose the Coercion Bill 'in strict accordance with the forms of the House avoiding all unnecessary obstruction; and should the Land Bill prove, in their opinion just and equitable, will not only support it in Parliament, but will endeavour to obtain its acceptance in Ireland'.[32]

When Henry rose to speak during the debate on the address in reply to the queen's speech he gave what the press described as, an 'elegantly-framed but unprejudiced speech . . . impartially blamed the Government, the Land League, and the Castle authorities for the present state of Ireland'.[33] The government, he told the House, had reneged on its promise not to re-instate the Coercion Act. They had failed to use existing laws effectively and had instead 'administered the law in Ireland in a weak and faltering spirit'. Parnell objected to Henry's assertion that the Irish people, 'through their Representatives', had worked to return a Liberal government to power. But now, it appeared 'the one object of hon. Gentlemen opposite (the Parnellites), was to discredit the Liberal Administration which they had just returned, and to prevent them from getting an opportunity of fulfilling any one of their promises'.

He appealed to the House not to pass Coercion Acts hastily, but instead to insist that the government bring forward its project of Land Reform, which would bring peace and reduce the necessity for such stringent measures. 'The organisation of the Land League is not secret', Parnell interjected, when Henry referred to secret organisations 'under the auspices of the Land League' existing in almost every parish, encouraging the people 'through bad influence and advice' to commit outrages.[34]

Following this the councils of the Loughrea, Ballinasloe and Athenry branches of the Irish National Land League passed resolutions calling for Henry's resignation.[35] Placards denouncing him were posted throughout the county:

> Mr Mitchell Henry has proclaimed to the world that the Irish people are nightly conspiring against law and morality. He has added the weight of his opinion as your representative to the slanders which have been cast upon us by the enemies of our people and multiplied through the agencies of the English press. In face of these circumstances it has been decided by the parent association in this county – namely the Ballinasloe Branch of the Irish National Land League – that a requisition shall be signed by you calling on Mr Mitchell Henry to resign.[36]

The Athenry branch called on Henry to sit with the members of the Irish party: 'we expect him to be an Irish member first and a Liberal afterwards'.[37] Hostility towards him was much stronger in the East of the county than closer to home in the West. However, his tenants were still withholding their rents, and this disappointed him greatly. But he attributed their actions to

> the secret agent of the Land League, whose doctrine of the "Land for the People" and direction to them to pay no rent are interpreted to mean, as indeed they are told, that every landlord is a robber and intruder. I have only 125 tenants, very few of whom have paid anything, although many would pay if they were not intimidated by a lawless confederation who have succeeded in completely changing the character and behaviour of the people, I trust and believe only temporarily.[38]

His attacks on the League and its leaders attracted criticism from Davitt to which he responded:

> I have a greater respect for Mr Davitt who has been abusing me, than I have for other persons of higher position. Mr Davitt makes no concealment of the fact that the objects he has in view are such as must prevent any honest man from taking the oath of Allegiance to the Queen at the table of the House of Commons, and he has consequently always refused to become a member of parliament.[39]

The persistent and prolonged bouts of obstruction adopted by the Parnellites during the debate on the first of the Coercion Bills, the Protection of Person and Property (Ireland) Bill, drew fierce response across the floor from Henry. He never understood the rationale behind repeated obstruction and when he spoke during such debates it was often to express frustration at the time-wasting behaviour of the Irish Members. On the fourth night of the debate the House sat for forty-one hours during which

Henry suggested that, for the future, 'instead of having Members of Parliament chosen from amongst gentlemen of position and education, they had better select them from amongst the coal-heavers of London and the Quay porters of Dublin'. How people 'who had to contend for the rights of a country by their intelligence, and not by their physical force, were to enter into these contests, he could not for the life of him understand'. And if the debate did not adjourn soon 'not being so young and enthusiastic as some of his hon. Friends, he should have respectfully and sorrowfully to take leave of Mr. Speaker for the night'.[40]

However, when on the following day, 2 February, the debate was suddenly brought to a close by the Speaker, Henry warned that he would 'jealously watch all attempts to abridge the liberties of debate' but noted the 'ill-considered and . . . ill-tempered action' which provoked the Speaker's decision. Butt's prophecy that 'obstruction would exhaust the patience of Parliament', had come true, he told them, to which T.P. O'Connor, the representative for Galway city, responded that Henry was thinking of England: 'The patience of the Irish people would never be exhausted by hon. Members who truly represented them'. But did Henry, he asked, 'truly represent any part of the Irish people?'[41]

This accusation was made again in the days that followed when Henry denounced Irish Members for inciting outrage. A.M. Sullivan taunted him with the reminder that at several public meetings held in his constituency resolutions had been passed calling on him to resign his seat.[42] As Henry continued with his attacks he was frequently reminded that he was living out his final days in the House. Such threats, however, did little to silence him.

Henry was of the belief that 'chronic misery' was the 'chief source of Irish discontent' and that the evils of Ireland were more social than political. And unless the government came to grips 'with the physical evils arising from poverty and hopelessness, no reform of the land laws [would] prevent the recurrence of periods of famine and disturbances'.[43] He had raised this argument in the House in the past and in March 1881 he sent a memorandum to Gladstone expanding on the theme that 'Ireland was an undeveloped estate',[44] in an effort to persuade the government to include some provision for the reclamation of land in the forthcoming Land Bill. The crux of the Irish question, he told the Prime Minister, was the 'miserable condition of a part of the population and the state of the country in which they live'. The number involved was small but yet their miserable condition 'gave the backbone to every Irish agitation'. The only way of dealing with this poor section of society was to 'thin it out'. State emigration to Canada and other colonies was one answer, but it must be backed up with State financed improvements to conditions at home. He recommended State loans for the construction of small branch railways and tramways for 'without State aid nothing will be done'. Another solution was for the State to purchase estates, such as the Martin Estate in Connemara, then the property of Berridge, to plant that section which was uninhabitable and to reclaim the rest. The reclaimed land then to be divided into forty acre farms and rented out to the people, encouraging them to build their own houses and farm buildings with local stone, while at the same time teaching them the fundamentals of 'practical agriculture'. By way of example he referred to the success of his own reclamation works at Kylemore.[45]

The Times accused Henry: 'a man of grand ideas[who] thinks it shabby to count the cost', of wanting the government to use public money to make Connemara habitable, when 'the prevailing idea of every tourist is that the whole region is good for nothing, except for a man to lose his money, or his wits, or his life in. The car rattles for miles and miles over a rough, natural pavement of stone, slightly varied with tufts of grass and pools of water'.[46] To which Henry replied that if one were to 'look at the whole question calmly, wisely, but at the same time boldly, there is nothing unreasonable in the suggestions in my memorandum':

> Ireland is saturated with water like a sponge, so that the atmosphere is poisoned and the spirits and physical strength of its inhabitants are depressed, and that this water can only be got rid of by works of arterial drainage on a large scale. I say, therefore, to the Government, it is a matter of Imperial policy for you to dry Ireland, for this cannot be accomplished by the unaided efforts of its inhabitants, and as long as such a state of things continues permanent prosperity is impossible.

At the time it took 'nearly 50,000 armed men . . . to hold Ireland in subjection, and hundreds of thousands of Irishmen in all parts of the world are longing for the opportunity to shake the British Empire to its centre'. Permanent peace lay in the development of the poorer regions and in improving the conditions of the people:

> We may theorize and reform as we like, but the common sense of mankind teaches us that loyalty and starvation are not compatible, and in my humble judgment the only hope that remains of producing permanent tranquillity in Ireland is to make a strong and well-directed effort permanently to increase the prosperity of the people.[47]

When the Land Bill was brought before the House in April Henry welcomed it as containing within it 'the elements of a radical settlement of the Land Question for all times'.[48], but felt the provisions for the reclamation of land were 'totally inadequate'.[49] The Bill allowed for the setting up of a Land Commission to arbitrate between the landlord and tenant on the subject of rent: it was felt that through the working of this Commission the three F's could be achieved, but it did nothing to address the question of rent arrears.

The Bill caused division in the Irish Party and on the second reading some Members voted in favour, despite Parnell's request for an abstention vote. Henry exposed the deep divisions among the Irish Members by drawing the attention of the House to a letter written by Patrick Egan, treasurer of the Land League, printed in the *Freeman's Journal* on 26 May 1881. The strongly worded letter took two Members, O'Connor Power and The O'Donoghue, to task for voting with the government on the second reading. Henry felt the letter was in breach of the Privileges of the House and put forward a motion to that effect. In the heated debate that followed O'Connor Power said that the letter was 'only a small part of the terrorism which has been practised . . . towards Gentlemen who dare to differ from the decrees of the Irish National Land League'. Unfortunately, he continued, 'Irish politics are in this position - that it requires greater courage to support a Government when they are right than to oppose them when they are wrong'. Despite protests from Parnell and others, O'Connor Power denied that there was any conspiracy between himself and Henry on the subject of the letter. Parnell refused to comment on the contents of the letter, but showed obvious annoyance at the exposure in the House of what he referred to as 'a question between Irishmen, and not a question between Englishmen'. A.M. Sullivan accused Henry of raising a scene 'which he knew well the enemies of Ireland would gloat over',[50] and one which would not be easily forgotten or forgiven.

Further clashes occurred during the debate on the Land Bill when Henry referred to the land agitation as 'the most dishonest, the most demoralizing, and the most un-Christian agitation that he had ever known'. In his own neighbourhood the people had until this 'treated him like a brother, and nothing but words of blessing had any member of his family received from them. But now that part of the country was stained by agrarian crime, and had been the scene of some of the foulest deeds'.[51] A little over two weeks earlier, on 24 April 1881, the murder of John Lydon and injury of his son Martin, which later resulted in his death, had taken place not far from

Kylemore. Lydon had no land of his own but was employed by the landlord Francis Graham, whose land bordered Henry's, as a caretaker and herd. The shootings took place in the middle of the night and were witnessed by Lydon's wife and children. A local man, Patrick Walsh, was later executed for the murders and his brother Michael was given life imprisonment for the murder of Constable Kavanagh, an investigating officer in the Lydon case, who was shot dead in Letterfrack village in February 1882.[52] Henry, himself, was of the opinion that the murders were committed by hired assassins, 'who were brought into the district by the secret societies',[53] and made very little reference to them in Parliament or outside.

The Land Act became law in August 1881.The major flaw in the Act was that it excluded leaseholders and those in arrears, their cause would have to be won by further agitation. Parnell spoke against the Act in public, but privately felt it was the best they could attain at that time. He advised the Land League to send test cases to the Land Commission. In October he gave a speech in Wexford which resulted in his arrest and incarceration in Kilmainham jail, where he remained until May 1882. Within days of Parnell's arrest the Land League issued a 'no rent' manifesto and the organisation was outlawed soon afterwards. The manifesto was condemned by the Catholic hierarchy and was not as effective as hoped. However, in the months that followed, evictions increased throughout Connemara, not because the tenants were responding to the League's call, but simply because arrears, accumulated in years of bad harvests, had left many destitute.[54]

Chapter 8
First Home Rule Bill

In February 1882 Henry had warned the House that the 'condition of things in Ireland was so bad that it was impossible to exaggerate it'. In Connemara there were large numbers of people 'encamped on the hillside, who had been turned out nearly naked in the cold and wet, to seek such shelter as they could get from the winds of heaven, because they could not, even if they gave their skins and their bones, pay their arrears of rent. These were the people whom Her Majesty's troops were engaged in evicting'.[1] None of these had the means to pay rent arrears, neither did they have the funds to take their case to court. Henry warned that until the issue of arrears was dealt with 'the troubles of Ireland would continue unabated, and undoubtedly they would get no benefit whatever from the working of the Land Act'.[2] In the two months of April and May 1882, 218 families were evicted in Connemara for non-payment of rent[3] and two gunboats, the *Redwing* and *Seahorse,* were lying in Clifden Bay with troops ready to support the bailiffs in even more evictions.

Although the tenants of Connemara were excluded from the protection of the Land Act, the provision for state-assisted emigration, allowed under the act, would facilitate many to leave behind the poverty and uncertainty of life as a tenant farmer and instead to seek out their fortune in distant lands. In May 1882 the *Galway Express* reported: 'The country is ruined, and the people find nothing can save them but emigration'.[4] A scheme was set up by James Hack Tuke, and others, to assist evicted tenants to emigrate to America and Canada. Between April and June 1882, 1,276 people left Clifden, Errismore, Roundstone, Renvyle and Letterfrack under the Tuke scheme.[5] And for those with means, the *Allen Line* was now offering direct service between Galway and Boston.

Henry, perhaps from personal experience within his own household staff, told the House that there was a very strong desire 'on the part of the Irish peasantry,

Emigrants gather at Clifden
Illustrated London News
21 July 1883

particularly those who were taken into service, both male and female, after they had learnt their duty, to emigrate to America; and there were very few of them who, when they were assisted to emigrate, did not make most respectable and worthy servants and members of society . . . They got excellent work and excellent wages, and were enabled to give very substantial assistance to their relatives and friends who remained at home'.[6] The training received at Kylemore Castle, and a reference from Mitchell Henry, must have set many a young man and woman on a successful path. But, Henry warned, 'Every emigrant who leaves these shores . . . goes away with hatred in his heart'.[7] Passing Coercion Acts and 'nibbling' at the question of emigration would not solve the problems of the West, he warned. There was in the West frequent crop failure which resulted in periodic famine and unless the government was prepared to institute public works in order to offer employment to the people, then 'those hovels from which the people were now driven out would be speedily refilled by others as miserable and destitute as their predecessors'.[8]

By 1882 the strain of political life was beginning to tell on Henry, who was then fifty-six. And it would appear from his letters to the press and speeches in the House that he was now not only disappointed but completely disillusioned with his tenants, fellow politicians and with events in general in Ireland:

Galway Express 7 April 1883

CLIFDEN.

FREE EMIGRATION.—Mr Tuke, with his deputies Messrs. Peter G. King and Andrew Lyden, have been busy for the past few weeks in preparing emigrants for the storied land of Washington and Franklin. Last week the elevated town of Clifden presented a very melancholy appearance. The main street was crowded to excess. From an early hour people of all classes began to pour into the town, under a heavy down pour of rain, as the floodgates of heaven seemed to be open to pour a last sprinkling on the exiles, who may never revisit the "Emerald gem of the western world." There were a good number of vehicles in readiness to convey the poor people to the emigrant ship, and the shouts of parting friends were heartrending in the extreme. One would imagine that the town was in a state of siege. Such yells could not be heard within the walls of a stormed city. As the loaded vehicles rattled through the streets, old men could be seen waving hats and handkerchiefs till they lost sight of the smokey chimney tops of Clifden;

Ireland is stained with blood and crime, and for the first time in the history of national movements Greed and Selfishness are proclaimed as national gods. Religion and Morality are openly scoffed at, and the Divine anger is justly roused against us by continued violence of the laws on which society is based. These things are the direct results of the present political policy, the exact opposite of that of the almost forgotten Isaac Butt. [9]

The Ballinasloe Town Commissioners accused him of voting for Coercion, to which he replied he had never voted for Coercion 'but always against it'. However, he denounced Coercion of another kind: 'boycotting, intimidation, and murder which has brought poor Ireland to ruin, and her people to disgrace. The insane and criminal conduct of men in public positions who have selfishly pandered to wicked passions which they excited in the minds of ignorant and reckless men, has roused a feeling in the Empire which cannot now be withstood, and the enslavement of our country will prove the direct result of the action of those who condemn me . . . My sympathies are still with the poor, the homeless and the friendless, and I claim to have given practical proof in my life and conversion of the reality of my convictions'. And having made plain his views he would, when Parliament would dissolve, 'confidently appeal for justification and support' from his constituents.[10]

Parnell was released from prison in May after reaching an agreement with the government on the matter of unpaid arrears of rent and the extension of the Land Act to cover leaseholders. In time things began to settle, but not before Connemara was to witness yet another horrific crime. This time it was the murder of the Joyce family at Maamtrasna in the heart of the Connemara mountains. The crime took place on the night of the 17 August when several men with blackened faces entered the house of John Joyce and brutally murdered himself, his wife, his aged mother and his daughter. They left his two sons wounded and dying, but fortunately they recovered. 'This murder was undoubtedly the most atrocious crime that had come under the notice of civilised Ireland or England during the present century, and was committed within 25 miles' of his own house, Henry told the House of Commons when the circumstances of the trial of the accused came up for debate: 'Such a concatenation of depravity and wickedness as had attended the circumstances of this murder – the perjury committed . . . the utter absence of knowledge of even the existence of a God on the part of some of the witnesses, filled his mind with perfect horror'.[11]

Galway Express
3 November 1883

In contrast to his early political career, when he was rarely away from the House when Parliament was in session, in the years 1883–85 Henry was frequently absent for long periods of time; whither this was from battle fatigue or for some more personal reason, is unknown. When the Glenamaddy Board of Guardians passed a resolution of confidence in him, in January 1883, his reply came from Algiers, where he was visiting his daughter Marie Waetjin. His response was one of heartfelt appreciation, pointing out that up until recent times he was 'thoroughly trusted by the Irish people', but now the motives and actions of representatives like himself had been 'systematically traduced and misrepresented'. However, he prophesied that before another general election 'common sense will again prevail, and those who have faithfully adhered to the policy of Mr Butt, will again be recognised in Ireland herself as the true friends of the people'.[12] It would appear that despite all that had been said and written, Henry was still hopeful of retaining his Galway seat.

Later in the year the Guardians of the Clifden Union passed a similar vote. Fifty voters from the town and surrounding district signed a declaration announcing their 'unabated confidence' in him and pledging their 'undivided and cordial support at the next election':

> we would consider ourselves wanting in gratitude to one of our best resident landlords, and his respected family, were we to give the public to understand by our silence that our feelings towards him had in any way changed since he was first returned and we endorse the complimentary vote passed unanimously by the guardians of this union.[13]

But there was no denying it, support for Henry had greatly diminished and he himself did little to retrieve it with his continuous attacks on Parnell. The Land League had been replaced by the Irish National League and the emphasis had again returned to Home Rule. The National League was working hard on the ground to secure suitable candidates for the next election and was winning support among the electorate. The fundamental differences between Parnell, the National League and Henry on the issue of Home Rule remained the same; for Henry it was some form of federalism, for Parnell and the League it was generally stated in more ambitious terms.

In a strongly worded letter to the *Pall Mall Gazette* in February 1885, in which he referred to Parnell's tactics in the House as 'Parliamentary ruffianism', Henry predicted that although Parnell may increase his party numbers at the coming election his influence would be curtailed by the British vote: 'England will never consent to restore to Ireland the Parliament of 1782 any more than she will agree to complete separation, and I am persuaded that Mr Parnell and his more intelligent followers fully appreciate these truths'.

Henry did not believe that Parnell would withdraw his party from Parliament, as he was threatening to do, because this would mean rebellion and he was of the opinion that 'of all men in the world the last to head a rebellion is Mr Parnell'. The Irish had, he felt, lost the sympathy of the British, and 'human sympathy is a powerful factor in the affairs of nations'. If one tenth of the sum 'wasted on repression' had been spent in draining the bogs as he had recommended, 'we should have advanced far towards the solution of the Irish question'. Once again he called for State aid to finance the construction of roads and railways, and for drainage works and land reclamation. The only true union that would cement these two islands together was, in Henry's opinion, 'mutual self interest, followed by mutual respect'.[14]

The *Freeman's Journal* reprinted the letter under the heading 'A Bid for a Baronetcy', but the *Evening Mail* believed it was an attempt to cheer up Gladstone and 'put some backbone into him in his coming troubles with the Irish Members'.[15]

The Liberal government fell in June and an election was called for November. The number of voters had trebled under the third Reform Act of the previous year and a rearrangement of the Electoral Divisions left the old County Galway seat divided in four, each returning one representative. Several names were put forward as possible candidates for the Connemara Division; Henry was not among them. Parnell was insisting that all candidates make a pledge of allegiance to himself, this Henry would never do.

Henry was invited to contest the Heywood division of South East Lancashire and other 'safe' seats in England, but declined.[16] Instead he planned, despite obvious opposition and his refusal to make the Parnell pledge, to go forward for the Connemara division of Galway. He wrote to the Archbishop of Tuam, John McEvilly, seeking his support, but this was refused. The Archbishop would use his influence 'only in favour of the Irish party'. Henry was deeply hurt by this rejection and wrote back:

> The last few years had many humiliations for those who have extolled the chivalry and the virtues of the Irish peasant, and who have made personal and pecuniary sacrifices for his benefit. One further humiliation was still possible, and your Graces defection has now supplied it. [17]

Passing both letters to the press for publication he added:

> I came home with the intention of again contesting this, the Connemara Division of Galway and had reason to believe that I

should meet with influential support. If there was any chance I would still go to the poll, but under existing circumstances there is no chance for anyone who will not take the degrading pledge to Mr Parnell, which was recently formulated at head quarters in Dublin. The Archbishop of Tuams attitude towards an agitation he has so often condemned throws an unpleasant light on the prospects of the future.[18]

On Monday 26 October 1885 Parnell presided over a Convention of the National League held at the Temperance Hall, Athenry, for the purpose of selecting candidates to contest the four divisions of County Galway. Representatives from Connemara were sent to Athenry to meet Parnell, but any suggestions or recommendations made by them were ignored. Parnell's men were selected; Colonel Nolan for the North Division; David Sheehy for the South Division; Patrick James Foley for the West Division and Matthew Harris for the Eastern Division.[19] All 'tried and trusted' men according to Parnell, but the *Galway Express* commented that 'no matter what the choice of the people might be, Mr Parnell's nominees must take precedence'.[20]

Turning away from Galway, Henry went forward as the Liberal candidate for the Blackfriars Division of Glasgow. He had previously turned down three other constituencies and had contemplated retirement, but on receipt of the invitation from Glasgow, where A & S Henry had a factory, he decided to 'see if there is any life in the old dog yet'.

However, his row with the Irish Party followed him even there. Irishmen, supporters of the Irish Party, thronged the hall where Henry was to speak and tried to disrupt the meetings. In the end admission was by ticket only but still when Henry got up to speak he was greeted with 'cheers, hisses and groans'. One Irishman in the body of the hall cried, 'Out you renegade'. Over twenty men were ejected before the meeting could continue. When asked if he would oppose Parnell and his party 'in bringing forward any measure to grant legislative independence to Ireland' Henry replied: 'I will oppose any measure which will have the effect of breaking up the unity of the Empire'.[21]

In an address to the electorate Henry summed up his political career as being 'one long plea for extending to [Ireland] the blessings of self-government'. And complaints now made against him by some 'extreme Irishmen' were made, he said, because he had 'stigmatised as degrading and insufferable the employment of threats to overawe the House of Commons and the Country', and because he had 'never hesitated to denounce with vigour crime and outrage, and especially the cruel and degrading practice of Boycotting'. Obstruction had paralysed Parliament and would be the cause of dissolving the Empire, he told them: 'The battle of the dissolution of the

Empire was begun in the House of Commons itself by an organised system of obstruction which has paralysed the best efforts of that assembly to carry out the people's will, and the first of all reforms must be such as will enable Parliament to regain its freedom'.[22]

However, despite all that had taken place it would seem that Henry still needed the approbation of his tenants back in Connemara: 'My time, my fortune, and my personal exertions have been given to the improvement of the neglected people of the West of Ireland, and if I am now calumniated, assuredly no words but those of blessing have ever come to me from my neighbours in Connemara'.[23]

Henry topped the poll with 3,759 votes,[24] the only election in his entire political career in which he did so. Afterwards at a rally held in the city he did little to hide his anger with what he saw as attempts by Parnell and his supporters to prevent him being elected for Glasgow. He predicted that Parnell and the Irish Party would return to Parliament with an increase in numbers. This was a 'very serious circumstance . . . a circumstance unparalleled in our Parliamentary history and it was eminently necessary that the Liberals should take stock of their own forces and also of the force of the enemy'.[25]

Back in Ireland Colonel Nolan was returned for North Galway and Patrick J Foley, described in the press simply as coming from London, for Connemara.[26] Foley was never acceptable to the people of Connemara and was frequently criticised in the press for showing little interest in local issues and for failing to take part in the campaign to establish a railway link between Galway and Clifden.

After the election the Liberals went on to form a government; it was, however, doomed to be short-lived. The Liberals' small majority over the Conservatives left the balance of power with Parnell and the Irish Party. Gladstone's decision to deal with the question of Home Rule in the first half of 1886 was causing further rifts in his already divided party. Speculation grew as to how far Gladstone would go to pacify the Irish Party and to what extent he would alienate members of his own party in doing so. Henry in a letter to *The Times* warned that those 'philosophical Radicals' who felt it their duty to 'satisfy Mr Parnell' should realise that 'he cannot be satisfied, for behind him, and towering over him, stands the stern paymasters, the Irish Republican Brotherhood of which the Church is in mortal dread and hopes to check' by its sudden support of Parnell. Instead of legislating to meet 'what we think [are] Irish sentiments', the government should assert the supremacy of the law while at the same time put hope into the hearts of the masses by offering them employment in the development of the country as previously outlined by him: 'The source of Irish disaffection and the strength of the revolutionary party are to be found in the empty stomachs of the unemployed agricultural population'.[27]

Gladstone introduced his Home Rule Bill on 8 April 1886. The Bill provided for an Irish parliament with limited powers; London would retain control over 'imperial, fiscal and security powers . . . foreign relations, currency, treason and the Post Office'.[28] Dublin would contribute one-fifth of the imperial charges but would have no vote on how it would be spent, as Irish Members were to be excluded from Westminster. The Bill was welcomed by Parnell and the Irish Party, but rejected by the Conservatives and many Liberals, the exclusion of the Irish Members being the latter's chief bone of contention.

Attached to the Bill was a Land Purchase Bill allowing for large scale purchase by the tenants of their holdings. As debate on both Bills filled the pages of the press, growing opposition in Gladstone's party left the public uncertain right up to the division on the second reading as to whether it would get through or not. Henry, like many other Liberals, supported Joseph Chamberlain's argument that the bill 'paved the way towards complete separation'.[29] It would, he stated in a letter to the *Galway Express*, be sheer folly to adopt a policy of expelling the Irish Members from Westminster and to 'expel or buy out' the Irish landlords. Such a policy would simply store up troubles for the future. Gladstone had introduced the Bill simply to rid himself of the Irish Members, so that Parliament could go about its business unhindered:

> The truth ought to be spoken, and the truth every impartial mind must acknowledge to be that the marvellous change of front which Mr Gladstone has executed has proceeded from his overmastering desire to restore the working of the Parliamentary machine by removing from it the Irish Members, whom in his heart he hates and despises. They, on their part, are perfectly willing to go because they know full well that to pay an annual tribute to Great Britain of upwards of three millions, without having the slightest vote in the expenditure, will provide them with a real grievance of overwhelming cogency, instead of sham grievances such as they have now.

Neither would depriving them of a vote on foreign matters silence them:

> Can any sane person suppose that Irish eloquence will in future be dumb, and Irish sympathy be dead, in all the great colonial affairs of this Empire, and in all the foreign questions, often involving Catholic Powers with whom they are united by religious faith. If Irishmen cannot discuss

these subjects at St Stephens, they will discuss them in their Assembly at home, whatever paper restrictions you may put upon them.

The Bill was, in his opinion, simply providing a platform for future agitation if 'Irish passion' were to become excited by some deed or omission perpetrated by Westminster; 'they will raise their Parliamentary standard, this time with a local habitation and a name, and beckon Irish soldiers in our regiments to rally round the cause of country and religion and strive in their own words "to make Ireland a nation once again"'.

He doubted Parnell's sincerity in accepting the Bill and felt that at sometime in the future he and his associates would be the first to 'repudiate it': 'Do we forget their pleas that leases of land ought to be broken because the contracting parties were on unequal terms, and the weaker party compelled to accept inequitable provisions? If such reasoning applies to individuals, how much more powerfully will it do duty in the affairs of a nation?' Gladstone would never have dared to offer to Butt 'this divorce from Imperial affairs as the price of any advantages, whether pecuniary or otherwise, to Ireland'.

If the Land Purchase Bill were to become law he warned that a new agitation would begin demanding the introduction of full State ownership: 'the moment you buy out the present race of landlords, many of them cultured persons who are centres of civilisation, and substitute for them the present race of tenants, there will be a renewed agitation on behalf of the labourers and of those who are not now tenants . . . to make the State the one universal landlord'.[30] The *Galway Express,* paying tribute to Henry's 'great experience, his great sincerity and his noble-hearted patriotism', suggested that all parties should consider the 'opinions and conclusions' put forward, whether they agreed with him or not.[31]

When it became clear to the dissenting Liberals that the government had no intention of making sufficient alteration in the Bill to meet their objections, Joseph Chamberlain called a meeting in Committee Room 15, which Henry attended, and it was agreed by an overwhelming majority to vote against the second reading of the Bill. The Bill was defeated on the 8 June by 343 votes to 313. Henry was among the 93 Liberals who voted against the government.

Following the government's defeat Parliament was dissolved. In the election that followed Henry again went forward for the Blackfriars and Hutchentown Division of Glasgow, but this time as a Liberal Unionist. His address to the electorate was, according to *The Times*, 'devoted entirely to the Irish question' and stating once again his belief that the Home Rule Bill would have 'weakened the unity of the Empire, subverted the Imperial

Parliament, and led to civil war and foreign complications'. It 'invited rebellion on the best grounds known to civilized nations, taxation without representation'.[32] Henry failed to be selected by the Liberal Association of the Glasgow Division, who selected a Gladstonian candidate in his place.

There were many back in Ireland who celebrated Henry's defeat, although the *Galway Vindicator* was of the opinion that 'when the country settles down' he could, if he so wished, once again represent Connemara. 'Had he, like others, taken matters quietly he could have remained an Irish Representative and Connemara would have been his stronghold', but being a man who always spoke his mind, 'a hard hitter', he was excluded from the Irish Party, 'but so was everyone else who did not follow Mr Parnell'. Parnell was, the editor accepted, 'an extraordinary man, a great leader', and he had 'selected men to suit his purpose'. Gladstone, on the other hand, 'admittedly the greatest man of Modern times', had failed to 'accomplish in England, what Mr Parnell has achieved in Ireland'.

Henry with his numerous interests and talents would have plenty to occupy his time and was, according to the Editor, 'more to be envied than pitied in being released from the turmoils and troubles of Parliamentary strife'. Being a 'gentleman of refined literary tastes, devoted to the Arts and Sciences', he had made 'the science of Agriculture his hobby', all of which had left him with 'abundant resources for the highest and holiest enjoyments of life'.[33]

Henry continued to serve the people in his capacity as Justice of the Peace and Deputy Lieutenant for Middlesex and Justice of the Peace for Westminster and Galway, although there is little evidence of his having attended many courts in Galway. And although he no longer occupied a seat in the House of Commons, he continued to participate in the broader arena of politics through the letters' page of *The Times* where he expanded on his theories relating to Irish politics. From his regular contributions it would appear that he recovered quickly from his rejection at Glasgow and was perhaps still open to the possibility of going forward yet again sometime in the future. His letters dealt principally with Irish matters and, recognised as an authority on the subject, he was given ample space to vent his criticism of Gladstone and the Irish Party. In one such letter he confessed he had at one time greatly admired Gladstone:

> in the outset of my House of Commons experience I was simply entranced by his eloquence and dexterity, but after the Ewelme ecclesiastical scandal and the Collier judicial appointment I lost my faith and with a pain not to be described, felt that language was habitually employed, not to declare his thoughts, but to conceal them.[34]

The two appointments referred to by Henry, an ecclesiastical appointment at Ewelme and the appointment of Sir Robert Collier to the Judicial Committee of the Privy Council, were pushed through by Gladstone, despite opposition, and caused many to question his judgment. He complained that Gladstone had ignored requests to visit the poorer regions of the West, during his few visits to Ireland, visiting instead the rich lands of the East, and that he constantly refused to avail of the advice given him by those with 'local' knowledge of these regions. Gladstone had, he wrote, 'a marvellous appetite for an Irish vote' when it was 'likely to enable him to return to power, but real practical sympathy with the poverty-stricken Irish tenant, I know from long and bitter experience, he has not'. Gladstone's early budgets, when he was Chancellor of the Exchequer, had brought high taxes to Ireland, drawing her deeper into poverty and this, he contended, was the cause of all of her difficulties: 'I do publicly and solemnly declare, not for the first time, that of all men now living Mr Gladstone has done more to deepen Irish poverty, and has done least to guard against Irish famines'.[35]

As the Liberals and Irish Party drew closer on the particulars of Home Rule, Henry wrote to *The Times,* declaring that a desire to 'remedy in a day the evils of centuries', was causing some politicians to prescribe drastic remedies for Ireland. He warned against the introduction of 'a ruthless and compulsory destruction of the relations of landlord and tenant', which would rob Ireland of the civilizing influences of an educated class and reduce the entire nation to 'one dead level of mediocrity'.

> A good landlord, and in Ireland good landlords are as numerous in proportion to bad ones as they are in England, becomes a centre of light and civilization in the midst of his tenants. No people was ever civilized except by example, and, therefore from above downwards. Education, culture, and fine arts, and all that raises men above the condition of mere hewers of wood and drawers of water, can come only through the possession of comparative wealth and comparative leisure in those whom, for want of a better term, we call the higher classes.[36]

There was, he pointed out, 'no Royal road to peace and prosperity in Ireland', but had his advice of past years been heeded and Ireland's 'woes' recognised as 'more social than political', they would have addressed the problem differently, as famine was addressed in India, and would not have had the 'social convulsions' experienced in recent times:

> An Indian administration would have put all to rights years ago, at a cost infinitely less than the money wasted on soldiers and police and gaols, and would have left us a contented people instead of a people

whom reckless and unscrupulous agitators have repeatedly lashed into deadly hatred and deadly crime.[37]

In the years that followed Henry would witness many of his suggestions for advancing and improving 'the neglected estate' implemented by the Conservative government, under the direction of Arthur Balfour's policy of 'Killing Home Rule with Kindness'. Early in his term as Chief Secretary Balfour's introduction and enforcement of tough measures to put down further agrarian agitation won him the name 'Bloody Balfour'. However, he was also responsible for the Light Railway (Ireland) Act (1889), under which funds for the construction of the Galway to Clifden railway were granted. Henry approved of Balfour's 'determination that whilst encouragement should be given to all classes, crime and outrage should be made amenable to the law' and praised him for inaugurating the construction of railways and roads in the most backward districts of the country. In October 1890 Balfour toured the poorer regions in the West, accompanied by his sister and local politicians, but without the customary armed escort. While in Connemara the party spent a night at Kylemore Castle, after which Henry praised Balfour for having the courage to visit the region without an armed escort and pointed out that: 'he who was represented as a fiend incarnate is at this moment the most popular man in the West and South of Ireland'.[38]

Chapter 9

The Closing Years

While Henry lived out his very active political life, the family business, of which he was Chairman, had provided him with a substantial income. The Henry family lifestyle befitted a man of his wealth and position. When the House of Commons was in session the family could be found at their London residence, Stratheden House, situated at Rutland Gate opposite Hyde Park. Stratheden House was ideally positioned for participating in the London social scene. Here, the family 'lived like Royalty; liveried footmen, gold plate for special occasions and carriages with two men on the box'.[1] During the fishing and shooting season, and for the Christmas holidays, the family were at Kylemore Castle, usually accompanied by a large group of friends. Henry entertained lavishly at both houses and Kylemore Castle was seldom without guests.

The Henrys were cared for by a large staff, both at Stratheden House and Kylemore Castle, with the principal members of the household, cook, butler etc., travelling with the family to both houses. The British Census Returns for 1881 gives the household staff at Stratheden House as follows: a German governess, an English housekeeper, three ladies' maids – two French, one English; a German seamstress, three kitchen maids, four housemaids, an English butler, a French cook, odd job man, an under butler, two footmen, Thomas Joyce and John Henehan, both from County Galway, as was the carpenter Martin Feeney. At Kylemore, as well as the household staff, there was also an extensive outdoor staff of gardeners, keepers, gillies, grooms, woodsmen and farm labourers.

While still young the children were accompanied by a nanny, maids and a governess. In later years there was Eton for the boys and tutors for the girls. Two of the sons attended university: John Lewis entered Oxford in 1869,[2] Alexander entered Cambridge in 1878,[3] both left without taking a degree. Indeed none of the children seems to have achieved

Henry Family Tree

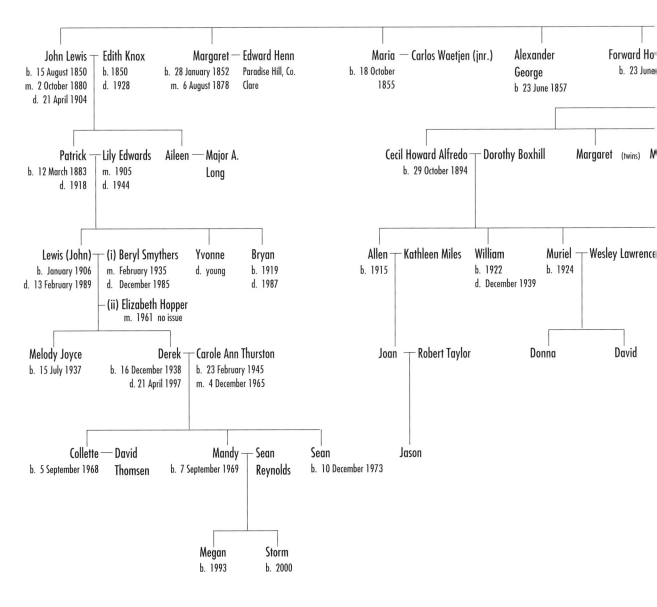

Mitchell Henry –
b 1826
m 30 August 1849
d 22 November 19⁻

John Lewis — Edith Knox
b. 15 August 1850   b. 1850
m. 2 October 1880   d. 1928
d. 21 April 1904

Margaret — Edward Henn
b. 28 January 1852   Paradise Hill, Co.
m. 6 August 1878   Clare

Maria — Carlos Waetjen (jnr.)
b. 18 October
1855

Alexander
George
b 23 June 1857

Forward Ho⁻
b. 23 June

Patrick — Lily Edwards
b. 12 March 1883   m. 1905
d. 1918   d. 1944

Aileen — Major A.
Long

Cecil Howard Alfredo — Dorothy Boxhill
b. 29 October 1894

Margaret   (twins)   M⁻

Lewis (John) — (i) Beryl Smythers
b. January 1906   m. February 1935
d. 13 February 1989   d. December 1985

Yvonne
d. young

Bryan
b. 1919
d. 1987

Allen — Kathleen Miles
b. 1915

William
b. 1922
d. December 1939

Muriel — Wesley Lawrence
b. 1924

— (ii) Elizabeth Hopper
m. 1961 no issue

Melody Joyce
b. 15 July 1937

Derek — Carole Ann Thurston
b. 16 December 1938   b. 23 February 1945
d. 21 April 1997   m. 4 December 1965

Joan — Robert Taylor

Donna   David

Collette — David
b. 5 September 1968   Thomsen

Mandy — Sean
b. 7 September 1969   Reynolds

Sean
b. 10 December 1973

Jason

Megan
b. 1993

Storm
b. 2000

On the death of Mitchell Henry his sons and Florence changed their surname to Mitchell-Henry.

Margaret Vaughan

daughter of George Vaughn, Quilly House, Co. Down

b. 1829
m. 30 August 1849
d. 4 December 1874

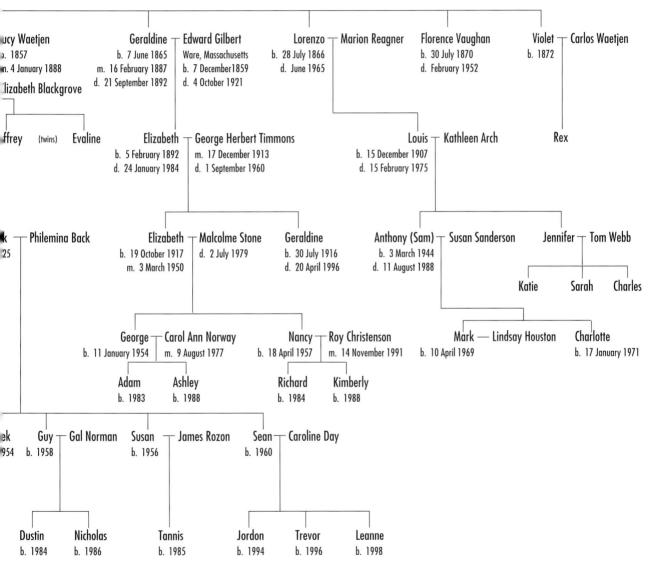

Lucy Waetjen
b. 1857
m. 4 January 1888

Elizabeth Blackgrove

Geraldine
b. 7 June 1865
m. 16 February 1887
d. 21 September 1892

Edward Gilbert
Ware, Massachusetts
b. 7 December1859
d. 4 October 1921

Lorenzo
b. 28 July 1866
d. June 1965

Marion Reagner

Florence Vaughan
b. 30 July 1870
d. February 1952

Violet
b. 1872

Carlos Waetjen

Jeffrey   (twins)   Evaline

Elizabeth
b. 5 February 1892
d. 24 January 1984

George Herbert Timmons
m. 17 December 1913
d. 1 September 1960

Louis
b. 15 December 1907
d. 15 February 1975

Kathleen Arch

Rex

Philemina Back

25

Elizabeth
b. 19 October 1917
m. 3 March 1950

Malcolme Stone
d. 2 July 1979

Geraldine
b. 30 July 1916
d. 20 April 1996

Anthony (Sam)
b. 3 March 1944
d. 11 August 1988

Susan Sanderson

Jennifer
Tom Webb

Katie   Sarah   Charles

George
b. 11 January 1954

Carol Ann Norway
m. 9 August 1977

Nancy
b. 18 April 1957

Roy Christenson
m. 14 November 1991

Mark
b. 10 April 1969

Lindsay Houston

Charlotte
b. 17 January 1971

Adam
b. 1983

Ashley
b. 1988

Richard
b. 1984

Kimberly
b. 1988

ek
954

Guy
b. 1958

Gal Norman

Susan
b. 1956

James Rozon

Sean
b. 1960

Caroline Day

Dustin
b. 1984

Nicholas
b. 1986

Tannis
b. 1985

Jordon
b. 1994

Trevor
b. 1996

Leanne
b. 1998

119

Courtesy of the Brady Family

The Henry Daughters

Forward Henry and his wife Lucy
Waetjen

Courtesy of the Brady Family

anything like the academic or professional success of their father, perhaps not having inherited his self-discipline, perseverance and earnestness; attributes Henry felt were essential if one was to achieve such success. All of the children were to benefit under the Marriage Settlement of their parents. However, under the terms of their grandfather's will, £20,000 was set in trust for the four oldest children; John, Margaret, Marie and Alexander. The remaining five children – Forward, Geraldine, Lorenzo, Violet and Florence – born after the death of their grandfather, were not included.

As previously mentioned, Henry's oldest daughter Margaret took over the running of the family on the death of their mother and she later married Edward Lovett Henn of Paradise Hill, Kildysart, County Clare. All of the remaining children, except Florence, married in the following years. By a happy coincidence three of the Henrys married into the same family, the Waetjen family from Algeria. Maria Catherine, Henry's second daughter, married Carlos Julio Waetjen, a widower, from Ghaba Kebira E Bier, Algiers, and they had a son named Harold. Later Maria's sister Violet married Carlos's son, also named Carlos, and the couple had a son, Rex. Forward, Henry's third son, married Inez (Lucy) Caroline Cecilia, Carlos's only daughter, in Algeria, on 4 January 1888. Forward and Lucy's marriage ceremony took place at the Church of the Holy Trinity, Algiers, and was performed by Rev. H.A. Boys, the British Chaplain.[4] Forward and Lucy had three children, a son, Cecil, and twin daughters, Margaret and Muriel. Cecil emigrated to Canada, where he married and had a family. Neither of the daughters married: 'Margaret was a member of the Voluntary Aid Detachment in the 1914 war and died of cholera nursing in the Middle East' and Muriel became a Director with the Elizabeth Arden cosmetic company. Forward married twice and his second wife, Elizabeth Blackgrove, also gave birth to twins; Geoffrey and Evelyn. Forward was said to have been an exceptional horseman, and, after what is believed to have been an eventful life, ended up working as an estate manager in England.[5]

Henry's oldest son, John Lewis, a Captain in the Royal Scots Greys, married Edith Maud Ancketill, widow of Thomas Knox, on 10 February 1880.[6] They had two children, Patrick, born in 1883, and Aileen. Henry's second son, Alexander, had a keen interest in photography and had his own dark room installed above the post office at Kylemore. He took some very fine photographs of the Castle, its interior and grounds, and many of the photographs of Kylemore reproduced in this book and held at the National Library Photographic Archive are attributed to him. Alexander is said to have enjoyed travelling and went to Africa in 1898, but little else is known of him.[7]

Another daughter, Geraldine, married Edward Hooker Gilbert of Ware, Massachusetts, U.S.A. Edward, a successful businessman, ran the George J. Gilbert Manufacturing Company which was started by his father. The marriage took place at St George's Church, Hanover Square, London on 16 February 1887. The marriage ceremony was performed by the Right Hon. and Rev. The Earl of Mulgrave, Vicar of Worsely. A mention in the *Galway Express* gives us a brief glimpse of the events of the day:

Courtesy of Elizabeth Stone

Geraldine as presented at Court, 1885

> The bride . . . wore a costume of rich ivory Bengaline, the front of the skirt and bodice being richly draped with natural exquisite old Brussels point lace. On the corsage was a garniture of orange blossoms, sent by her sister from Algiers. Her ornaments consisted of a magnificent diamond necklace, the gift of her father, and a diamond star from the bridegroom.

Her sisters Violet and Florence acted as bridesmaids. Their dresses were of 'pale blue satin trimmed with fawn-coloured *dentelle degaze,* with hats *en suite.* They wore a diamond and pearl brooch, the gift of the bridegroom'. Forward, the bride's brother, acted as best man. After the ceremony 'the bridal party drove to Stratheden House....where the wedding breakfast was served. Subsequently the bride and bridegroom left town by the night mail for Paris en route for Spain. The Bride's travelling dress was of dark blue and red serge, with hat and jacket to match'.[8]

Ellen M. Blake, granddaughter of Henry Blake of Renvyle House, in her memoir *My Connemara Childhood* gives a glimpse of life as experienced by those fortunate enough to count themselves among the guests of the Henrys at Kylemore Castle. The Henry family were particularly kind to the Blakes after the death of Ellen's father in 1884, which brought about a decline in the family circumstances. Every Christmas Ellen's mother and her three children were invited to stay at the Castle. Ellen became a great friend of Florence Henry.

Courtesy of Elizabeth Stone

Geraldine in her wedding dress, 1887
Described by Henry as *'the flower of my flock'*

Florence owned three large white donkeys brought from Egypt, which drew a low carriage like a "Victoria". Over-fed and little exercised, these animals were very lazy. She, being tender hearted, could hardly bear to use the whip so progress was slow.

For Ellen, Kylemore Castle was a magical place 'with its many staircases and corridors'. She and Florence got up to all sorts of mischief:

Courtesy of the Brady Family

John Lewis Henry

> One of our favourite amusements was to lower a basket by a long cord from her bedroom window, which was over the kitchen department, with a note to the chef who would fill it up with good things such as meringues or fruit; then we would pull it up again. Once, in a bad temper, he sent up bones which was a bitter disappointment!

On Christmas Day the Ballroom held the Christmas tree and she recalls 'proceeding there after lunch to find presents around it for the family, guests, and all the staff':[9]

> They generally had big house parties at Kylemore. On these occasions a small dining-room was used for the schoolroom party, which consisted of a couple or more governesses, English and French, the two younger (Henry) girls and ourselves, waited on by a minor footman. When we dined in the state dining-room we tried our best to make the old butler laugh, and often succeeded in doing so. Every night, just before dinner, a maid would go round to all the bedrooms bearing a tray of small and very stiff bouquets for each of us to wear at dinner.
>
> The guests had what you would now think a dull time. After breakfast all the women collected in the library, looked at the *Illustrated* and other papers arranged in rows . . . and did fancy work until twelve oclock, when a short walk was taken before luncheon: then another walk or drive before tea: after dinner billiards was sometimes played, and perhaps there was a little music. I do not seem to remember any other games. We met there at various times quite a number of interesting people.

Courtesy of the National Library
Kylemore Collection 11

Lorenzo, Alexander and John Henry

To help ease away the chill of a damp day spent on the lake, or crouched on the mountain side waiting for the pheasant to rise, an added luxury for the guests was the fully-equipped Turkish Bath, with hot, intermediate and cooling rooms, all lined with white glazed brick and containing white marble and mahogany fitting. This was situated on the eastern end of the Castle, right next to the lean-to orchard house and small rose house. On Sundays the household staff drove 'in state' to the Parish Church. 'I can see the long procession of maids, led by the housekeeper, walking into church clad in black dresses and wearing bonnets'.[10]

All of the family enjoyed Kylemore, but by far the most attached to the place were Henry's youngest son and daughter; Lorenzo and Florence. Lorenzo renowned for his skills with a rod and gun, was from an early age, his son Louis later recorded, 'a remarkable shot both with a shot-gun and rifle: shooting from the left shoulder, as his left eye was the stronger'. After attending Eton he was commissioned into the Royal Monmouthshire Regiment (Militia) Royal Engineers. He followed this with a spell in Heidelberg, where 'he did not actually attend the University but had a tutor and learned to speak very good German', and somehow managed to combine his studies with various sporting expeditions. After Germany Lorenzo returned home and divided his time between Stratheden House, 'where he used to drive a four-in-hand and where he lived a life of the greatest fun and luxury in society and clubland, and Kylemore Castle, where he had his own steam yacht, the "*Ida*" (which he designed and had built at Plymouth) with a crew of four, and the run of a vast sporting estate . . . In the 1890s he took to motoring and was one of the first to make the run from London to Brighton and back in one day . . . He was also one of the first members of the Royal Automobile Club and one of the first to take a car to Ireland where not only animals but also people took to their heels!'[11]

Lorenzo liked to invent things, but seldom took the care to patent his invention with the result that many of his inventions were copied by others and brought no commercial success to himself:

> One invention he did make money with was the *Henrite* shot-gun cartridge. By that time, he was internationally known as a champion "pigeon shot"[12] taking part in competitions all over Europe and various centres in England. The cartridge was one of the first "smokeless" and the main principle was that the charge was constant and the same for each cartridge . . . A company was formed and the *Henrite* cartridge became very popular among sportsmen.

Henry gave Lorenzo Bunnaboghee, in Letterfrack, where he had built a substantial Lodge with a small building on the grounds known as the Powder House. Here Lorenzo could conduct his experiments at a safe distance from Kylemore Castle. Attached to Bunnaboghee Lodge was the fishing rights to that section of the Dawros river bordering the land and where the river entered the sea.

© Kylemore Abbey

Ida Lorenzo's yacht

The years away from politics would have given Henry more time to spend with family and friends in the beautiful surroundings of Kylemore Castle, and more time too, perhaps, to reflect on the more pleasant things in life. Such reflection is evident in the tone of his letter to *The Times* in September 1891, in which he eulogised the benefits of wine in old age: 'Wine is in truth the milk of old age, and you should take enough of it just to enable you to eat a little more food than you would care to touch under the cold inspiration of *aqua pumpaginis*'. But alcohol, he warned, 'is a poison to the young and vigorous, who do not require it; but it is a beneficent creature to the over-wrought mental or bodily labourer'. However, as always a man of advanced views, he warned that an even greater danger 'lies in youthful smoking, especially of cigarettes, but how that is to be stopped . . . your present correspondent has not an idea'.[13]

In 1889 A & S Henry, after eighty-five years as a private firm, was converted into a public liability company, with Henry remaining on as Chairman for a further four years.[14] Henry was then aged sixty-three and at the time was in possession of 12,615 shares valued at £10 per share; his brother, John Snowdon, held 2,300 shares. In the same year he was made High Sheriff of Galway (1889–90),[15] but the position was chiefly an honoury one. Maintaining his 'Imperial' view he wrote to *The Times* on 3 September 1892 pointing out the values and advantages to the British navy of Killary Harbour, all of which would be lost if Gladstone's 'infatuation' was to persist. Killary, a deep fjord not far from his home, had that summer played host to the British navy while on manoeuvres along the West coast. Pointing out Killary's suitability as a starting point for liners crossing the Atlantic, he suggested the construction of a branch line linking Leenane with the Galway to Clifden railway, then under construction.[16] A similar suggestion had been put before the Galway Grand Jury in 1890 by engineers, Edward Townsend and Arthur E. Joyce, in a proposal for the Galway to Clifden railway recently sanctioned by government. The proposal, entitled 'The Galway and Clifden "Via Oughterard" Light Railway, Recess & Killary Branch', was one of five put forward for consideration in that year, and was based on the plan first drawn up by Samuel Ussher Roberts over twenty years before. It allowed for a branch line running from Recess to Killary through the Inagh Valley, parallel to the main road and terminating at the boundary of Tullyconor and Derrynacleigh, beside the main road from Leenane and close to the deep water of the fjord.[17] The letter was reprinted in the *Galway Express* under the title, 'The Discovery of Killary Harbour'; a week later the same newspaper carried the sad tale of the accidental death of Henry's fourth daughter, Mrs Geraldine Gilbert.

Geraldine had been living with her husband in America, where the couple had lost two children in infancy. When the third child, a daughter named Elizabeth, was born, Geraldine brought her to Kylemore in the hope that she would thrive there. On Wednesday afternoon, 21 September 1892, the Henry family and friends were taking one of their regular drives around the estate. The main party had gone ahead in the big four-in-hand, Geraldine following behind in a phaeton, driven by a very spirited horse. She was accompanied by her daughter, Elizabeth, and her Nanny. On approaching Derryinver Bridge, just three miles from the Castle, the pony became agitated and by the time Geraldine had reached the bridge she had lost control and the phaeton overturned, throwing her over the bridge and into the water. The Nanny and baby, aged eight months, were thrown out on the road, but were not seriously hurt. Geraldine died instantly, however; according to the newspaper, her body was not discovered until two hours later.[18] Geraldine's husband brought her body back to America for burial next to the couple's two children.

Courtesy of the Brady Family

Geraldine with her daughter Elizabeth

Given Henry's reaction to the death of family and friends in the past, and his deep love for all of his children, one can only imagine the devastating effect the loss of Geraldine would have had on him. However, putting his own feelings to one side, he wrote to Edward offering praise, assurance and advice. The letter reached Edward at Kylemore, before his departure to the US. In it Henry informed him of his high regard for him both as a husband and son-in-law; he thanked him for his devotion to Geraldine and recommended that, in time, for his own sake and for the sake of his daughter, he should remarry:

> For myself I have only this to say; You were to my Geraldine an ideal husband. You made her intensely happy in spite of her many sorrows.

You gilded her life and she adored you, as few women adore a man. Therefore I, if for no other reason, shall for the years, or days or hours, that remain to me ever look on you as a true man, and as a model husband, and a model son.

Come back as soon as you can, but remember this you must not pass your life alone, for she would not have wished that, and your child will need a brother.

You will think it odd that I should say this, but what ever time may bring about, remember that nothing can dim my affection, or diminish my gratitude for what you have proved yourself to be to my Geraldine, the flower of my flock . . . Yes it is true, work, hard work is the only . . . now and you and I have plenty of it – I feel very lonely and very solitary but that is natural –

Ever your affectionate friend and relative.[19]

Geraldine's death seems to have precipitated some major changes in Henry's life. The following year he resigned as Chairman of A & S Henry and a year later Kylemore Castle and Estate were put up for sale. Descriptive illustrated particulars, with a detailed map of the estate and conditions of sale, were drawn up by E. & H. Lumley of London, and put on sale at 10s 6d per copy. *The Times* carried notice of the auction to be held in London on 3 July 1894: 'There are about 25 bed rooms, four bath rooms, four sitting rooms, ball room, billiard room. library, study, and many offices inside and out. It would be impossible to find a more habitable, luxurious and comfortable residence than Kylemore Castle. Among the advantages attached to this estate is its accessibility, for the railway station at Recess [soon to be opened] . . . will be only 11 miles from the castle . . . a person may leave London by the evening mail of one day and dine at the castle on the next'.[20] The Estate had, according to the Book of Sale, one hundred and ten tenants who paid a rental of £600 a year: 'whose families supply the labour necessary on the Estate at weekly wages'. And added Henry's proud boast: 'The present proprietor and his family have lived on his estate for the last thirty years at peace with all men, and has never evicted a tenant or raised a rent'.[21] The auction however failed to attract the price sought and so the property was withdrawn.

Henry was also, it would appear, experiencing financial difficulties. In the eight years since A & S Henry had gone public he had divested himself of a large portion of his stock and by 1897 had reduced his holding to 4,490 shares.[22] In July of the following year, in an attempt to capitalise on his assets, he began negotiations with a building contractor to build residential flats on the site of Stratheden House. However, it soon transpired that the builder was bankrupt and Henry withdrew, but was later taken to court by the builder and his associate for loss of fees and other payments. Henry settled his case with the associate; the case with the builder was eventually thrown out of court.[23]

Henry's last letter to *The Times* was written from Kylemore on 18 July 1900. The subject was on the advantage of shooting from the hip. This was not a metaphor for Henry's behaviour in the House of Commons, although one might be forgiven for thinking so, but was in this case a statement of fact. Young recruits in the army, he argued, ought to be trained to shoot their guns from the hip, since a rifle discharged from the standing position tends to fly over the head of the enemy. 'If however, the recruit is taught to reserve his fire, and then to fire from the hip' he will, Henry elaborated, reduce the effects of kick back and increase his chances of hitting the target: 'in early life I belonged to two corps of Volunteers and have long taken an interest in rifle shooting'.[24] Needless to say this piece of advice does not appear to have been acted upon.

Little was heard from Henry after this; it would seem that he moved quietly out of Kylemore and into retirement in England. Lorenzo remained on at Kylemore and took over the running of the estate. By then it was becoming evident that Henry's financial circumstances were beyond redemption. In December 1901 outstanding mortgages and interests on Kylemore Castle and Stratheden House amounted to £165,422. The mortgage on Stratheden House was £93,564.5.0 and on Kylemore Castle it was £57,071.5.0d. Henry had a life policy for £300,000 which was perhaps expected to rescue the family homes in the event of his death. However, he was having difficulty meeting the payments, along with the mortgage repayment, with the result that the mortgagees foreclosed on both houses. Stratheden House was then pulled down to make way for redevelopment and Kylemore Castle was back on the market.

There are many theories as to the cause of the decline in Henry's fortune. The Benedictine Nuns, who later purchased the Castle, were told that Henry had lost his fortune through a series of set-backs: 'First the loss of a

THE DOMAIN

Extends in a direct line from North to South a distance of about 7½ miles and from East to West about 6 miles, including within its limits several Loughs, Rivers, Mountains, Valleys and Glens in addition to a

Stretch of 3 miles of the Atlantic Coast

Here broken by numerous inlets and in parts extensive tracts of sand.

The entire Estate is in the

PARISH OF BALLYNAKILL

And embraces within its borders the whole of the following

Twelve Town Lands

DAWROSMORE, CURRYWONGAUN, BARNANANG, LETTERGESH WEST, TOOREENA, MULLAGHGLASS, LEMNAHELTIA, MWEELIN, ADDERGOOLE, LETTERGESH EAST, POLLACAPPUL AND SHANAVEAG

In the Heart of Connemara

COUNTY GALWAY, IRELAND

From London by the Royal Irish Mail Service, Dublin is reached by the direct and accelerated route via Holyhead, whence by fast boats Kingstown is reached in about 3½ hours. Thence the Midland Great Western Railway of Ireland run a fast service of trains in connection with the cross channel traffic and from Dublin there are through trains to Recess and Clifden Stations, both equi-distant about 13 miles from Kylemore.

The whole journey from the Metropolis occupying about 16 hours and from Dublin about 6 hours.

Driving from Recess Station, the road to Kylemore, which has a very easy gradient, passes through the Valley of Lough Inagh, skirting the Lough for the greater part of the way, and affording a Grand View of the ranges of Mountains which shut in this fine Valley. Continuing, the road leads to the Entrance of

The Beautiful Kylemore Pass

Justly renowned for its picturesque natural formation, with the Loughs of Kylemore, Pollacappul and Maladrolaun following in quick succession, bounded on either side by mountains, rising from the water's edge to heights approaching 3,000 feet.

© Kylemore Abbey

Kylemore Book of Sale 1902

lawsuit over his London home, then the failure of some Australian gold mines in which he had invested heavily, then the Boer War broke out, wrecking his mining interests in South Africa'.[25] Contributing factors were Henry's extravagant lifestyle, the heavy mortgage on Stratheden House, his indulgence in technical and agricultural experiments; and added to this the numerous expenses associated with his political career. There is also little doubt that the enormous expense incurred in the construction of Kylemore Castle, the improvement works carried out on the estate and the continuous demand for its upkeep were a heavy drain on his fortune.

However, never at any time did Henry voice complaint or regret over the monies spent on Kylemore. Indeed on one occasion in the House of Commons he casually dismissed his efforts as 'simply his hobby', explaining that, 'having a taste for agriculture, he had spent his money in that pursuit to amuse himself'. However, anyone familiar with Henry's political career knew that the development of Kylemore Estate was more by way of an agricultural and political experiment, set out to show what a man with capital and the courage of his convictions could achieve. But Henry was a rarity among men, few at the time possessing his extraordinary energy and tenacity, and even fewer were prepared to invest so heavily in the waste lands of Ireland.

Henry's development of the Kylemore Estate from wasteland to a place of great beauty was an extraordinary feat given the many disadvantages and obstacles confronting him. But being a true Victorian he believed that nothing was impossible, it was simply the lack of will that made it so, and taking advantage of available expertise and new innovative ideas he set to work with energy and enthusiasm and succeeded where lesser men would have failed.

No doubt his family background had a tremendous influence on his success. His early education and religious training in the Unitarian Church would have helped to shape his personal and political attitudes and left him open and tolerant of others; stories of the early struggles of the Manchester Unitarians would have been known to him and must surely have influenced his dealings with his Roman Catholic neighbours and his views on the political question of denominational education. Coming from a middle-class manufacturing background his purchase of Kylemore moved him into the landlord class, bringing new responsibilities and challenges which he met with an innate sense of justice and fair play. His tenacity as a politician left him to the end holding fast to his original ideals that Ireland's troubles stemmed from social rather than political causes and that Home Rule should be granted along the lines of that sought by Isaac Butt and the Home Government Association and not in the restoration of 'a Grattan

Parliament'.[26] His efforts to win political ground for his theories left him on the fringe of the Liberal Party, eventually abandoning the Irish Party and towards the end praising Conservative policy in Ireland. And yet, despite the many derogatory comments written in the newspapers and those fired at him from across the House, Henry viewed his experiment at Kylemore as a success and was aggrieved that, given his experience on the ground, Gladstone and the Liberal Government did not take his advice and develop the entire country along the same lines.

For the people of Kylemore, Henry's departure brought to an end a period of advancement and development that would not be equalled for many years. From generation to generation stories would be passed down telling of this extraordinary man who built a castle in the wilderness, out of love for his wife and for Connemara, and lost a fortune in the process. As always with folklore not all the stories would be accurate and not all of them flattering, but the fact remains that, for a small man, Mitchell Henry cast a long shadow. And his wealth, generosity, sensitivity and judicious decision-making, which helped to make him so popular in life, have made him a legend in death.

Down through the years the Henrys had entertained the aristocracy, politicians, members of the diplomatic corps, men of commerce, wealth and reputation at Kylemore Castle. However, when the Castle's most distinguished guest, King Edward VII, came to call in 1903 he was met, not by a member of the family but by the agent, Henry A. Robinson. The King was touring the Congested Districts of the West and was accompanied by the Queen and Princess Victoria. The group arrived by Royal Yacht at Leenane on 29 July 1903 where they were met by a nine-car motorcade which carried them through Connemara. Their route took them through Tully, Letterfrack and

King Edward VII at Kylemore

Kylemore, where they made a brief stop at the Castle. At the entrance to Kylemore Castle the Royal party was welcomed by the Agent and the Queen was presented with a bouquet by Miss Clementina Browne, the niece of Lord Kilmaine. The group next travelled to Recess where they lunched at the Railway Hotel and later alighted a train for Galway.[27]

Almost immediately rumours spread that the King was considering purchasing Kylemore Castle as a Royal residence. For years pressure was mounting on the King to purchase a residence in Ireland, the only part of the British Isles that did not have one. The King himself, it was said, was in favour of the idea and 'expressed strong admiration for the scenic beauty of the sister-isle and real appreciation for the rugged splendour of the West coast'. Several properties were suggested but one newspaper, the *Daily Express*, pointed out that the 'most suitable of all was the superb modern castle of Kylemore'. But because of the 'enormous size of the house and the immensity of the grounds and park . . . it is considered too expensive for His majesty, as no less than £40,000 a year would be required for its upkeep'.[28] This figure was considered by many to be an exaggeration.

While public attention was focused on the possibility of the King becoming the new owner of the Estate, private negotiations were well underway between the mortgagees, Friends Provident, and the Duke of Manchester. The Castle and lands, now reduced to a little over 13,000 acres, was eventually sold to the Duke for £63,000 and possession was handed over on Tuesday 22 September 1903.[29] The Manchesters were friends of Lorenzo, and had visited him at Kylemore some months previously. A court case was later taken by Lorenzo against Friends Provident for £1,260 commission, which he claimed was due to him for introducing his Grace as a possible buyer to the mortgagees. Under an agreement reached between Lorenzo and the Institution, Lorenzo was to receive three per cent of the sale price on completion of the sale, and a further two percent if completed by 15 May 1903. However, because the sale was not completed by that date, Lorenzo missed out on his two per cent and was seeking it through the courts. The case came before the King's Bench in London two years later, but the court found in favour of the mortgagees and Lorenzo lost the case.[30]

Florence, Henry's fourth daughter, moved to Bunnaboghee Lodge, which Lorenzo signed over to her in 1904, and where she spent the remainder of her life until her death in 1952. Lorenzo stayed on at the Castle for a year or two, as a guest of the Manchesters, and helped in the running of the estate. Lorenzo later married Marion Reagner, the daughter of a wealthy New York lawyer, Louis Christian Reagner. The couple settled in London and in 1907 they had a son, their only child, Louis Mitchell Henry, one of whose god-fathers was the Duke of Manchester.

Mitchell Henry died in Leamington, in England, on 22 November 1910, aged eighty-four. Local and national papers gave coverage to his death, mentioning his political career and some paying tribute to his great contribution to the West and in particular to the people of Connemara. His body was cremated and his ashes brought back to Kylemore and laid to rest next to Margaret's remains in the mausoleum in the Castle grounds. On his death in 1910 Henry left just £425, the remainder of his assets having previously been disposed of.

Following the death of his father, Lorenzo, who was frequently referred to as "young Mitchell Henry", changed his surname to Mitchell-Henry and was followed by other members of the family. Later he won fame as a fisherman. He was the first man to catch a tuna fish on a rod and later published a book on the subject. In 1933 he held the world record for a tuna caught off Whitby weighing 851 lbs.

Lorenzo continued with his inventions, two of which were purchased and used by the Government: 'a machine-gun mounting for coastal patrol boats and a rocket-like missile attached to thin steel cable for becoming entangled in propellers of enemy bombers'. Old age found Lorenzo still scoring a perfect bull's-eye in a target shoot at the age of eighty-eight, and without glasses. Lorenzo died just one month short of his ninety-ninth birthday, in 1965.[31]

Cover of Lorenzo Mitchell-Henry's book on tuna fishing, showing him with his 851 lb. world record catch.

Caught on the Improved Mitchell-Henry Reel on a line of 152 lb. breaking strain, Mitchell-Henry Hook. Bait, mackerel; Time, 1 hour 17 minutes; Boatman – Harry Wray; Tender, "Success"; Place, 40 miles off Whitby; Date, 11 September 1933.

The best remembered of the Henry family in and around Connemara was Florence. Florence lived at Bunnaboghee Lodge and farmed over 195 acres of land. She also held the fishing rights to the lower section of the Dawros river and the estuary, and frequently played host to other members of the Henry family. Her sister Geraldine's granddaughters, Elizabeth and Geraldine Timmins, spent almost a year there in 1925, attended the local national school and made friends with the children of the neighbourhood. Lorenzo's son, Louis, remembered Florence with great fondness:

> She was a most remarkable woman and a very great character. She was an exceptional salmon angler and once in her prime caught forty in a fortnight, all on the fly . . . She was also an exceptional bridge player. She was very much a "loner" and never married although I believe she had an admirer for many years whom she was unable to marry. He remembered her generously in his will and she became reasonably well-off.[32]

Florence turned Lorenzo's Powder House into a cottage which she rented out with the shooting and salmon fishing of Bunnaboghee. She employed former workmen of the castle as farm hands and gillies and their families as household staff. Florence had as a companion, Lena Murray, an English woman who had been her maid at Kylemore when they were both young. Lena remained with Florence to the end, living well into her nineties though completely bedridden in her final years. Florence herself suffered from severe arthritis for the last fifteen years of her life. Following her death, in February 1952, Bunnaboghee and its contents was sold at public auction, thus bringing to an end the Henry presence in Connemara.

Chapter 10

The Manchesters

William Angus Drogo Montague, the 9th Duke of Manchester, took possession of Kylemore Castle on 22 September 1903. The Duke was twenty-six years of age and already had a well earned reputation as a playboy and gambler. Three years earlier the Duke had married the beautiful American heiress, Helena Zimmerman, and there were many who speculated that the recent acquisition was financed by his wealthy father-in-law, Eugene Zimmerman of Cincinnati, Ohio. The purchase was indeed made in the name of the Duke and Duchess of Manchester and a mortgage of £54,500, with the Friends Provident Institution, was taken out in the Duke's name. But the remainder of the purchase price, £8,500, and the cost of the lavish refurbishment of the Castle that followed, it seems safe to assume, was provided by Zimmerman.

At the time of purchase the Kylemore Estate covered a little under 13,400 acres and included the following townlands: Lettergesh East, Lettergesh West, Mullaghglass, Lemnaheltia, Tooreena, Shanaveag, Pollacappul, Currywongaun, Dawros More, Adrigoole, Barnanaugh and Mweelin. Along with 'the Mansion House, known as Kylemore Castle, the church, farms, houses, homesteads cottages, stables, outbuildings and all other' buildings and erections standing on the above listed lands. Excluded from the sale was Bunnaboghee, which was retained by Florence Henry. The only section of the Kylemore Estate that the Manchesters purchased directly from Mitchell Henry was the licence to farm and plant oysters at Ballynakill and Barnaderg Bay on 21 November 1904, for £50.

The *Galway Express* reported that the Duke was expected to take advantage of the new land act of 1903 and sell off the farms and small holdings. The enormous upkeep of the Estate was cited by the Duke as his reason for considering such a step. He planned to retain the castle and a small shooting, thus leaving him a more economical holding. This plan, however, came to nothing.[1]

William Angus Drogo Montague, 9th
Duke of Manchester in his Coronation
robes at the Coronation of King George V,
June 1911

The Manchester title was created in 1719; a further title, Baron Montague of Kimbolton, dated back to 1620. Born on 3 March 1877, the Duke was educated at Eton and Trinity College, Cambridge, and succeeded his father in 1892, when he was still a minor. His inheritance included Kimbolton Castle in Huntington, England, once the residence of Catherine of Aragon, and Tanderagee Castle, Co Armagh: the combined acreage of which was about 27,400. The Duke also inherited a collection of paintings by such artists as Vandyke, Titian, Holbein, Reynolds, Reubens, Lely and Lawrence.[2] However, the Duke's inheritance was heavily indebted and, because of his age, his estate was for many years administrated by trustees, whom he claimed robbed him. Because of the heavy charges levied against it the income from the estate was insufficient to meet the outgoings, with the result that, until he came of age, the Duke's personal income was provided out of the residuary estate of his grandfather.[3] This, however, came nowhere near meeting his needs and so the Duke began borrowing on the strength of his inheritance.

On coming of age in 1898 there was still insufficient funds to provide the Duke with an income. A relative came to his rescue and granted him an allowance of £70 a month, but as his expenditure was from £1,500 to £2,000 a year, he was forced to resort to further borrowings to make up the difference. Although still young, the Duke was fast developing a taste for the high life: he enjoyed travel, high society, gambling, hunting and shooting, all of which proved expensive for a man with no income. The consequence of this high lifestyle left the Duke bankrupt at the age of twenty-three and it was becoming obvious that he would have to go down that well travelled route of the British aristocracy and marry a rich woman. This he did in 1900 when he married the Cincinnati heiress, Helena Zimmerman.

The couple met in France, where Helena was staying with her aunt, Miss Effie Mackenzie Evans, a journalist on the staff of the *New York Herald* in Paris. The couple were attracted from the beginning and, following a successful courtship, encouraged by Miss Evans, the Duke followed Helena to America. While there he succeeded in obtaining employment as a journalist with Randolph Hearst. Helena was the only child of Eugene Zimmerman, an oil and railroad tycoon, with extensive interests in coal and iron mines. Zimmerman was President of the Cincinnati, Hamilton and Dayton

Railroad, and, along with other assets, was said to hold a quarter of a million dollars worth of railroad stock in his own name. This self-made man was not impressed with his daughter's choice in a prospective husband and it was rumoured that he opposed the match. However, despite this, Miss Evans and Helena returned to Europe in the autumn, where, on 14 November 1900, without parental consent, she married the Duke and news of the marriage was cabled to Zimmerman in Cincinnati.

Ten days later *The Times* newspaper announced that the Duke of Manchester, with liabilities standing at £37,794, was declared bankrupt and 'certain live and dead farming stock', and all his goods and chattels, were to be sold. Farming stock at Kimbolton had previously been sold for £12,700 to satisfy creditors[4], but on this occasion his assets were not expected to produce more than £7,545.[5]

The marriage, however, having taken place, there was nothing left for Zimmerman to do but to accept the situation. When the newlyweds came to Cincinnati shortly afterwards, Zimmerman hosted a large reception for the couple in his twenty-eight roomed mansion at the corner of Auburn Avenue and McMillan Street. In return, the Duke and his father-in-law were honoured at a dinner at the Queen City Club, and the Duke and Duchess were guests of honour at two parties at the St Nicholas Hotel.[6]

At the time of their marriage the gossip columns in the American newspapers were alive with comment and innuendo, much to the annoyance of all concerned. The Duke writing later in the *New York Journal* gave 'novelty' as the reason why 'English noblemen or men of position marry American wives' and not money, as was so often quoted: 'Most of the marriages were for love, no doubt. That is what Americans always marry for, isn't it?' American girls were, in his opinion, 'the most beautiful and fascinating in the world. They have all the qualities of all the other girls put together . . . they are beautiful, witty, graceful, high-bred, original, innocent, audacious, intellectual and practical'.[7]

In his memoirs, *My Candid Recollections,* published in 1932, the Duke freely admits to being 'unrepentantly addicted' to gambling and incapable of handling his finances: 'Some of the biggest thrills of my life have been at the tables, and though I have lost a great deal of money at various times I

Courtesy of
National Library of Ireland

Helena, Duchess of Manchester
Illustrated London News 26 June
1909, 935

have also won a great deal'. The Duke's golden rule in life was never to keep accounts, instead he would simply say, 'I had my money's worth'.[8]

The Dowager Duchess of Manchester, also an American, whose family had plantations in Cuba and Louisiana, was for years a friend of Edward, Prince of Wales, and, under her influence, the Duke and Duchess were welcomed into that most prestigious of social circles. The Prince was said to have been 'most impressed by the improved behaviour' of the Duke following his marriage to Helena. Later, when the Prince became King Edward, he frequently dined at the couple's home and, at one time, 'the Duchess of Manchester had the rare distinction of entertaining the King of England and the King of Spain at the same time'.[9]

The Manchesters' lifestyle was typically aristocratic Edwardian: an endless round of country house parties in the shooting and fishing season and balls and dinner parties in London:

> When one came to London for the season then, one came prepared
> for an orgy of parties, and ivory cards fell like snowflakes. One could
> count on being two or three deep every evening in balls, to say
> nothing of having a choice of dinner-parties before-hand, as well as
> luncheons and even breakfast-parties.[10]

The Duke's godfather was William K. Vanderbilt, Senior, and this, coupled with his wife's connections, meant time spent in America would have drawn the Manchesters into an equivalent social circle there. The Duke liked to boast that it was his mother who had 'helped to launch the W.K. Vanderbilts on the social sea', and 'despite their immense riches' they were, according to the Duke, 'glad to accept' her help.[11]

A year after their marriage the Duchess gave birth to the first of four children, Mary Alice, and in the following year, a son and heir was born, Alexander George Francis Drogo. One of the first alterations to be undertaken by the Manchesters at Kylemore Castle was the conversion of some of the rooms into a special suite of apartments for the nursery and play-rooms.

King Edward was planning another visit to Ireland in April 1904 and by February of that year the *Galway Express* announced that the King and Queen were expected to spend a weekend as guests of the Duke and Duchess at Kylemore.[12] Arrangements were well underway for their reception and extensive alterations were being carried out on the Castle, making it more suitable to accommodate the Royal party.

Journalists from English and New York newspapers visited Kylemore on 7 April to see the preparations and were met by the land steward, John Couper, a Scotsman, who had been with the Estate since the time of

Mitchell Henry. They found 'myriads of workmen flitting about fashioning things in wood and plaster and stone', and the Duchess, 'whose intelligence and admirable management are praised by everybody in the district', was, they wrote, 'determined that nothing shall be wanting to make Kylemore quite equal, if not superior, to any Royal palace'. In all, the alterations were said to have cost £16,000.

The Duchess wished to modernise the Castle by remodelling almost all of the interior, enlarging the rooms and completely re-arranging the bedroom apartments. The Royal couple were to occupy the aptly named Royal Suite; which was beautifully decorated in white and pink, with a communicating corridor to the Royal dressing-room and bathroom. Each apartment was 'large and lofty, and the decorations are in keeping, and nothing could exceed the quiet sumptuousness of the whole arrangements'. Adjoining the Royal apartment were two suites of rooms 'only a little less splendid than the state rooms, and each has its distinctive scheme of decoration: but the Duchess's general decorative taste [seemed] to run in a cheerful white and pink'. And in all cases the effect, we are told, was 'very pretty'.[13]

On the ground floor more dramatic changes were underway and many of Samuel Ussher Roberts's fine Gothic features were ripped out to make way for a more austere interior. The magnificent marble arches in the hallways were torn down and the entire area was panelled in mock Jacobean style. The wall between the morning and breakfast rooms was removed, and the solid outside wall pulled down and replaced with two Ionic Columns, making the drawing-room twice its former size. The library and study were transformed into one large reception hall and the fernery, constructed to conceal the joining of Kylemore Lodge to Kylemore Castle, was roofed and transformed into a conservatory.

But most drastic of all was the conversion of the Gothic Ballroom into a kitchen. This beautiful room, which in the past echoed to the soft tones of chamber music and the happy laughter of family and friends enjoying an evening's entertainment, was now to echo to the sound of pots, pans and crockery.

A large mirror in the hall which reflected the light from the stained glass window on the stairway, was ordered to be destroyed, the workmen protested, but in the end carried out the order. The stained glass window too was removed and replaced by plate glass. The Henry coat of arms, positioned just above the main entrance, was for some reason retained and is still there to the present day. Much to the disappointment of the Manchesters the King's itinerary did not allow for a return visit to

Kylemore, but the publicity had certainly drawn attention to their arrival in the neighbourhood.

The Duke's memoirs give little information on his time at Kylemore Castle, except to say that they were very fond of the place and that their youngest child, Louise, was born there on 6 January 1908. A study of the 1901 and 1911 census for the Estate shows some changes in staff under the new owner. The steward, John Couper, and head gardener, William Comfort, had by 1911 left the Duke's employment. Couper purchased his own farm in The Neal, Co. Mayo, and Comfort retired to England where he died in 1912. Perhaps an indicator of where the Duke's priorities lay is revealed in the fact that the gamekeeper no longer resided, as in former times, in a house near to the model Home Farm but now resided in the former steward's house and the number of assistant gamekeepers had increased from one to four. By contrast the number of gardeners was reduced, from five in 1901 to two in 1911. An indication that the walled garden was already under threat is shown in that by 1911 the Duke no longer employed a stoker to attend to the boilers, necessary for maintaining and controlling the heat in the glasshouses.

The Castle, in the absence of the owner, was in both years left under the care of Martin Feeney, a widower born in County Galway, who did not appear to have a family. This is perhaps the same man listed in the 1881 census for Stratheden House. Martin was listed as an electrician and in 1901 he oversaw a staff of four, three housemaids and a pantry boy: also living in the house at the time was Mary Simpson, a telegraphist. In 1911 Martin was accompanied by three staff: the housekeeper Lizzie Daly, Ellen Joyce, a housemaid, and Martin Coyne, the hall boy. David Anderson, the Scottish born coachman, lived with his wife and three children in a two story house next to the coach house in 1901, and by 1911, when the coach was replaced by a motorcar, he remained on as driver and mechanic. Patrick Hastings, born in Co. Galway, remained on as forester and resided in a house at Model Home Farm along with his wife and family. Thomas Aspell, born in Co. Wexford, and his wife Anne, born in Co. Monaghan, also lived at the farm staff quarters. The Aspells had four children, all of whom worked on the farm in 1901, but by 1911 they had retired and Willie and Bridget Aspell, a young couple recently married, were the only members of the family left working on the estate.[14]

The contrast between the Manchesters and Mitchell Henry could not

Obituary.

WILLIAM COMFORT. — We regret to record the death of Mr. William Comfort, which occurred on the 15th inst., at the age of 65. He was one of five brothers, all of whom, like their father and grandfather, followed gardening as a profession. He served his time in his native county of Aberdeen, and afterwards became foreman at Altyre, near Forres. Mr. Comfort served as head gardener at Maryhill, Elgin; Aberlour, Banffshire; Farnley Hall, Otley, Yorkshire; Knowle Hall, near Birmingham; and Kylemore Castle, Co. Galway, first under the late Mr. Henry, M.P., and latterly under the Duke of Manchester. About seven years ago he retired from service, and has since resided in Berwick-on-Tweed, where he carried on a business as fruiterer and seedsman. He leaves a widow, but no family. One of his brothers, Mr. Charles Comfort, is gardener at Broomfield, Davidson's Mains, Midlothian.

William Comfort Obituary
The Gardeners Chronicle 27 July 1912

have been greater. The Duke, by his own writings, would appear to have been a conceited snob, whose delusions of grandeur led him to believe that his title entitled him to a respect which neither his attitude nor behaviour warranted. There was little room for Henry's Liberal philosophy of 'The greatest happiness for the greatest number' in the Duke's notions of superiority. Neither did he hold his Irish tenantry, particularly those in the West, in any regard. There were, in his opinion, three distinct races in Ireland. The first being the Scottish-Irish of Northern Ireland: stern, with a 'laborious perseverance' and a religious zeal, 'verging at times upon fanaticism', who were also blessed with 'gifts of imagination and humour [and] . . . an unquenchable desire to get something for nothing'. The second race was the 'wholly lovable child . . . "the real Irish"'. This was the Irish of the West and South:

The workmen responsible for laying down the hard-surface tennis court.

The men came from Lettergesh and Mullaghglass, only a few names survive.

Back Row: (1) Phil Conroy.

Second Row: (5) John Lydon, (6) Keane, (7) Martin Coyne.

Front Row (1) Anthony Keane, (2) Mike Gibbons, (3) Miley Walsh.

> completely lacking the sterner characteristics of the first type, but making up for this deficiency by the richer texture of his imaginative life. Treat him as a gentlemanly child, and you will find him one of the most charming people on earth: cross him or approach him with an air of superiority, and his native obstinacy will prove the most formidable of barriers. Well fed, with his body and brain sufficiently nourished, this Irishman is capable of the most astonishing achievements. His energy is boundless – witness what he has done and is still doing in America . . . but in his native mountains, and in some of the cities of the South, semi-starvation and indescribably bad housing conditions have induced in him a lethargy for which I have found no parallel among any of the so-called "depressed" classes of the world. The will seems paralysed, except for rare spasms of energy, usually, alas! of a destructive nature.

The third 'race' he called 'the mongrel', 'a cross between the native Irish and some foreign race', perhaps the Spanish:

The "mongrel" Irish is sly, cruel, deceitful, lazy; he is a born plotter and intriguer. He is at heart a coward, despite his ferocity, and it is he, not the true Irish either of North or South, who has been responsible for the cowardly outrages that have been a blot on the escutcheon of one of the most charming races in the world.

If protected from the influences of the 'mongrel' and treated 'kindly – though when necessary firmly – the Irishman, both as an individual and as a nation, is altogether delightful and tractable'. But he recommends that the reader remember that the Irishman 'is a child, and like a child responds to being trusted and taken into the confidence of those who are in the position of employers or landlords'.[15] There is no mention of the dignity of the individual, of mutual respect, or of the mutual responsibility of landlord and tenant towards the land and each other, in the writings of the Duke. Neither did there appear to be any long term plan for development, improvement or advancement in his management of the estate. It was his property, purchased to provide him with a degree of pleasure and recreation, and seemed to carry with it no responsibilities whatsoever except for the burden of having to finance the mortgage.

To demonstrate how best, in his opinion, to treat the Irish labourer, he related the following story:

Once when I was at Kylemore Castle, our other Irish estate, I heard that two walking delegates were on their way through Connemara to urge our labourers to strike for higher wages. Now, I frankly admit that if anyone ever did a full and fair days work in Connemara, the labourers wages would be a crying shame; but as it takes at least two men and a boy to do the same amount of work as one English or Northern Irish labourer, the rate of pay is, proportionately, not unduly low – especially as landlords keep on through the winter a good number of men who are wholly useless when they happen to have no work to do about their own small-holdings. These walking delegates were of the "mongrel" class . . . [and had] succeeded in causing strikes on three neighbouring properties, and one fine Monday morning I got wind that they were coming to me. So at breakfast time I went down to the farm and met these gentlemen at the gate. I asked them where they were going and what they wanted, and they answered truculently that they were going to "make my labourers strike on me." I told them to go ahead, and offered to take them to my labourers; and so we went round to where the men were seated at breakfast (provided by me) and I then spoke to them.

"Look here, boys," I said, "here are two men come to tell you all to strike for double pay. Before they start I want to tell you one thing: I have just so much money I can afford to spend on labour this winter, and it does not matter in the slightest to me whether half of you do the work at double the wages, or whether you all stay on, each doing half a mans work at the present rate of pay. But if you decide on the first plan there is one thing I will make you do, and that is decide for yourselves which half of you are going to be kept on and which are going to be turned off. Now these walking delegates can come and talk to you, but if, when they have finished, you all decide to stay on, the first thing Ill tell you to do is to take these lazy, loafing trouble-breeders and throw them into the lake."

There was a roar of laughter from the men, and . . . those walking delegates very soon became running delegates, and were last seen covering in record time the seventeen miles to Recess station. The Connemara labourers strike died an inglorious death.[16]

By all accounts Eugene Zimmerman never did grow to love his son-in-law, but he did come to enjoy his visits to the family estates in Ireland and England and took a keen interest in their operation. And when, yet again, the Duke was experiencing financial difficulties, he was, apparently, quite happy to come to the rescue. He took up a twenty-one year lease on the entire Kylemore Estate, including all fishing rights, on 20 July 1907, at the yearly rent of £2,160. A year previously the Duchess had given birth to her second son, Edward Eugene, named for his godfather, King Edward, and his grandfather, Eugene Zimmerman. It was believed that it was for this grandchild that Zimmerman eventually took over the entire mortgage on the Kylemore Estate on 1 November 1910.[17]

Eugene Zimmerman

The Manchesters appear to have had little impact on the area. The Duchess did lend her patronage to the Women's National Health Association set up by Countess Aberdeen, wife of the Lord Lieutenant of Ireland, and was elected president of the Letterfrack branch on 26 September 1909.[18]

The Duke, as a father of four children, was determined to be 'a little less drastic' in their training than his own father had been with his. However, there are some who would question the Duke's definition of drastic when reading in his memoirs the following anecdote. To illustrate his theory that a child should learn by experience, the Duke recounted an incident which took place at Kylemore Castle. One day Mary, the oldest daughter, stood in a room in the Castle screaming at the top of her voice that she would not do something she was ordered to do, and 'added the awful threat: "I would rather sit on the fire than do it!" 'The Duke, who claimed to be 'an active believer . . . in the principle of never uttering a threat unless first prepared to put it into execution' decided that Mary should be taken at her word and taught a lesson. The fire was, the Duke observed, only smouldering at the time and so he told Mary, ' "By all means sit on the fire if you want to." ' Mary ignored his suggestion and continued to scream. The Duke then picked her up and sat her on the fire. To reassure the reader he added: 'Of course it did not really hurt her or I should not have done it; but it taught her not to be self-willed in the future, and more important still, never to threaten unless she was prepared to act'.[19]

In another anecdote, told to illustrate how imaginative and quick the Irish can be with a response, the Duke tells the tale of an English Queen's Counsel, disappointed that the fishing stream he had rented for a season had not yielded anything like what he had been promised. He was making a quick departure from a North of Ireland railway station when accosted by three local beggars. The beggars' tales of 'huge families to support, and bare cupboards and hungry little ones weeping for bread', were proving too much for the disgruntled QC, so he confronted them:

> "Look here, you rascals, I've heard nothing but lies since I came to this damned country, and Ill give five shillings to the one of you that tells me the biggest lie now." . . . so quick as lightning the dirtiest of the three beggars held out his hand and said:

> "och, yer Honours a gentleman!"

> He went away enriched by five shillings!

Further down the same page the Duke tells the reader that despite Mitchell Henry's good work for Home Rule and 'spending a tremendous lot of money on the peasants in the West of Ireland, he never seemed to get on very well with them or to succeed in winning their confidence'. The Duke was of the opinion that Mitchell Henry was still viewed in the neighbourhood as 'a stranger', while he, on the other hand, was not. Talking to an old woman on the estate, the Duke seeking an explanation, asked:

> "Tell me why all of you are so nice to me when I spend nothing on any of you, and why all of you are so different to Mr Mitchell Henry when he lets you off paying your rent (something I have never done), and gives you money besides?"

> "Ah, well, your Grace," she answered, "ye see, old Mitchell Henry is not of the ancient families like yeself."[20]

And he seemed happy with the answer: which only goes to show that an English QC is far more astute than an English Duke.

Not all of the Duke's anecdotes were restricted to the poor Irish; the rich Americans too were subjected to his close study. The attempts of Americans to enter English society were held up to ridicule for their lack of knowledge regarding Court and social etiquette, but since his memoirs were published in 1932, one year after his divorce from Helena, perhaps the barbs were a deliberate snub to the Duchess and her friends.

Zimmerman died on 20 December 1914, leaving over a million dollars in trust for his daughter, the income from which was to be put at her disposal at the discretion of the trustees. Should she die before the children reached the age of twenty-one, the income of the trust was to be divided among them: one third was to go to her son, Alexander, heir to the title, and two thirds to the remaining children.[21] The Duke, it would seem, was left out in the cold. Zimmerman's will did specify that the Duchess could change the terms in relation to the disposal of the trust after her death if she so wished. This she did on two occasions, causing a legal wrangle which was not settled until twenty years after her death. At the time of Zimmerman's death the mortgage on the Kylemore Estate was still outstanding, and although there was sufficient funds to redeem it, it would appear the Duchess and the trustees were not prepared to do so. The result was that, in 1914, Kylemore Castle and Estate fell to Ernest John Fawke, who had taken over the mortgage some years before. Fawke, a banker and property speculator from London, never took up residence in the Castle and only visited it on occasion. The Castle and management of the estate was left in the hands of caretakers until a new owner could be found. As already mentioned, the Duke and Duchess divorced in 1931. The Duke remarried in the same year, and he died on 9 February 1947. Helena remarried in 1937, the 10th Earl of Kintore, Scotland; she died on 15 December 1971, at the age of ninety-one.

At the departure of the Manchesters all furniture, livestock etc., were left in place and life for the small number of staff and farm workers remaining went on pretty much as before, under the stewardship of a series of caretaker-managers. However, beyond the estate things were taking a dramatic turn, as war and rebellion changed life and politics in Connemara as elsewhere in the country.

In the years since Mitchell Henry had left Irish politics the Irish Parliamentary Party had continued its struggle for Home Rule. Parnell faced a crisis when his affair with a married woman, Catherine O'Shea, became public knowledge. Following her divorce the couple married but Parnell died soon afterwards, in October 1891. Conciliatory measures brought into place under Conservative governments were producing a positive effect on the ground in Connemara. The Congested Districts Board (1891), set up to assist in the development of agriculture, fisheries and small industry, and the Local Government Act (1898), addressed many of the issues raised by Mitchell Henry in the House of Commons and the people were enjoying a degree of prosperity. Land legislation had resulted in the break up of many of the larger estates throughout the country and the division of their lands among the former tenants. The Congested Districts Board further assisted the tenant in the purchase of his holding by spreading the cost over a number of years.

The tenants at Kylemore, however, were not so fortunate. The workings of the Congested District Board were often slow and cumbersome, and frequently estates were left on the market while the tenants were clamouring for their break up. At one time Fawke called a meeting with local anglers and potential investors in an attempt to persuade them to form a co-operative and purchase the Estate, but they declined. The political climate at the time was making it increasingly difficult to find a buyer. A successful political campaign had won the Sinn Féin party a majority in the 1918 general election, bringing about the demise of the Irish Parliamentary Party. Refusing to take up their seats at Westminster, Sinn Féin set up Dáil Éireann in Dublin in January 1919, eventually drawing the country into a state of war. However, in the midst of this chaos, in December 1920, the Castle and Estate at Kylemore were sold to the Irish Benedictine Dames of Ypres, for a little over £45,000. And in the months that followed Kylemore Castle would cease to exist and Kylemore Abbey would come into being. The arrival of the Nuns was greeted with great delight by the local community. It was viewed as a new beginning for everyone, Kylemore itself, its community within and its dependant community without.

Part II

History of Kylemore Abbey

Chapter 11
The Irish Dames of Ypres

The Irish Benedictine Nuns were refugees from Ypres, Flanders, and had fled from their monastery in 1914 during the bombardment of that city by the advancing German army. They were first given refuge in Oulton Abbey, Staffordshire, England, and later spent nine months at Highfield House in London, before arriving in Ireland in February 1916. With the help of supporters and friends they established a monastery and school at Macmine Castle and Merton House in County Wexford, but the Castle was old and in bad condition, and so they were forced to seek out more suitable accommodation elsewhere. For almost a year the Lady Abbess 'made many fatiguing journeys'[1] in her efforts to find a property large enough to accommodate the community and school, before finally settling on Kylemore Castle.

The Abbey at Ypres

The Nuns, because of the nature of their foundation, were known as the Irish Dames of Ypres and were referred to as such in the press of the day. Their history was a long and eventful one reaching back to the community's foundation in 1665. The community had maintained strong links with Ireland since its foundation and its return to Ireland at this time was seen as a homecoming.

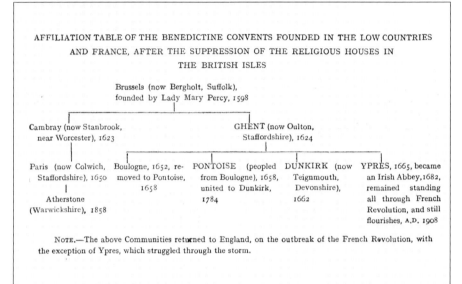

AFFILIATION TABLE OF THE BENEDICTINE CONVENTS FOUNDED IN THE LOW COUNTRIES AND FRANCE, AFTER THE SUPPRESSION OF THE RELIGIOUS HOUSES IN THE BRITISH ISLES

Brussels (now Bergholt, Suffolk), founded by Lady Mary Percy, 1598

Cambray (now Stanbrook, near Worcester), 1623

GHENT (now Oulton, Staffordshire), 1624

Paris (now Colwich, Staffordshire), 1650
Atherstone (Warwickshire), 1858

Boulogne, 1652, removed to Pontoise, 1658

PONTOISE (peopled from Boulogne), 1658, united to Dunkirk, 1784

DUNKIRK (now Teignmouth, Devonshire), 1662

YPRES, 1665, became an Irish Abbey, 1682, remained standing all through French Revolution, and still flourishes, A.D. 1908

NOTE.—The above Communities returned to England, on the outbreak of the French Revolution, with the exception of Ypres, which struggled through the storm.

Affiliation Table.
Dom Nolan's *The Irish Dames of Ypres*

The Benedictine Order was founded by St Benedict of Nursia, Italy in the 6th century. It is a Monastic Order; this means that the first duty and principal occupation of the Benedictine monk or nun is prayer. Five times a day 'the Benedictines meet in choir, according to the rule of their founder, to sing the praises of God in the Divine Office, the official Psalmody of the Church'[2] : the Divine Office is the singing of psalms and the reading of the scriptures at given hours throughout the day. The Irish Benedictine nuns had lived this life of prayer enclosed within the walls of their monastery at Ypres for almost two hundred and fifty years. Their secondary occupation was the education of young girls.

'The Benedictine, or monastic, Order is neither essentially contemplative nor essentially active'.

Dom Nolan's *The Irish Dames of Ypres*

In common with other monastic orders, the community was made up of Choir Dames, the traditional title of a Benedictine nun, and lay sisters. To be a Choir Dame one had to have enough education to read and sing the Latin Office, and one needed a dowry. Choir Dames alone were members of the Chapter, for purposes of voting on any business and in the election of an Abbess. Once elected, an Abbess reigned for the duration of her life and could only be replaced if considered unfit due to ill health. Lay, or

Converse, sisters did most of the manual work of the community. They said a simple Office in the vernacular, or if they could not read, certain prayers, and they did not have to have a dowry.

The Abbey at Ypres was an affiliation of the Abbey at Ghent, one of the English monasteries which recognised Lady Mary Percy, daughter of the Earl of Northumberland, as its founder. At a time of religious intolerance in England, Lady Mary Percy founded a Benedictine house for English women in Brussels in 1598, out of which grew the foundations at Ghent, Pontoise, Dunkirk and Ypres. At the time, all Benedictine Abbeys were independent and subject only to the Diocesan Bishop. The Abbey at Ypres was set up at the request of the Bishop of Ypres, who provided a house and the promise of financial support for the community. The first Abbess, Dame Marina Beaumont, was elected in 1665. However, within a year the Bishop of Ypres died leaving the fledgling community struggling to survive.

Over the years Lady Abbess Beaumont had great difficulty attracting novices to her house. She requested and received assistance from the Abbesses of Ghent, Pontoise and Dunkirk, all of whom sent nuns to try and bolster her community, but none of these would stay. On the death of Lady Abbess Beaumont there were just two nuns remaining in the Abbey: Dame Flavia Carey and a lay sister. The Lady Abbess of Ghent, who had always intended that Ypres become an 'Irish' house, requested that Irish nuns be sent to Ypres to elect an Abbess for a community of Irish. Dame Flavia Carey, who had been at Ypres since its foundation, was accordingly elected the second Abbess of Ypres on 19 November 1682. She is, however, recognised as the first Abbess of the Irish community: 'Lady Flavia Cary . . . was the first who, jointly with the communities of Ghent, Pontoise and Dunkerque gave this house to the Irish for a refuge to keep as such for ever'.[3]

The Abbey was dedicated to the Immaculate Conception of the Blessed Virgin, under the title of *Gratia Dei*. More Irish nuns from the other monasteries were sent to increase the numbers at Ypres and from then on the community became known as *De Iersche Damen* – the Irish Ladies or the *Irish Dames of Ypres*. For almost two hundred and fifty years the Abbey at Ypres would remain the only Irish Abbey of the Order of St Benedict. The purpose of the Abbey was to provide an education and religious community for Irish women, although other nationalities were also welcome. During the 17th and 18th centuries, when anti-catholic laws were in place in Ireland, the Abbey attracted the daughters of the Irish nobility, both as students and postulants, and enjoyed the patronage of many influential Irish families living in exile.

Lady Abbess Flavia Carey died on 20 February 1686. The community elected, for their third Abbess, Dame Mary Joseph Butler, a cousin of the Duke of Ormond. Lady Abbess Butler was the first Irish Abbess of Ypres and would be followed by six more of Irish birth: it would be over one hundred and fifty years before an Abbess of any other nationality would take up the position. Within a year of her election Lady Abbess Butler received a request from the Lord Lieutenant in Dublin, the Duke of Tyrconnell, on behalf of James II, King of England, Scotland and Ireland, that she come to Ireland and establish her monastery there. The King, a convert to the Roman Catholic faith, wished to establish a Royal monastery in Dublin and was offering his patronage to Lady Abbess Butler. With the consent of the Abbess, a house was taken in Great Ship Street for herself and her community. However, conscious of the opposition that existed towards the King, Tyrconnell wrote to the Grand Vicars of Ypres requesting that they preserve the Abbey there for the Irish nuns, in case they should be obliged to return. The community at Ypres was still small in number and nuns from the sister house at Pontoise were sent ahead to Dublin to prepare the house for the arrival of Lady Abbess Butler.

In 1688, Lady Abbess Butler 'departed from Ypres accompanied by some choir Dames' and a lay sister. On her way through London the Abbess was presented to Queen Mary of Modena, wife of King James II, in Whitehall, 'in the great habit of her order, which had not been seen there since the fall of religion'.[4] After leaving London she arrived in Dublin on 31 October 1688 and, according to Ypres manuscripts, was presented to the King, 'who received her most graciously, and promising her his royal protection'.[5] Lady Abbess Butler went immediately to Great Ship St and entered her enclosure 'where the Divine Office, Holy Mass, and all the regular observances were daily performed, to the consolation and edification of the nobility and gentry of Ireland, who hastened to place their children for education, under the care of the venerable Abbess, who excelled in piety, virtue, and every branch of good education'.[6]

Lady Abbess M. Joseph Butler (1686–1723)

Thirty young girls enrolled at the school and of these eighteen expressed a wish to join the community. However, James II's brief reign as King was quickly coming to an end. In February 1689 William of Orange and his wife Mary, James's daughter, with the support of the British Parliament, were crowned joint sovereigns and James fled to France. With an air of uncertainty hanging over Dublin, the Abbess wisely decided not to accept any postulants 'until more peaceable times'.[7]

Supported by French and Irish troops, James returned to Ireland and decided to make a stand against William and the English parliament. In Dublin on the 5 June 1690 he made good his promise to Lady Abbess Butler and drew up a Royal charter establishing his 'first and chief Royal Monastery of Gratia Dei', of the Order of St Benedict, with Lady Abbess Butler as its Abbess, and granted the foundation one hundred pounds sterling a year and freedom from rates and taxes.[8] Within a month James was defeated by William at the Battle of the Boyne and had fled the country.

King James's Charter

Lady Abbess Butler, having already sent her students home, collected whatever possessions she could manage and, along with her small community, took refuge in a neighbour's house while the Williamite forces ransacked the monastery. One young nun, Sister Mary Placida, removing her habit and disguising herself in secular clothes, returned to the monastery and managed to save some of the most 'sacred and precious' objects from the looters.[9] The violence and the confusion that followed left Lady Abbess Butler in no doubt as to where her future lay and, despite promises of protection given by her cousin the Duke of Ormond, on behalf of King William, she made up her mind to return to Ypres. The Duke then obtained a pass from King William for the Abbess and the community 'to leave the kingdom, without any molestation being made to them from his troops'.[10]

The Abbess arrived back in Ypres and was immediately abandoned by the nuns from Pontoise, who returned to their own monastery. Finding herself with just four lay sisters and no choir Dames, the Abbess lived out the next five years in extreme poverty. The community could only be saved if she could succeed in attracting postulants, but in such poor circumstances there seemed little hope of her doing so. Seeing the hopelessness of her situation the Bishop of Ypres tried to encourage her to dissolve the monastery, sell the house and retire to another convent, but she would not hear of it. Eventually postulants did arrive and financial assistance was received from Pope Innocent XII, the King of France and Queen Mary of Modena. The Queen retained a keen interest in the welfare of Lady Abbess Butler and her community at Ypres and was most anxious that it continue to thrive. However, vocations were few in the years that followed and numbers were always low.

It was at this time that the community received a curious gift; the Flags of Ramillies. The flags were left in the Abbey by members of the Irish Brigade and were hung in the choir where they remained for the next hundred years. The Irish Brigade was made up of Irish soldiers who left Ireland after the defeat of James II and were then fighting in the French army. For centuries controversy has raged over the exact battle in which these flags were taken and as to the regiment to which they belonged. Tradition among the nuns maintains that the flags were captured by the Irish Brigade from a British regiment at the Battle of Ramillies, in 1706, and deposited at the Abbey by Murrough O'Brien, the Lieutenant-Colonel of the regiment of Clare:

The regiment of the Irish Brigade under Lord Clare took part, along with the French cavalry, in covering the retreat of the French at the Battle of Ramillies in 1706. In one of the rearguard actions the Irish captured two and probably three flags from the enemy. These flags were deposited by the Brigade in the Irish Convent at Ypres.[11]

Military historians disagree with this explanation, and with each other, as to the true origins of the flags.[12] However, whatever their origin, the flags and their place of rest attracted symbolic significance for the Nationalist cause, as shown by the Young Irelander, Thomas Davis, in his poem *Clare's Dragoons*:

The Flag of Ramillies

> When, on Ramillies' bloody field,
> The baffled French were forced to yield,
> The victor Saxon backward reeled
> Before the charge of Clare's Dragoons.
> The Flags we captured in that fray
> Look lone in Ypres' choir, they say,
> We'll win them company to-day,
> Or bravely die like Clare's Dragoons.

Lady Abbess Butler died in 1723 at the age of eighty-two. Dom Patrick Nolan in his book, *The Irish Dames of Ypres,* comments: 'Thus passed away the first and greatest of the Irish Abbesses of Ypres'.[13]

For the next forty years, during the Abbacies of Lady Abbess Xaveria Arthur (1723–1743) and Lady Abbess Mary Magdalen Mandeville (1743–1760), the community suffered great hardship: 'poverty and trials and afflictions were the daily lot of the Irish Dames . . . So great, indeed, were the trial and difficulties that assailed the community at this period that they seem to have seriously thought of leaving Ypres and transferring themselves to the French King's dominions',[14] but this was later abandoned. Religious vocations again were down, only two nuns being professed under Lady Abbess Mandeville.

Things were better under Lady Abbess Mary Bernard Dalton (1760–1783); numbers increased and conditions for the nuns improved. Lady Abbess Dalton had great devotion to the Sacred Heart and had all of her community enrolled in the newly

Lady Abbess M. Bernard Dalton (1760–1783)

established Confraternity of the Sacred Heart at Bruges. This devotion to the Sacred Heart had enjoyed a long tradition among the nuns; indeed, 'they claim the honour of having been the first to introduce this devotion into Flanders'.[15]

Choir at Ypres

The seventh Abbess of Ypres, Dame Scholastica Lynch (1783–1799), endured the terrifying experience of having her enclosure invaded by about forty or fifty armed soldiers during the French Revolution. The soldiers were members of the invading French army who, on 13 January 1793, threatened 'to point their cannon against the house' if not admitted. Once inside they began placing seals on the door to the Church Sacristy and anywhere else where they hoped to find anything of value. As the day wore on, and after drinking their fill, the soldiers were eventually persuaded to confine themselves to the parlour for the night and allowed the 'divine sacrifice to be celebrated in the choir'.[16] Next morning, on learning that the General in Chief of the army was in fact an Irishman, thought to be 'the Republican general, James O'Moran', the Abbess sent word informing him of conditions at the Abbey and requesting his help. Shortly afterwards the Commander of the town came 'to make excuses, took off the seals, and paid the damage caused by his unruly soldiers, whom he withdrew from the Convent'. Before leaving, the Commander suggested that the nuns take advantage of the 'liberty granted by the French nation', break their vows and return to the outside world, 'but the proposition was rejected with disdain, as might have been expected'.[17]

Later that same year the French were forced to withdraw from Belgium but returned the following year and during the ensuing battle for Ypres the monastery, situated close to the ramparts, came under attack. Bombs fell in the garden and set fire to neighbouring houses, killing some of the occupants. The French took possession of the town on 19 June 1794 and under the new regime a decree was issued ordering the expulsion of the religious orders. The Irish Dames were given a reprieve, for a time, on the grounds of their members being foreigners, but were subjected to continuous harassment: 'domiciliary visits and at unseasonable hours on the most ridiculous pretexts, taking inventories of all that belonged to them, placing a guard to inspect all that came in or went out of the house, threatening them frequently to drive them out of doors without any previous warning, and other ill usages'.[18] In the years that followed the Abbey at Ypres was the only monastery left in the Low Countries; the mother house Ghent and the other English Benedictine houses had been driven out in the early years of the French Revolution.

In the midst of this intimidation Lady Abbess Lynch died, on 22 June 1799; she was just forty-six years of age. The community chose her sister, Lady Abbess Bernard Lynch (1799–1830), as her successor. Towards the end of the year, the order came for the nuns to leave the house: the Abbey had been sold over their heads and they were to be forced out, taking with them only what was in their cells. The date for departure was set for 13 November, the Feast of All Benedictine Saints. However, when that day came and the nuns were gathered at the doors, ready to depart, a violent storm prevented them from leaving. The following morning, the Feast of All Benedictine Souls, news that there had been a change of Government reached the town, 'and the Irish Dames remained in their Monastery to extol the mercies of the Almighty, who made the very elements serve them so favourably'.[19] The new owner of the property, however, could not be so easily disposed of and the nuns were forced to sell some of their church plate to buy back their monastery.

The financial burden of trying to restore and maintain the Abbey, which was almost devoid of furniture, fell heavily on the community. Once again reduced to 'dire straits of poverty – one result of which was that for a whole year, not having a bedstead in the house, they were obliged to sleep on the floor' – the nuns struggled on. Despite the severity of their living conditions, the nuns never forgot their primary purpose in life and 'regular discipline was not relaxed, nor had it been during the whole period of revolutionary troubles; and it [was] one of the proudest boasts of this community that, during the whole reign of terror they performed the divine office with an exactitude worthy of their order'.[20]

Things seemed to have greatly improved by 1810 and the community, consisting of ten choir Dames and four lay sisters, was able to record the following:

> These religious women are now, in every respect, by the blessing of divine Providence, comfortable situated in their own Convent, which is well furnished, in a retired part of the town, with a large garden, and in a very good air; they have no debts, and enjoy in perfect union with one another every advantage this holy state affords. Nothing would be wanting to their wishes for this world had they a greater

number of companions to share in their happiness, and perpetuate this establishment for the glory of God, and the honour of the adorable Heart of Jesus, whose holy will be done. *Amen*.[21]

Lady Abbess Bernard Lynch (1799–1830)

Lady Abbess Bernard Lynch died in 1830 and was succeeded by Lady Abbess Mary Benedict Byrne (1830–1840), the last of the Irish Abbesses of the Irish Dames of Ypres. She in turn was succeeded by Lady Abbess Elizabeth Jarrett (1840–1888), who was born in London. Over the years the Abbey had deteriorated and was no longer the comfortable building described above, but was, by all accounts, falling to ruin. Lady Abbess Jarrett took it upon herself to rebuild the monastery, 'replacing the old building by a fine specimen of Flemish Gothic, built of red brick with limestone dressing, and having the square cloisters'.[22] She was greatly assisted in her work by Dame Mary Scholastica Bergé, Cellarer and Prioress, who 'thanks to her great economy [she] was able in a few years to rid the Abbey of all the debts occasioned by the new building'.[23]

At one time during the regime of Lady Abbess Jarrett there was not a single Irish nun left in the monastery. It was at this time that the Abbess ordered the removal of the Flags of Ramillies from the Choir, to be placed elsewhere. Some time later, not knowing their history or value, two German lay sisters 'wishing to honour the feast of St Martha . . . picked up the colours and proceeded to cut them up for decorations;'[24] fortunately one of the other nuns intervened and succeeded in saving a remnant. The remnant was then moved to a safe place and has remained in the possession of the nuns right to the present day. The link with Ireland was reestablished with the arrival in the House of Mary Josephine Fletcher, in 1854. The young

Old Monastery & New Monastery

156

Irish woman was just nineteen years of age and it would be another sixty years before she would again set foot outside of the monastery's enclosure. In later years Dame Josephine was fond of reminding the nuns that her arrival in Ypres had united the community again 'to old Ireland'.[25]

The passage of time, old age and infirmities caused Lady Abbess Jarrett to resign in 1885, and the management of the House was passed to her Prioress, Dame Mary Scholastica Bergé. On the death of Lady Abbess Jarrett in 1890, Dame Mary Scholastica Bergé was elected Abbess.

Lady Abbess Bergé (1890–1916), was born in Tournai, Belgium, and entered the monastery in 1850, at the age of twenty. According to Dom Patrick Nolan, whose book *The Irish Dames Of Ypres* was published in 1908, Lady Abbess Bergé

> although not Irish by birth, she is, like so many of her compatriots, in full sympathy with Irish aspirations, and may be said indeed to be *ipsis Hibernicis hibernior*, more Irish than the Irish themselves; so that the destinies of the Abbey are safe in her hands; indeed the Convent of the Irish Dames has, perhaps, never been so flourishing as under her admirable sway, and the prospects for the future of the Abbey are more encouraging.[26]

No one could have foreseen the dramatic changes that would befall the community in the reign of Lady Abbess Bergé, or that she, along with her community, would be driven from her homeland and forced to take refuge in Ireland, the titular home of the community.

Under Lady Abbess Bergé the number of vocations had increased and included women from Ireland. The Abbess arranged for the community to take up the recitation of the Benedictine Office, instead of the Roman Office which had been said until then, and, under her supervision, devotion to the Sacred Heart was as strong as ever. In July 1902 the Golden Jubilee of the Abbess's Holy Profession was celebrated, 'and the happy years under her maternal rule continued in regular succession till June 23th 1912'.[27] On that day Lady Abbess Bergé suffered a severe stroke which left her partially paralysed, unable to speak and confined to a chair for the rest of her life. Mother Prioress, Dame Irma Mary Maura Ostyn, took over the responsibility of running the monastery and it was to her would fall the onerous task of leading the community out of Ypres during the early days of the Great War in 1914.

Lady Abbess M. Scholastica Bergé (1888–1916)

Garden at Ypres

Chapter 12

Leaving Ypres

In the early months of the Great War the nuns would be forced to abandon their ancient Abbey and seek out refuge in other lands. Priding themselves on having survived war and expulsion in the past, the nuns were reluctant to give in, but the powerful German guns soon pounded home the inevitable. The community's' final days at Ypres were recorded by the nuns and later published, entitled *The Irish Nuns at Ypres*. The material was gathered from personal diaries kept by individual nuns during their terrible ordeal and edited by Dame Columban Plomer, and it is from this that the following story is reconstructed. The introduction to the book was written by John E. Redmond M.P., then leader of the Irish Parliamentary Party, whose niece, Dame Teresa (Dora) Howard, was a member of the community. John Redmond had visited the Abbey at Ypres and had presented the community with a statue of St Patrick.

In 1914 the community consisted of Lady Abbess Mary Scholastica Bergé, Mother Prioress Mary Maura Ostyn, eight choir Dames, eight lay sisters and a novice. Lady Abbess and Mother Prioress were both Belgian, as was the novice, Sister Mary Odilon Allaeys; the remainder was made up of four Germans, three English, one from Luxembourg and seven Irish.

Soon after the outbreak of the war a law was passed expelling all German nationals from Belgium. On 7 September an officer came to the monastery to inform the Abbess that the four Germans nuns: one choir dame and three lay sisters, would have to leave within thirty-six hours: 'We were all stunned. Benedictines! Enclosed nuns! All over twenty-five years in the convent! What harm could they do? Surely no one could suspect them of being spies. Telegrams flew to Bruges, even to Antwerp, to obtain grace – all was useless and at 3.30 p.m., September 8, we assisted at the first departure from the Abbey, which we innocently thought would be at the worst for about three weeks, little dreaming what we should still live to see'. The German nuns were taken by the chaplain to the Bishop of Bruges, who placed them in a convent 'just over the frontier in Holland'.[1]

Ypres Noviceship

Towards the end of September, 'vague rumours of the enemy's approach reached us at Ypres', by the afternoon of the 7 October the effect of the German big guns could be felt by the town, and word reach the monastery that the Germans were indeed in the town. The nuns, fearing that at any moment their enclosure would be invaded, and that they would be arrested or perhaps killed, congregated in the choir and began reciting the rosary; 'after the rosary, we recommended ourselves to the endless bounty of the Sacred Heart, the Protector of our Monastery . . . And putting all our confidence in the double protection of our Divine Spouse and His Immaculate Mother, we awaited the issue of events'.[2] For six hours German soldiers, followed by guns, cars of ammunition and provisions, passed through the town. A small presence was left to hold the town but, after some skirmishes with the Allied forces, they retreated. Then, 'just one week after the coming of the Germans, the troops of the Allies poured in', and 'amid the enthusiastic cheers of the people, 21,000 soldiers filled the streets'.[3] But the cheering would not last for long. John Redmond in his introduction gives the stark facts of what the *Irish Dames* witnessed over the next six weeks:

On October 11, what may be called the battle of Ypres began in real earnest; but the town, defended by the Allies, held heroically out; and by November 20, the utter failure of the attempt of the Germans to break through towards Calais by the Ypres route was acknowledged by everyone.

During the interval, Ypres was probably the centre of the most terrible fighting in the War.[4]

With the presence of such large numbers in the town and continued fighting in the countryside, the first problem encountered by the nuns was food shortages; meat, milk and bread were difficult if not impossible to find and would remain so for the duration of their stay in Belgium. Ypres became the headquarters for the British troops and activity on the streets was unceasing. The sky too carried a menacing promise of events to come, as the Germans surveyed the town from the air.

Their enclosure prevented the nuns from following the 'exciting events of those troubled times, but friends usually kept [them] supplied with the most important news'. [5]

Inside the walls the nuns prayed fervently for an end to all fighting and the restoration of peace. They began making badges of the Sacred Heart for the soldiers: 'We set to work with good will – some cutting the flannel – others embroidering – others writing – till at last we had finished . . . we then tried, in every way possible, to find a means of distributing out handiwork; but all in vain', until a local girl named Hélene, who worked at the monastery, came to beg prayers for her brother at the front. Mother Prioress promised to pray for the young man and gave her some badges to send to him and for any others who might want them. Hélene soon returned for more, and soon the devotion spread through the town and everyone came flocking to the monastery door to get badges for a relative or friend at the front. One young girl, 'hearing of the devotion', brought dozens of badges to 'St. Peter's parish (where an Irish regiment was stationed), impressing on each man, as she pinned the badge to his uniform, that it was made by "the Irish Dames!" '6

Library at Ypres

Being cut off from the outside world and totally dependent on others for news, the monastery was alive with rumour: 'Each day brought its item of news . . . As often as not, what we heard one day was contradicted the next, and what was confirmed in the morning as a fact, was flatly denied in the afternoon; so that one really did not know what to believe. We could at least believe our own ears, and those told us, by the ever-approaching sound of firing, that the danger was steadily increasing for the brave little town of Ypres. It was therefore decided that, in case of emergency each nun should prepare a parcel of what was most necessary, lest the worst should come and we should be obliged to fly'.7

Members of Ypres community

The nuns began to prepare hiding places for the many 'precious treasures and antiquities' held by the community. Three walled-up hiding places were created in the cellars into which were placed as many of the treasures as was possible. Among the treasures preserved at the Abbey was a silver Abbatial crozier dating from 1721; four valuable medallions, representing the Immaculate Conception, St Joseph, St Scholastica, and the Martyrdom of St Thomas of Canterbury; a church vestment,

made of the gold horse trappings of James II; a second vestment made from the dress of Archduchess Isabella of Spain; the royal patent of James II; a large portrait of James II, presented by the King to the Abbey; voluminous correspondence from the King, his Queen and their descendants; a large border of lace worked by Mary Queen of Scots, also presented by James II. The treasures also included portraits of some of the Abbesses and, of course, the Flag of Ramillies.

As more and more towns fell to the Germans, Ypres began to fill with refugees, and, despite the shortages of food, dinner and supper were daily distributed to some thirty or forty at the Abbey doors. Soon all communication with the outside world was cut, however, the nuns had but to listen to know that the Germans were coming closer: 'The roar of the guns in the distance scarcely stopped a moment. From the garret windows, we could already see the smoke of the battle on the horizon; and to think that, at every moment, hundreds of souls were appearing before the judgment-seat of God!' On 21 October they received the news that the town 'would probably be bombarded in the evening. We had already prepared our parcels in case we should be obliged to fly and now we were advised to live in our cellars, which were pronounced quite safe against any danger of shells or bombs'.[8]

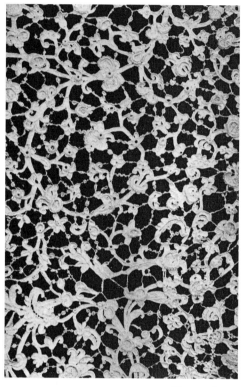

Lace by Mary Queen of Scots

Forty thousand Indian troops arrived in the town and the ambulances 'continually brought in the unfortunate victims from the battlefield, till at last the town was full to overflowing'. Throughout the night a nun kept watch while the others slept, and during the day prayers continued as usual: 'Despite the danger and anxiety, we strove to keep up religious life, and the regular observances went on at the usual hours. Instead of distracting us, the roar of the battle only made us lift up our hearts with more fervour to God'.[9]

One wing of the monastery, housing 'the class-rooms, children's dormitory and refectory, the library, noviceship and work-room' [10], was cleared to make way for French wounded, only to be told later that they had found a more suitable place closer to the battle-field. Later the school was taken over by the British ambulance service, and the nuns were asked to provide bandages for the French:

All our recreations and free moments were spent in "rolling" bandages, for which were sacrificed sheets and veils, and in fact anything that could serve for the purpose – to all of which we of course added dozens of badges of the Sacred Heart . . . One day [a French deacon] brought a little souvenir, by way of thanks for our help. It consisted of a prayer-book found on a German wounded prisoner, who had died. The prayers were really beautiful, being taken mostly from passages of the Psalms, adapted for the time of war; while the soiled leaves showed that the book had been well read.[11]

As the bombardment continued, towards the end of October it was decided that for her own safety the Lady Abbess should be moved to Poperinge, a town lying nine miles to the west, but it proved almost impossible to obtain a carriage to convey her there. At last a cab was secured. However, because of her condition, the Lady Abbess found it impossible to ascend the stairs and was in need of assistance. It took four of the nuns to carry the Abbess to the ground floor, and out 'into a world that she knew not and had never wished to know', and place her safely in the cab.[12] Although the Constitution of the Order of St Benedict allowed for breaking of the enclosure 'in times of war, and in other cases provided for',[13] Lady Abbess Bergé had, in the sixty years since her profession, never once stepped outside the door of the Abbey and it was only with much persuasion and pleading, and with assurances that the rest of the community would soon follow, that she agreed on this occasion to do so.[14] The Lady Abbess was accompanied by two elderly nuns: Dame Josephine Fletcher, then aged seventy-nine, and Sister Magdalen Putte, aged seventy-three. All were placed in the care of Dame Placid Druhan, who had herself entered the monastery twenty years before:

> our beloved Abbess drove out of the enclosure, the great door soon hiding her from our sight. Sad, troubled, and anxious, we turned back, wondering what would become of our dear absent ones. Would they arrive safely at their destination? Would they find kind faces and warm hearts to welcome them? Only the boom of the guns mockingly answered our silent enquiries.[15]

The nuns were, however, given little time for such contemplation, as there was work to be done. Yet another rumour had reach them that the Germans 'might penetrate into the town that very evening', and requests from 'strangers'; two priests and five ladies, to be given refuge in the safety of the cellars, had to be accommodated. Before long a hastily written note from Dame Placid arrived from Poperinge, saying that they had succeeded in obtaining a room for the Abbess, but that all other rooms were full, and they were left standing out in the rain with nowhere to turn to. The note also included a list of necessities required by the nuns.

Despite the rumours of invasion, the nuns passed an unusually quiet night and woke in the morning to gather in the choir for meditation at 5.30 a.m.,

> and at 6 recited lauds – prime and tierce. At 7, the conventual Mass began; when, as though they had heard the long-silent bell, the guns growled out, like some caged lion, angry at being disturbed from its nights rest. The signal given, the battle waged fiercer than before, and the rattling windows, together with the noise resounding through the church and choir, told that the silence of the night had been the result of some tactics of the Germans, who had repulsed the Allies. [16]

As the bombardment continued 'all the inhabitants who were able were leaving the town, abandoning their houses, property – all'. Food was even more scarce than before and it was proving impossible to send the provisions requested by the nuns to Poperinge. Over thirty people now took shelter in the convent, bringing their own mattresses, and many others sought entry:

> In the end, no fewer than fifty-seven persons came for a night's lodging. Numberless poor came also during the day for food, for they could not find anything to eat in the town; bakers, butchers, grocers – all had fled to save their lives. We were in the greatest necessity ourselves, but still gave to all who asked. We experienced the truth of our Lord's words, "Give, and you shall receive," when, a few days later, we were in the streets – without a house, without food, without money. It was then, indeed, that we received a hundredfold the charity we showed towards those who applied to us in their distress. [17]

Once again Hélene, the girl from the town, came to the aid of the nuns and agreed to travel with her brothers to Poperinge and deliver the parcels to Dame Placid and the Abbess. However, before they could leave, the community received word that the Abbess and nuns were attempting to return to Ypres. After two days spent at Poperinge, seeing that the rest of the community had not yet joined her, as they had promised, the Abbess insisted that a carriage be found to bring her back to Ypres. Mother Prioress decided that she must make the dangerous trip to Poperinge to prevent them returning. She was accompanied by Hélene: 'leaving the community in a state of anxiety impossible to describe . . . We were now truly orphans, deprived both of our Abbess and our Prioress, and not knowing what might happen to either of them'. [18]

In the Abbey Mother Prioress was a figure of authority and power, but now, out in the world, filled with apprehension and fear, she found herself dependent on her servant Hélene:

> When I heard the door shutting behind me, and the key turning in the lock, in spite of all my efforts, the tears came to my eyes. I was then really out of the enclosure – back again in the world – after twenty-seven years spent in peaceful solitude. The very sight of the steps brought back the memory of the day when I mounted them to enter the Monastery. I hesitated . . . There was still only the door between us, but no! my duty lay before me. I must prevent Lady Abbess returning; so, taking courage, I started off with Hélene, who was trying all she could to console me.

The road was crowded with refugees, Allied soldiers, motor cars and bicycles. 'I was stupefied, and thought at every moment we should be run over; but my companion, amused at my astonishment, assured me there was nothing to fear'. [19]

The Prioress intended to prevent the Abbess returning and then seek out a convent which would receive the entire community at a future date. She managed to intercept the Abbess and the other nuns at Vlamertinghe, a village about half way between Ypres and Poperinge, where her cab had stopped on its journey to Ypres. They tried to persuade the cabman to turn back but he insisted that Ypres was far safer than Poperinge and drove away, leaving the Prioress 'in consternation'. A past pupil of the Abbey school came to her rescue and gave the Prioress and Hélene the use of their carriage to take them home. Halfway to Ypres they came across the Abbess's cab, which was held up by a British officer who was talking to the nuns inside and eventually persuaded them to return to Poperinge. The Prioress, unable to stop their own cab, was forced to continue to Ypres. However, Dame Placid got out of the Abbess's carriage before it turned back and continued her journey to Ypres on foot. After relaying her story it was decided that Sr Romana King should accompany Dame Placid back to Poperinge to assist the Abbess. They set out from Ypres at 4 o'clock in the evening. They brought with them a hand cart, 'a kind of bath-chair, filled with packets and parcels for Lady Abbess and the old nuns' which they were forced to abandon at Vlamertinghe, and continuing on they reached Poperinge before nightfall.

D. Patrick.   D. Columban.   D. Bernard.   D. Teresa.   D. Walburge.

D. Placid.   Mother Prioress.   D. Aloysius.

Irish Dames who fled Ypres

There was at this time a cessation of hostilities and Mother Prioress decided that now was the time for the community to leave Ypres. Dame Columban Plomer and Dame Bernard Stewart were sent out into the town to try to find a workman, previously employed at the monastery, to help them carry their possessions: 'Mother Prioress gave us her blessing, and let us out of the enclosure door. Oh dear! What a sensation! Happy prisoners for so many years, we now found ourselves in the streets. With a shudder, we started on our errand'. The moment they left the monastery the shells began to fall. Experiencing real danger they continued through the streets searching for the workman, only to discover that he had already left the town that morning. They returned to the monastery. Edmund, their handyman 'an honest, a fearless, and a reliable retainer, with certainly a comical side to his character',[20] tried to persuade the nuns not to leave the safety of the cellars, if the monastery was bombed it would be God's will, he reasoned; 'Why not die here as well as anywhere else?'[21] The Lady Abbess of Oulton Abbey in England, formerly of Ghent, had offered, 'from the very outset of the War, to take the whole community, but the great question was how to get so far'.[22]

When, in the morning, the priest failed to arrive to say Mass the Prioress assembled the entire community at the enclosure door and putting down their veils, they made their way to the Carmelite Convent, situated a little way down the street. In those few steps the entire community had broken their enclosure, for many of them it was the first time outside the monastery door in many years, but the dangers of war left them little time to reflect on this momentous step. At the Carmelite Convent they learned that the nuns had left the previous day, but determined not to miss Mass at any cost, and fearing it may be their last, they continued to the Church of St James and arrived in time to receive Holy Communion. The next day,

Friday 6 November, they again attended Mass at St James's, their cellars being now almost entirely deserted, 'for all those who could possibly leave the town had already done so'.

As the day wore on and the bombardment continued, in the space of thirty minutes twenty shells burst quite close to the monastery; it became clear that it was their side of the town that was under attack. Mother Prioress made up her mind and 2 o'clock was set for the time of departure, she instructed the community that they should take only essentials and the clothes in which they stood. The final leave-taking of the Abbey, that had been home to the community for almost two hundred and fifty years, is best described by the nuns themselves:

> We went about, looking – perhaps for the last time – at the dear old scenes, which we had thought to leave only when death should knock at our door.
>
> We had already placed on every window of the convent a paper badge of the Sacred Heart, and lastly erected a niche outside one of the garret windows, in which we put the miraculous statue of Our Lady of the Angels, which had remained unhurt outside the Monastery in the siege of Ypres, in 1744. We had done all we could and must now abandon all, leaving everything under the double protection of the Mother and the Son.
>
> A little after 2 oclock the hand-cart came round to the door . . . The enclosure door was then fastened on the inside, and all other important rooms or cupboards being likewise locked, we passed with a last farewell through the long-loved choir, which had known the joys and sorrows of our whole religious life.
>
> We then went through the outer church into the sacristy, locking the door of the grille behind us. There was but one more door which separated us from the outside world – one door more! and we should be out of our enclosure, perhaps never more to return! There was a pause in our sad procession – the key was not there. Our Lord watched over us once more; for, had we then continued in our procession, some of us would inevitably have been badly hurt, if not indeed killed. After a few minutes waiting, the key was brought, and already placed in the key-hole, when a loud explosion, accompanied by a terrific crash which shook the entire building, laid us all prostrate . . . Bewildered, rather than afraid, we arose, and saw through the window, a shower of bricks and glass falling into the garden. The first – though not the last – shell had struck our well-loved Abbey . . . The door was opened, and with an indescribable feeling of horror, mingled with uncertainty, we went out. In the street we raised our eyes in one

sad farewell to our beloved Monastery; and there, out of the cell
windows, principally that of Mother Prioress, a cloud of vapour and
smoke told us of the passage of the shell . . . A cry of anguish arose
from our hearts as, hurrying along the deserted street, we saw our
convent thus apparently burning.[23]

Taking the road to Poperinge, the noise of the shelling of Ypres still audible
in the distance, they again shared the road with refugees and marching
troops. However, what left the deepest impression in their memories 'was
the thick slimy mire we had to wade through. In some places it was so bad
that it was almost impossible to get on – we seemed to slide back two steps
for every one that we made forward. We trudged bravely on, but before we
had gone a quarter of the way some of us were already *au bout*. We, who for
years had not walked more than six or seven times round our little garden,
were certainly little fitted to go some nine miles in that dreadful mud, and
carrying parcels which, by this time, seemed to weigh tons . . . We could
hardly push through the crowds of fugitives, each with his or her bundles of
different colour, shape and size . . . We passed through the village [of
Vlamertinghe] and on, on on! always in company of troops, motor-cars,
and refugees'. It was dark by the time they reached Poperinge, where they
remained for a fortnight at the convent La Sainte Union.

The convent where they lodged was already crowded with three other
religious communities, wounded soldiers and some refugees. During their stay
the nuns spent their time making badges of the Sacred Heart for the wounded
French soldiers and visiting them daily. As time went on contradictory stories
arrived as to conditions in Ypres, but the sound of guns drew ever nearer.

In the midst of all the confusion Dame Josephine Fletcher, then feeble
and infirm, caught a cold and on 15 November she passed away. She was
laid to rest in a private vault in the cemetery, having been first placed in a
double coffin, so that in the event of the nuns being able to rebuild the
monastery at Ypres, 'we shall then lay dear Dame Josephine with her other
religious Sisters'.[24]

Attempts were made by some of the community to return to Ypres to
check on the monastery, but these met with little success. Mother Prioress
then set about finding a way to get her community to England.
Accompanied by Dame Teresa, the niece of John Redmond M.P., who it
was felt might be 'specially useful', she set out to seek help from the British
military authorities. With the assistance of the Belgium Commandant of
police, the two nuns succeeded in reaching the appropriate British authorities and were eventually promised transport to the coast.

However, before departing, the nuns decided to make a further attempt to visit Ypres. The journey needed to be done quickly as transport might become available at any time; an English officer, Captain Liddell, was making every effort to secure ambulances through the Chief Medical Officer.

Dame Placid, Dame Columban and Dame Patrick, accompanied by two local women, volunteered to attempt the hazardous journey. Along the way they were advised on several occasions to turn back – even the Allied soldiers had been forced to abandon the town because of the continuous shelling – but they refused. Progress was slow however and they were forced to spend the night in a roadside house. Next morning, with the assistance of the older children of the house, and an Irishman named Mr Walker, they reached Ypres. The monastery looked in reasonable condition from the outside, but once inside the 'whole building seemed but one ruin'. [25] Here and there holes in the roof were to be seen and debris of cement, mortar, wall-paper and bricks could be found everywhere. The nuns collected up their 'breviaries, great-habits, and other things which the other nuns had recommended to us'. Leaving the monastery with a hand-cart over-loaded with books and clothing, stuffed into white pillowcases, and with the aid of their helpers they set out through the deserted streets stunned by the devastation that sur-rounded them.

At one point they met up with a British cavalry regiment coming from the trenches: 'They looked at us and shouted: "Who are you, Sisters, and where do you come from?" Dame Columban answered: "We are English

D. Teresa.   D. Placid.   D. Columban.   D. Patrick.

Mother Prioress.

Mother Prioress with Dame Teresa, Dame Placid, Dame Columban and Dame Patrick

nuns from the Benedictine Convent of Rue St. Jacques." This was too much for Dame Patrick, who called out: "We are no such thing. We are *Irish* Benedictines!" "Irish!" shouted half a dozen of them, "and so are we," and they all began singing, "It's a long way to Tipperary," and thus escorted, we took a long, last look at the dear old town. Needless to say, it was an Irish regiment – every man wore the harp and shamrock on his collar and cap'. [26]

169

On their return journey they were forced to take a country lane, 'which had the double inconvenience of being twice as long as the straight road and, indeed, of being also almost impassable', no carts, except those belonging to the army, were allowed on the road.[27] Along the way they managed to find some men to help with the cart and succeeded in arriving back in Poperinge just in time to be loaded, along with the rest of the community, on to two ambulances for transportation to the coast.

The Lady Abbess had to be lifted on to the ambulance by the soldiers. For although 'able to walk fairly well when helped on both sides, it was almost impossible for her to mount the two small steps' to the ambulance. Edmund, the handyman, travelled with them, along with a 'young Irish girl, Miss Keegan, who had been trying to get home since the war broke out, and had now begged to be allowed to make the journey with us'.[28]

Their journey to the coast was broken by a two nights stay with Ursuline nuns at St-Omer. On the first morning the Nuns attended a Military Mass in the cathedral, celebrated by an Army Chaplain and attended by over seventy soldiers, members of an Irish regiment. Next day three ambulances carried the group to Boulogne. An Irish priest, Father Flynn, was sent to accompany them on their journey, he was, he told the nuns, the first Catholic Chaplain to arrive with the troops in France.[29] The British officer, Lieutenant Stuart-Hayes, who was responsible for securing their passage, gave them a parting gift of a bottle of light wine and a box of biscuits. At Boulogne the Lady Abbess was carried by stretcher on board ship and placed in her cabin:

> The passage was very calm, but cold and frosty. For more than one of us it was the first crossing, Lady Abbess having up to this time never even seen the sea; and, sad to say, nearly all proved "bad sailors" except, curiously enough, Lady Abbess. Happily, however, the passage only lasted 1 hr. 20 min., so we were soon at Folkestone.

They took the train to London where Dame Patrick's aunt, Mrs Jessop, had arranged lodgings for them. They 'steamed into Victoria Station' at 11 p.m. on 23 November, and received a warm reception from some women on the platform who were intrigued to discover the details of the nuns journey and their encounters along the way: 'A bath-chair was brought for Lady Abbess who was wheeled out of the station, Mother Prioress holding her hand'.[30]

Lady Abbess and seven other members of the community were taken to SS. John and Elizabeth hospital, Dame Patrick, Mother Prioress and Dame Columban, along with Edmund, were received at Mrs Jessop's home. Dame Teresa, Dame Aloysius and Dame Walburge were received at the Sisters of Hope. All attended Mass the following morning, having never missed Mass or Holy Communion 'in spite of all the dangers and fatigues of the past weeks'.[31]

Next morning they were

> all motored from our different lodgings to Euston Station . . . and at
> 10.30 we entered on the last stage of our never-to-be-forgotten journey.
> We had three reserved compartments at our disposal, by the kind inter-
> vention of a gentleman at Victoria Station, who had given a signed card
> to Mother Prioress, telling her to show it to anyone who should
> question her. And so we travelled safely from Ypres to Oulton. How
> strange it seemed, for more than one of us, to pass by those scenes
> which we had thought never more to see in this life! We had left our
> country, home, and all, to shut ourselves up in the peaceful solitude of
> Ypres Abbey; and here we were, forced to retrace out steps and to return
> temporarily to the world which we had willingly given up.[32]

The nuns arrived at Oulton Abbey in Staffordshire on 24 November and were welcomed by Lady Abbess Laurentia and her community. The Benedictine community at Oulton Abbey was formerly at Ghent. It was from Ghent that the house of Ypres was funded, and so for the Irish Dames of Ypres it was almost as if they were coming back to their mother house. The Ypres nuns would remain eternally grateful for the welcome they received and for the hand of friendship that was extended to them at their time of great need:

> No one save those who have suffered as we have suffered can realise
> the joy which we experienced in finding ourselves once more in the
> calm and quiet of monastic life, where Holy Mass and Communion,
> the singing of the divine Office, meditation and spiritual reading, suc-
> ceeding the varied duties of the day, tend to soften the memories of
> the scenes of bloodshed and wretchedness which can never be
> forgotten.[33]

But the stop at Oulton was to be only temporary, and the future for this tiny community of just fourteen was still uncertain:

> And now, what has God in store for us? We know not! When shall we
> return to brave little Belgium, and how shall we rebuild our
> monastery which, . . . should this very year celebrate its 250th
> anniversary? God, in His own good time, will raise up kind friends
> who will come to our assistance – of this we cannot doubt. In confi-
> dence, patience, and prayer we shall therefore await the moment
> chosen by Him.[34]

The Mother Prioress of Ypres.

The Lady Abbess of Oulton.　　　The Lady Abbess of Ypres.

Abbesses of Oulton and Ypres, with
Mother Prioress M. Maura Ostyn

News of the nuns' safe arrival in England was reported in the *Freeman's Journal* on 30 December 1914. The newspaper announced that William Redmond M.P., brother of John, had received a letter from his niece, Dame Teresa Howard, details of which were published three days later, telling of the community's safe arrival in England. William was later killed in action in 1917, but John would prove an invaluable friend to the community up to his death in 1918. The newspaper also announced that the nuns had succeeded in bringing with them the Flag of Ramillies: 'which has been their cherished possession for so long, and which the Irish public will be rejoiced to hear they have saved'.[35]

The rest of the community's treasures still lay in the cellar of Ypres Abbey, hidden behind a brick wall, but no less vulnerable all the same. A Jesuit priest, Henry V. Gill, stationed in France with the 2nd Royal Irish Rifles, found himself in Ypres in January 1915, and being acquainted with the history of the Irish Abbey and of its famous flag, he decided to see how the building had fared. He was met by the old caretaker who still inhabited the kitchen and, wandering around, he found that the chapel was badly damaged and some French soldiers were billeted in the convent:

> At this time the Convent was by no means a complete wreck. The upper rooms appeared to be intact. They were locked up and were filled with the nuns belongings.

In April and May, 'the second and more severe bombardment' of Ypres took place, 'and continued with more or less intensity during the summer and autumn'. Every citizen was ordered to evacuate the town, 'Ypres became a city of the dead'. Father Gill returned to Ypres on 26 May 1915, in the company of M. Delaere, the Cure of St Pierre, Ypres, who had been in contact with the nuns in England and been informed of their hiding places in the cellars and was anxious now to retrieve their treasures. This was the first of many trips made by the men in their quest to save the treasures. By then the monastery had been completely gutted by fire: 'All the inner rooms and flooring had been burnt away. The walls still remained, but nothing else'. The men climbed down to the cellars and eventually found what they had been looking for: 'Gold and silver chalices, ciboriums and monstrances, blackened and destroyed by fire, half melted glass vessels, blackened pieces of an ivory crucifix, and such like remnants were found. Other objects, such as half-buried books and manuscripts, were also found. These were carefully collected and forwarded in a tin box to Paris', and were later restored to the nuns.

At one time the building was hit by shells as the men continued their work. Fr Gill was convinced that the Flag of Ramillies was still in the cellars and searched desperately for it: 'It was, therefore, impossible to do more than save objects of special value. One modest little paper parcel which I passed out was labelled "Lace of Mary Stuart"! But no trace of the flag could be discovered'.

He entered into correspondence with the community in England and, contrary to the newspaper report, it would seem that they too expected the Flag to be with the rest of their treasures. Fr Gill left Ypres convinced that the Flag was lost. His last visit to Ypres was in May 1918 and he again visited the Abbey: 'Some of the walls were still standing, but the cellars were full of water. It was a time of real anxiety, and the silence and gloom of desolation hung over the dust of the once beautiful town'.[36]

In time the Flag of Ramillies materialised, exactly when or how is unclear, and its image was used in a postcard published by the community to help raise some badly needed funds, an advertisement for which appeared in the *Freeman's Journal* in November 1915. The community was, at the time, almost entirely dependant on a small weekly allowance made to them by the Belgian Refugees' Committee in London.[37]

In 1915 the nuns compiled the account of their departure from Ypres and had it published the following year. It was still their plan to return to Belgium and restore their Abbey and the publication of their book was looked on as the first steps in a fundraising drive to that end. In his introduction John Redmond kicked off what was to become a nationwide appeal, headed up by himself and Barry O'Brien, with the following plea:

> This little community is now in exile in England. Their Abbey and beautiful church are in ruin . . . what is their future to be? Surely Irishmen, to whom the subject especially appeals, and

THE NUNS OF YPRES.

HOW THEY ESCAPED.

NEWS FROM MR. REDMOND'S NIECE.

HISTORIC IRISH FLAG SAVED.

Mr. Redmond has heard from his niece, who was one of the Irish Benedictine Community of Ypres, the famous Irish Convent founded some 250 years ago. The Community lived in the cellars until the convent and church were both struck by shells. They then escaped on foot, and after strange adventures found their way to England, where they are the guests of the Benedictine Abbey of Oulton in Staffordshire. They were unable to take any of their property with them, except the flag of the Irish Brigade, which has been their cherished possession for so long, and which the Irish public will be rejoiced to hear they have saved.

Freeman's Journal 30 December 1914

IRISH NUNS OF YPRES.

A WEEK IN THE CELLARS.

Saved by almost a Miracle

LETTER TO Mr. Wm. REDMOND, M.P.

The following is an extract from a letter to Mr. William Redmond, M.P., from his niece, Sister Mary Teresa, one of the Irish Nuns of Ypres:—

Oulton Abbey, Stone, Staffordshire.

We have been here since the 24th of November. The Right Hon. Lady Abbess of Oulton had invited us ever since the beginning of the war, but we thought it would not have been necessary to leave. However, the times became so bad that, after living in the cellars for a week, it was decided we should go.

Just before leaving the dear old Abbey the first bomb fell on it, quite close to us, only about a yard or two away, and we escaped almost by a miracle.

Freeman's Journal 2 January 1915

English sympathisers who appreciate courage and fortitude, will sincerely desire to help those devoted and heroic nuns to go back to Ypres – the home of the Community for over two centuries – to rebuild their Abbey and reopen their school, to continue in their honourable mission of charity and benevolence, and to resume that work of education in which their Order has been so long and so successfully engaged.[38]

After spending six months at Oulton Abbey, the community moved to Highfield House, Golders Green, in London, where they remained for a further nine months. Throughout this time contributions towards their National Fund were coming in from every county in Ireland but their future was still undecided.

Chapter 13
Benedictines Return to Ireland

As the war continued to rage in Europe the nuns, encouraged by the example and support of the Benedictine monk, Abbot Dom Columba Marmion, decided to move to Ireland. Abbot Marmion had himself been forced from his monastery at Maredsous in Belgium and was then living with his monks at Edermine House near Enniscorthy, Co Wexford. Close to Edermine was a property which Dom Marmion felt would suit the community, and with the assistance of John Redmond, M.P., he succeeded in winning the consent of the Most Rev. Dr Browne, Bishop of Ferns. Funds for the transfer were raised by the National Fund and the nuns took up residence in Merton House, Macmine, Co Wexford, in February 1916. A tall Georgian building with three stories over a basement, Merton House had thirty acres attached and was leased by the nuns from the Richards family.

Once established the nuns began to attract novices. Ten nuns were received into the monastery between the years 1916 and 1920; five went on to become choir Dames and five lay sisters. The young novice who had accompanied the nuns from Ypres, Dame Mary Odilon Allaeys, took her final vows at Merton in 1916, far from her native Belgium. In later years Dame Odilon would prove to be a tremendous asset to the community in her capacity as bursar. One of the nuns who travelled out of Ypres, Dame Patrick, left the Order entirely.

The first profession of Irish novices in Ireland took place in August 1916 and was cause for great joy within the community. The reception of Kate Magner and Maggie Josephine Curtis into the Order afforded great hope for

Dom Columba Marmion's letter to John Redmond

the future of the community. The ceremony was performed by the Lord Bishop and attended by local clergy, Dom Aubert Merten O.S.B., Prior of the Benedictines at Edermine since the departure of Dom Marmion in February, and friends and family of the two women. Miss Kate Magner, who was given the name Sister Agnes in religion, was a B.A., graduate of Cambridge University. Originally from Blackrock in Cork, Sister Agnes was a niece of Mr Timothy M. Healy, K.C., M.P., later to become the first Governor-General of the Irish Free State, and a relative of Terence McSweeney, Sinn Féin Lord Mayor of Cork, who later died while on hunger strike in Brixton prison, London, in 1920. Miss Josephine Curtis was given the name Sister Mary Benedict. The Curtis family were neighbours of the nuns and had been especially helpful when they first arrived, providing accommodation for some weeks while negotiations for the lease of Merton were underway. Their support continued after the setting up of the monastery, often supplying fresh food from their farm when community funds were low. Later in 1918 Sister Martha Kilgannon from Moylough, Co Galway, joined the community as a lay sister.

Courtesy of Ibar Carty ©

Macmine Castle

The nuns were anxious to reopen their school and were given permission to do so by Bishop Browne. To accommodate both monastery and school a second and much larger property, Macmine Castle, with over one hundred acres of farm land, was leased, again from the Richards family. Macmine, formerly a 13th century towerhouse, was enlarged in the 1850s and converted into a twenty-eight roomed baronial castle with a two acre walled garden.[1] The nuns transferred the monastery to Macmine Castle and opened the boarding school at Merton House. While some of the community were occupied in the classrooms, the younger nuns worked long days on the farm, tending the animals and vegetables.

Although large and roomy, Macmine had been neglected for years and was cold and damp. Because of her frail condition and advanced age it was decided to leave Lady Abbess Mary Scholastica Bergé at Merton, under the devoted care of Sr Romana. However, later that year, on 10 November 1916, almost two years to the day of her departure from her native Belgium, the 11th Abbess of the Irish Dames of Ypres, passed from this world, 'in the 86th year of her age, the 64th of her Religious Profession and the 26th of her Abbatial dignity'.[2] High Mass for the repose of her soul was held at the oratory at Merton House and was presided over by the

Lord Bishop. The celebrant was Prior Dom Merten and the music for the Requiem Mass was chanted by the nuns in choir. Interment took place immediately after in the new cemetery in the monastery grounds: 'The nuns of the Community chanted the "Benedictus" at the grave side. The last absolution was pronounced by the Lord Bishop'.[3]

There was never any doubt as to who would succeed Abbess Bergé. Mother Prioress, Dame Maura Ostyn, had been acting Abbess now for four years. But the formalities had to be attended to and an election was held on 12 December 1916. Bishop Browne presided at the election and pronounced Dame Maura duly elected. Sadly, the Bishop died shortly afterwards and the ceremony of Abbatial Benediction had to be postponed. Lady Abbess Maura Ostyn (1916 – 1940) was later blessed in the oratory at Macmine Castle by Bishop Brown's successor, the most Rev. Dr. Codd, on the 21 March 1918. Lady Abbess Maura was born in Belgium and was professed in 1888, at the age of twenty. In the early years of her religious life she was employed as a mistress in the school and was greatly loved by her students. A woman of deep religious commitment, her love of community life was only surpassed by her love of God. Her strength of character had already been tested; as acting Abbess she had seen the community through some of the most traumatic years of its history, and the experience gained would stand her in good stead in the still more difficult years to come. Already events of the future were beginning to take shape. Since the community's arrival in Ireland the country had witnessed a rebellion, the Easter Rising in April 1916, and the subsequent arrest, imprisonment and execution of some of the participants had heightened tensions throughout the country which would culminate in revolution and civil war.

In August 1918 Mademoiselle Delourme, later given the name Dame Margaret Mary, arrived at Macmine Castle seeking admission as a postulant. A native of Roubaix in France, she had made a difficult journey through a war-torn country to take up the life of prayer and sacrifice. Dame Margaret Mary spoke very little English, but her presence in the community was immediately felt when a flu epidemic hit the district in October and many of the nuns and pupils were taken ill. The young novice was immediately put in charge of the laundry, replacing the stricken Dame Aloysious Rossiter. She also acting as Infimarian to the school, where she worked tire-lessly nursing the pupils, day and night. Two members of the community grew dangerously ill. Sister Agnus Magner, so recently professed, was one of

© Kylemore Abbey

Lady Abbess M. Maura Ostyn
(1916–1940)

the first to be struck down and sadly died on 16 November; she was laid to rest in the cemetery at Merton. Dame Aloysious Rossiter, too ill to be nursed in the cold confines of Macmine Castle, was removed and placed in the care of the Convent of the Sisters of Mercy, at Our Lady of Lourdes, outside Dublin, and later died there in February 1919.

With the signing of the Armistice in November 1918 the nuns were forced to come to a decision; should they return to Ypres or remain on in Ireland. Prior Dom Aubert Merten, a good friend to the nuns at Macmine, was encouraging them to remain on in Ireland. A similar debate was going on at Edermine. Dom Marmion, Abbot of Maredsous Abbey in Belgium, was anxious to retain Edermine as an Irish foundation of that house, as was Prior Dom Aubert Merten. The Benedictine monks living there, however, were having difficulty with Dom Merten's authority and a good deal of unrest had developed within the monastery.

Unrest of a different kind was developing in the outside world. Following their success in the 1918 general election, the Sinn Féin M.Ps., intent on establishing an Irish republic, set up an Irish parliament, Dáil Éireann, in Dublin. Simultaneously the Irish Republican Army began waging war on the British Army, and as reports of skirmishes between the two reached the convent it must surely have seemed to the nuns that they had simply swapped one war for another.

Two more nuns were professed in 1919; Sr M. Columba Egan, a lay sister professed at the age of twenty-two, and Dame Elizabeth Magdalen Lee. Dame Magdalen was born in England and raised a Protestant; she worked for some years as a governess in Europe and was received into the Roman Catholic Church in 1897. Two years later she entered the Ursuline Convent in Lierre, Belgium. In 1914, along with other members of the community, she was given refuge at St. Mary's Benedictine Priory, in Princethorpe, England. Within the cloistered environment of the Benedictine Abbey, the young Ursuline nun plucked up the courage to inform her superiors of her long held desire for a more contemplative life within the church. After some delay she was eventually sent for one year to Macmine to test her vocation and to assist the nuns establish their school. In her memoirs, written late in her life, she described her early days in Co Wexford and her joy at last at being accepted into the Benedictine Order:

© Kylemore Abbey

Dame Elizabeth Magdalen Lee

> When I arrived in Ireland I found it snowbound, as England had been. The Lady Abbess received me most kindly, and I felt at home. In my heart there was great joy and peace; the outcome of perfect surrender. This time there had been no self-seeking. I had come to strangers in a

strange country. This time it was God alone I sought . . . I lived with the community, but did not go to the Divine Office. I continued the Ursuline prayers and the Little Office, and worked hard in the school and in the garden, and often in the fields . . . The Community was very poor, and great poverty was the order of the day.

After a few months, the Lady Abbess told me she and the Community were ready to receive me if I still wanted to join them. Of course I did, and at once I applied to the Holy See for permission to enter the great and venerable Benedictine Order. After waiting for several months, the rescript came from Rome allowing me to enter the novitiate.

Because she had her Ursuline vows, she was exempt from the temporary vows and admitted at once to perpetual vows on 21 March 1919, the feast of St Benedict. She was given the name Dame Elizabeth Mary Magdalen and chose for her motto *Deo Gratias* (Thanks be to God):

> And oh! the pride and joy of receiving the holy habit, the Benedictine Breviary, and my own place in the monastic choir! there to take my part in the "*Laus perennis*" – the never-ending praise, which day and night, the Benedictines are privileged to chant to their Lord and King, praying too for their brethren in the world who pray not. Surely no woman could have a higher vocation than this! And to think it is mine!.[4]

The ceremony was officiated by the Bishop of Ferns, Dr Codd, and attended by Dom Columba Marmion, who was in Ireland on a brief visit. During his stay Dom Marmion learned that Bishop Codd had requested that, since the war was now over, the Benedictine monks at Edermine should return to their house in Belgium. Following the subsequent sale of Edermine House, Dom Aubert Merten was allowed remain on in a small house close to Macmine as chaplain to the nuns.

For the Benedictine nuns circumstances made their decision easier. Reports were reaching the community, telling of the total destruction of their Abbey at Ypres. The nuns finally abandoned any hope of returning to Ypres and rebuilding their Abbey; instead it was decided that the community should remain in Ireland. Macmine Castle was considered by some members of the community to be totally unsuited to their needs and they recommended that they seek out a more suitable building, perhaps in a more hospitable diocese; in this the nuns were strongly influenced by Dom Merten.

Ypres Abbey Ruins

179

But there were others who felt that, with some expenditure, Macmine could be made more habitable, thereby preventing the necessity of yet another move. When it was put to a vote the majority returned in favour of leaving Macmine, and the rest were obliged to concede.

The Lady Abbess began searching the country for a property large enough to accommodate the community and school. The guerrilla war, waged throughout the country over the previous year, along with the passing of the compulsory land purchasing acts, had resulted in a flood of such properties coming on to the market, but finding one in a diocese that was willing to accept the nuns was quite another matter. Kylemore Castle had been on the market for seven years and was supervised by caretakers who reported back to the owner Ernest Fawke in England. When the nuns first came to inspect the property it stood silent and forlorn. The cold and unwelcoming appearance was in stark contrast to the days when this happy house resounded with the presence of the family and guests of Margaret and Mitchell Henry. And yet, like the Henrys before them, the nuns were drawn to the beauty of Kylemore Pass, the idyllic setting of the Castle and the many attractions of the estate. Dr Thomas Gilmatrin, the Archbishop of Tuam, in whose diocese the Castle stood, was approached and found to be welcoming. Having won his consent, the nuns went ahead and an agreement was drawn up for the purchase of Kylemore Castle at £45,000.

However, the ruination of the Abbey at Ypres, and the refusal of the British Government to allow War Reparations, left the community strapped for funds. It was decided that Lady Abbess Maura and Dame Teresa should travel to London to plead their case. Their friend and supporter, John Redmond, had died in 1918 and so the Abbess turned for help to T.P. O'Connor M.P., Lord Fitzalan, Sir John Lavery and other sympathetic Irishmen with political influence. All efforts on their behalf, however, met with little success and the nuns were forced to fall back on their own resources, which by now were little more than courage and conviction. However, in time Lady Abbess did succeed in attracting guarantors to assist in raising funds through the banks and the purchase went ahead. From London the nuns decided to re-visit Ypres and see for themselves the extent of the damage. They also hoped to collect whatever possessions they could from friends and religious who had managed to salvage some items during the bombing. The visit took place in June 1920 and photographs taken show the Abbess among the rubble of their former home.

© Kylemore Abbey

Lady Abbess Maura in the garden at Ypres Abbey Ruins 30 January 1920

Chapter 14

From Castle to Abbey

The nuns took possession of Kylemore Castle and estate on 30 November 1920. The estate comprised eleven townlands covering almost 10,000 acres. Excluded from the sale was the townland of Barnanang and other small holdings which had been previously sold. Also excluded was 2,200 acres of Addergoole, including Diamond Hill (Binn Ghuaire), lying west of Model Home Farm, which had been previously sold to James B Joyce, Clifden; this was later bought back by the nuns. The purchase also included the fishing and shooting rights and the oyster beds in part of Ballynakill and Barnaderg Bay outside or adjacent to the townland of Dawros More. However, the oyster beds were already worn out and the licence to plant beds had been allowed to lapse.[1]

Before leaving Macmine Castle two more nuns were professed; a lay sister, Sr Aiden Casey, and Dame Scholastica Murphy. Sr Aiden a native of Roscommon, was twenty years of age, while Dame Scholastica from Kerry, had studied in London and was a late vocation at the age of thirty-two. The community then stood at twenty-three; this included three novices who were later accepted into the community at Kylemore as lay sisters and the three German nuns who had not yet been re-united with the community. Dame Columban Plomer, the author of *The Irish Nuns at Ypres*, would later leave the community to join the Benedictine community at Minster in England.

On Friday, 3 December 1920, the community left Macmine Castle for what they hoped would be their final destination, Kylemore Castle. The *Wexford People* recorded the event reporting that the nuns were very popular among the local people, 'and their departure [was] very much regretted'. A large group accompanied them to the railway station, and 'the leave-taking from their old friends was a very pathetic scene'. The nuns made the journey to Galway in a first-class saloon carriage provided by the Midland Railway Co and special provision had been made so that they were

Connacht Tribune 16 Oct. 1920

able to make the journey to Galway without the inconvenience of changing trains.[2]

Local press in Galway had previously announced the purchase of Kylemore Castle by the Benedictine Nuns; on 23 October the *Connacht Tribune* carried the following notice:

> Last week, in London, Mr. R.W. Mackie, of the firm of Joyce, Mackie and Co., Galway and Dublin, in conjunction with Mr. P.J. Wemys, Mullingar, concluded the sale of Kylemore Castle Estate to the Irish Benedictine Dames of Ypres, for a sum of just over £45,000 . . . the vendor in the present sale is Mr. Ernest J. Fawke, of Norfolk Square, London, who has extensive interests in London, Liverpool, and elsewhere . . . [the nuns] had, prior to the war, a beautiful convent at Ypres, and only left when German shells were actually falling on the building. They travelled on foot for miles, until the British Red Cross rendered them assistance, and they finally landed in London, where friends assisted them to secure Macmine Castle, Co Wexford, in which they established themselves. They have now decided on the purchase of Kylemore, where they expect to be established in a short time.[3]

The contents of the estate were not included in the sale and these went on sale at a public auction which ran for three days from 26–28 October. Among the 1,000 lots on sale were 'antique and modern furniture, oil paintings, prints, bronzes, carpets, curtains, farm machinery, saw mill, poultry houses, vehicles, cattle and horses'.[4]

Converting Kylemore Castle into Kylemore Abbey would prove to be an enormous task, and one which would require tremendous effort on the part of the entire community. In Ypres the community had lived within the confines of their convent wall in the town; now they had taken ownership of 10,000 acres of land, a large portion of which was occupied by tenants. They were expected to farm the remainder, as well as cultivate and maintain the extensive grounds surrounding the Abbey itself, including the six acre walled garden with glasshouses and orchard. There was also the renowned Kylemore Fishery to be considered, along with the welfare of the tenants, all new challenges for a heretofore enclosed order of nuns. The previous four years at Macmine had given the nuns some practical experience in fruit growing and farming, but little else. Added to this was the ongoing War of Independence.

Undaunted by the obvious obstacles facing her, Lady Abbess Maura gathered her community around her and with the assistance of her Council faced into the work at hand. The experiences of the past six years had shown Lady Abbess that she had about her a very willing and gifted team of women, all were blessed with individual talents which would prove very necessary if the community were to survive the final stage of their journey from Ypres to Ireland. The division in the community, brought about by the move to Kylemore, had to be healed quickly. Kylemore must be accepted as their permanent home, it was here that their future lay. On the request of Lady Abbess Maura, on 1 March 1921, the Sacred Congregation for Religious granted permission for the rights and privileges of Ypres Abbey to be transferred to Kylemore, thus bringing Kylemore Abbey into being. As at Ypres, Kylemore would retain its autonomy as an individual house, subject to its own Constitutions and with the Archbishop of Tuam as their immediate superior. Kylemore Abbey then became the first Benedictine monastery established in Ireland since the Reformation. In thanksgiving for their delivery to Kylemore, Lady Abbess Maura promised to erect a statue to the Sacred Heart as soon as funds became available.

One of the first difficulties presented to Lady Abbess by her new Abbey was the question of enclosure. In Ypres the community practised strict Papal enclosure. This required a high wall to enclose the monastery, but such a thing would be impossible at Kylemore. Dr Thomas Gilmartin, Archbishop of Tuam, suggested that, instead of a wall, the nuns take the mountains surrounding the Abbey as their enclosure; this left them free to live out their lives in the less strict environment of monastic enclosure.

The next obvious problem was the very structure of the building. Kylemore Castle was designed as a family residence, with suitable accommodation for entertainment. It was never intended as a monastery and school. The interior, now sparsely furnished, was in a shocking state of neglect. In the kitchen the ranges had been pulled out for sale in the auction and the oak floor was destroyed. The bedrooms were too large to act as cells and too small to act as dormitories. The Gothic Church, although considered a treasure by the nuns, was too far away to act as a private chapel, given the frequency with which the nuns were called to prayer.

Dame Bernard, always a practical person, set about adapting the Castle to a monastery. She acquainted herself with all the practical details of the building; the drains, pipes, electricity, and advised the community on how best to utilise the rooms. The room which in Mitchell Henry's time was the elegantly dressed ballroom, and more recently the kitchen, was recognised by the nuns as ideally placed to act as the community Chapel. They arranged for a new floor to be put down and the walls replastered and painted. The kitchen was then relocated on the ground floor.

The very heart of the building was adapted to the nuns enclosure, large rooms were partitioned into small cells and dormitories were laid out for the novices. Four months after their arrival the nuns suffered the loss of Sr Rosalie Madeleine Putte. Sr Rosalie, a lay sister born at Baal in Luxembourg, died on 2 April 1921 at the age of eighty. Since their arrival, she liked to refer to herself as the 'foundation stone' of Kylemore Abbey, being the oldest member of the community.

Two of the three novices who had travelled with the community from Macmine were professed at Kylemore in 1921; Sr Mary Patrick Mannion from Glenamaddy and Sr Gerard Judge from Headford, both in Co Galway. The third, Sr Oliver Greally, was professed in 1925.

The nuns' desire to reopen their school was hampered by the war. Military activity in the district was intensified and regular searches were carried out on the homes of Sinn Féin supporters by the Royal Irish Constabulary, backed up by the Black and Tans. In March two RIC men were shot dead on the streets of Clifden by the IRA, and the British forces responded by burning down fourteen houses in the town, killing one civilian and seriously wounding another. On two occasions British army lorries pulled up in front of the Abbey and, despite the protests of the nuns, the entire building, including the enclosure, was thoroughly searched by the soldiers. During one such visit, Dame Magdalen went out on the terrace to talk to the soldiers and seeing the machine guns she asked what they were, and 'the soldiers said they would give her a demonstration, so they fired across the lake, thus warning every Republican for miles around of their presence'.[5]

Not knowing how long hostilities would last, the nuns decided to persist with their intention of having the remains of Abbess Bergé, Dame Aloysios Rossiter and Dame Agnes Magner exhumed from their resting place at Merton House and brought to Kylemore for re-burial. Abbes Bergé was the first to be transferred, and it would seem that her last journey across Ireland was to be as eventful as any of those taken while she was still alive. Dom Sweetman, a Benedictine priest who ran a school, Mount St Benedict, in Gorey, Co Wexford, came to the nuns' assistance and assured them that they need have no worries, he himself would take charge of the entire operation. Dom Sweetman hired a lorry to transport the coffin from Wexford to

Kylemore. The Sweetman family were well-known republicans and the driver, knowing this, was, from the outset, a little suspicious of what lay hidden in the coffin but decided to ask no questions. However, when on his journey, he saw what appeared to be a British army checkpoint up ahead, he turned off the main road and dumped the coffin in the first available farm building. The owner of the farm, equally suspicious, decided that "what you don't know can't hurt you", and turning a blind eye, left the coffin untouched until, as he assumed, the "boys" would return to collect it. In the meantime Dom Sweetman phoned Kylemore Abbey to know if the Abbess had arrived safely, only to be told that she had not. On learning the truth from the driver an all-out search of the countryside was instigated to try and track down the exact shed in which the Abbess was deposited. The coffin was eventually located and transported to Kylemore, where, much to the relief of all concerned, it was laid to rest in the crypt of the Gothic Church. The Abbess was later joined by the remains of Dame Aloysios Rossiter and Dame Agnes Magner. These three were the only members of the community to be buried in the crypt; a plot of ground next to the Gothic Church was railed off as a cemetery for future community use.

The War of Independence came to an end in July 1921 and was followed by the signing of the Anglo-Irish Treaty, which resulted in the setting up of the Irish Free State. Disagreement over the terms of the Treaty eventually brought the country to a civil war, which ran from June 1922 to May 1923. During this time the nuns too learned to "turn a blind eye", as men from both sides moved through the countryside in the dead of night. Once again the nuns learned of unfolding events through rumour and speculation. Clifden was at the centre of serious fighting in the district and little was witnessed by the nuns except for the sound of rifle shots ringing out from distant hills. When the war eventually came to an end and the railway line was repaired and fully operational, three of the four German nuns expelled from Ypres at the outbreak of the war were re-united with the community in 1924; Dame Gertrude, Sr Baptiste and Sr Catherine Margaret. The fourth, Sr Helen, had died in exile in Holland in 1920.

The community's presence in the locality, was, from the time of their arrival, recognised as a blessing. The nuns brought with them knowledge and expertise which would prove most useful in what was still a very remote region: young mothers brought their sick children to Dame Walburga, the community Infimarian, for advice, and she would help dress their wounds. The tenants too had found a sympathetic landlord and hopes were high that the Land Commission would purchase their holding. Lady Abbess Maura took a keen interested in all aspects of the estate and she visited the farm and garden every few days, driving herself in a donkey and trap. She was concerned for the welfare of the employees and their families and for the needs of the neighbourhood. Under her direction the community extended a helping hand when ever, and where ever, it was needed. Conscious of the poor circumstances of many of their neighbours, each Christmas the nuns wrote to manufacturers and large shops throughout Ireland, requesting items for distribution to the less well off in the district. In the weeks leading in to the festival, boxes upon boxes would arrive filled with clothes, material, sweets, chocolates and biscuits. These were divided up and parcels were prepared and distributed locally. Very early in their life at Kylemore the nuns began a tradition which was to continue for many years. After Mass on St Stephen's Day all of the people of the parish were invited to visit the tall Christmas tree erected in the main hall. The entire community came out to greet them, offering tea and cake to the adults, and the children were encouraged to pick a gift from the tree, usually fruit or sweets.

With the return to normality the community reopened their boarding school as quickly as possible. The principal reception rooms and bedrooms in the Abbey were converted into classrooms. Other rooms were converted into dormitories, but there was little to fill them. Some items of furniture had been purchased at the auction, but this still left empty rooms and insufficient beds and bedding. Gifts of furniture and fittings began arriving from shops and factories in Westport and Galway; it would seem there were many who were anxious to assist the war refugees settle into the West.

Pupils were accepted almost immediately, but the school was not formally opened until the 11 September 1923. A small number of lay teachers were employed from the start, but the majority of teachers were members of the community who had themselves been educated at Ypres. The school had a junior school and secondary school and the headmistress, Dame Scholastica, enrolled thirty pupils on the appointed day, ranging in age from eight to eighteen. The students had come to receive an education 'drawn up in accordance with the principles of Benedictine education and on the lines

Lawrence, Photo., Dublin.   Copyright.

Benedictine Abbey,
Kylemore
6 March '21

My Dear Cousin
I hope you will like this photo of our school. I love to be here. It is a beautiful place. We have great fun climbing the mountains we are going to put a statue of the Sacred Heart up on one of the Mountains next week. You know it was the S. Heart that got Kylemore for the nuns.
When will you come over to Ireland again? I hope soon.
Sister Maura told me that she wrote to you some time ago. She sends her love to you.
With much love from your little Irish cousin
Becie Scally

Becie Scally was a student at Kylemore School in 1921

of a public secondary school'.[6] From the beginning it was seen as 'a high-class school 'offering 'all the advantages of a Continental education without the necessity for lengthened travel'.[7]

The school was visited by an Inspector from the Department of Education on 25 March 1924. Following the Inspector's report, which praised the 'excellent organisation and the high standard of the work being achieved', the school was officially recognised by the Department of Education.

On 5 April the choir was examined and judged to be 'above the Dublin record'. In the music examinations in piano and violin, which took place in June, all pupils passed, some with honours. The year 1923–24 was the last year of the old system and it was decided not to present the pupils for the intermediate examinations. Only one girl sat the matriculation and she passed with high marks and continued her studies at the university.

In 1924 the number of students increased to forty-nine and the curriculum included Irish, English, Mathematics, Geography, History, Music, Choir, French, Latin, Christian Doctrine and Apologetics. A good deal of work had gone on in the intervening year and several new rooms had been added; a new study hall, library, a spacious refectory, a 'technical' kitchen and a laboratory. And a new dormitory now made it possible for the school to accommodate ninety pupils.[8] In fact in the following decades the number of boarders at the school would average in the thirties.

On 20 December 1924 the school hosted its first concert and prize giving ceremony. In attendance was Archbishop Dr Gilmartin, parents and friends, and eleven members of the clergy, mostly from the neighbourhood: Right Rev. Monsignor McAlpine, P.P., V.G., Clifden; Very Rev. J.S. Canon Walsh; Rev. Ed. O'Malley, C.C., Cleggan; Rev. W.. Diskin, P.P., Letterfrack; Rev. G.J. Prendergast, C.C., Castlebar; Rev. W. J. Heaney, P. P.,; Rev. J. O'Dea, Bishop's Secretary, Galway; Rev. M.A. MacHale, B.A., Vicksburg, U.S.A.; Rev. M.J. Morris, C.C., Tullycross; Rev. L. Lyons, C.C. Letterfrack; Rev. W.M. Kelly, C.C., Errismore.

Connacht Tribune 20 December 1924

FIRST PRIZE DAY AT KYLEMORE ABBEY.—A group taken outside the main entrance to Kylemore Castle after Prize Day on Monday. His Grace the Archbishop of Tuam is in the centre, and on his left are Right Rev. Monsignor McAlpine, P.P., V.G., and Very Rev. Dr. Mereton, Prior of the Benedictine Fathers. Note the beautiful carving on the doorway.
("Tribune" photo).

SOME OF THE STUDENTS AT KYLEMORE.—A group taken after Monday's concert and presentation of the court scene from " The Merchant of Venice " Miss Hession, who sung Gounod's " Ave Maria " so well, and Miss Clodagh Moore, who played " Portia," are standing on the running-board of the motor-car in the background. There are now over 40 students at Kylemore.   ("Tribune" photo).

Connacht Tribune 20 December 1924

The *Connacht Tribune* reporter commented that the concert programme was 'ambitious and varied. Perhaps the best item was the singing of Gounod's "*Ave Maria*" by Miss Hession, of Tuam, a young lady with a smiling stage presence and a voice of singular purity and charm'. Also receiving praise was a daughter of Mr. Walter McNally, the Irish baritone, and Miss Clodagh Moore, who played the part of Portia, in the *The Merchant of Venice*. Dom Merten, in his capacity as Chaplain to the nuns, welcomed his Grace the Archbishop and the other guests to Kylemore, and the Archbishop in response paid tribute to the performers and to their teachers. Kylemore would in time, he told them, become a famous school: 'The Benedictine Dames had great traditions behind them. These traditions had been handed down from the earliest monastic times in the history of the Church; and they hoped that these traditions would live in the country to which the Dames had now come'.[9] Photographs of the students and visiting dignitaries were published in the *Connacht Tribune*, along with the names of the recipients of prizes.

The prize giving ceremony become an annual event and Archbishop Gilmartin was back again at Kylemore on 3 June 1925. Among the prizes distributed on this occasion was a gold medal awarded by Professor Whelehan of Dublin to Lelia Mangan, for English Essay. Along with the usual attendants of clergy, parents and friends, there was, according to the press, some notable dignitaries: William O'Malley, former M.P,. for the district; Col. Fritz Brase, 'the well-known musician', who was on a short visit at the Abbey; Miss Cashel, County Counsellor, Acting Professor of

CONCERT BY KYLEMORE ABBEY STUDENTS.

GROUP OF LADY STUDENTS at Kylemore Abbey School, photographed with Colonel Fritz Brase, Conductor of the No. 1 Army Band, seen on the extreme right. The pupils recently gave a highly meritorious concert at which his Grace Most Rev. Dr. Gilmartin was present.   (Photo, Hofberton).

Connacht Tribune 27 June 1925

Education, U.C.G.; Miss W. McNally, Galway; Mrs MacHale, Clifden; Mr and Mrs Philip O'Gorman, Galway; Mr B Stanton, Westport; Mr D. Waldron, Tuam; Mr W. Irwin and Mr H. Palmer. After the concert, which preceded the prize giving, Col. Fritz Brase, who paid tribute to the 'great musical talent in the school', gave a piano solo of his "*Second Irish Fantasia*", and was heartily thanked by Dom Merten and His Grace the Archbishop. The Archbishop once again paid tribute to the 'high character of the education given in Kylemore Abbey'.

William O'Malley wrote about his visit in a letter to the *Connacht Tribune*, in which he proclaimed that 'Yes! Kylemore Abbey has come to stay and I have no doubt whatever that in a short time it will be one of Ireland's most famous colleges, and be an added glory to the Benedictine Nuns. It would be impossible, I think, to find anywhere a situation for a ladies' college so beautiful as Kylemore, or a house so suitable as the famous Kylemore Castle. The scenery is simply superb and it is well-known that grand mountain scenery has an ennobling effect on the character of those who are fortunate to enjoy it'.[10]

The school was already attracting foreign students, many of whom came to study English, but the majority were drawn from Galway and the neighbouring counties. This international 'mix' added to Kylemore's already growing reputation and attraction, and, on the evening of a school concert in 1931, resulted in shopkeepers' daughters from Clifden sharing the limelight with Indian Princesses. The Princesses, Rajkumari Rajendra Kumari and Rajkumari Manher Kumari of Jamnagar, were the nieces of the His Highness Maharaja Jam Ranjit Sinhji Sahib Bahadur of Navanagah. The Maharajah, a renowned cricket player, had a residence in Connemara, Ballynahinch Castle, where he spent several months of the year fishing salmon and entertaining his many guests. The concert was in aid of the Christmas Tree Fund for the poor, and was well attended by local clergy and dignitaries. At the conclusion of the concert Monsignor McAlpine, P.P., Clifden, when thanking the nuns and students for a most enjoyable evening, added that, 'from a scenic standpoint, not only has Kylemore its own peculiar charms and attractions, but that it is a veritable paradise in itself. Perhaps in the past some might [have been] inclined to regard it as a *Paradise Lost*, but since the advent of the Benedictine Sisters' it was recognised as 'nothing less than a *Paradise Regained*'. They were, he concluded, fortunate to have such 'a splendid school and such a religious community in their midst', and his hope for the future was that, 'nothing will happen, nothing can happen, that will in the smallest shorten their stay, curtail their

PAX

KYLEMORE ABBEY
SCHOOL

Programme of Concert

In aid of the Christmas Tree Fund. Sunday, 22nd November, 1931.

1. CHORUS .... "Veni, Sancte Spiritus" .... *Plainsong.*
2. PIANO SOLO ... "Sunday Morning at Glion" .... *F. Bendel.*
   MISS KATHLEEN HEADON.
3. .... (a) "Nursery Rhymes"
   (b) "Balloon Dance"
   THE MISSES MARY & BEATRICE CASEY AND
   HELEN STEWART
4. VOCAL SOLO ..... "The Fairest Flower" .... *D. Slater.*
   MISS RITA KING.
5. VIOLIN SOLO ...(a) "In the Morning Sunshine"......... *Wecker.*
   (b) "A Visit to Poland"
   MISS NELLA CARLEY.
6. CHORUS .... (a) "Autumn Leaves" .... *Anon.*
   (b) "Spailpín Fanac" .. *(Jacobite Song).*
7. DANCE .... "Fisher Girls" ....
   THE MISSES KATHLEEN HEADON, MARY NAGLE
   AND NELLA CARLEY.
8. VOCAL SOLO "Elisabeth's Prayer" (from *Tannhäuser*) .. *R. Wagner.*
   MISS EVELYN MURRAY, L.L.C.M.
9. PIANO SOLO ...... "Rustle of Spring" .... *Sinding.*
   MISS EVELYN MURRAY, L.L.C.M.
10. "The Greek Mother"
    (Episode of the Turkish Conquest of the Ionian Isles).
    CHARACTERS :
    THE MOTHER .... K.S. MANKERKUMARI OF JAMNAGAR.
    IRENE (her daughter) .... MISS RITA KING.
    ALEXIS (her son) .... MISS HELEN STEWART.

    Piano Accompaniment :
    DR. KARL SEELDRAYERS.

11. VOCAL SOLO .... "Die Loreli" .... *German Folksong.*
    MISS MARY NAGLE.
12. PIANO CONCERTO........ — .... *Handel.*
    DR. CARL SEELDRAYERS & MISS EVELYN MURRAY, L.L.C.M.
13. BALLET .... "Fountain Dance" .... —
14. VOCAL SOLO ..... "Berceuse de Jocelyn" .... *Godard.*
    MISS OLGA GAILLARD.
15. VIOLIN SOLO ... "Spanische Tänze, N. 2 & 3" ..... *Moszkowski.*
    MISS EVELYN MURRAY, L.L.C.M.
16. CHORUS .... "The Sabbath Morn" .... *Mendelssohn.*
17. RECITATION ...... "Ex Ore Infantium" .. *Francis Thompson.*
    MISS HELEN STEWART.
18. PIANO SOLO ..... (a) "Third Phantasia" .... *P. Benoit.*
    (b) "Symphonic Poem" .... *P. Benoit.*
    DR. KARL SEELDRAYERS.
19. SAYNETE.. "Une Cure Extraordinaire"
    CHARACTERS :
    MADEMOISELLE PIMPRENELLE .. MISS OLGA GAILLIARD.
    MADEMOISELLE SENE .... MISS EVELYN MURRAY.
    MARGOT (bonne) .... MISS MARY NAGLE

    [FINIS]

PRINTINGHOUSE GALWAY

endeavours, or lessen their activities. *Prospere Procede! Macte Virtute!*[11]

Anxious to improve conditions for the young girls of the district, the nuns opened a Domestic Economy school for day pupils at St Maurs, formerly the steward's house, on the west avenue. Three nuns were placed as teachers in the school; Dame Teresa, Dame Bernard and Dame Magdalene. Here the girls were taught cooking, sewing, knitting, lace making and other crafts. The girls attending St Maurs travelled many miles over mountain and bog, and in all weathers, to reach Kylemore. The Irish government was proving no better at creating employment in Connemara than their British counterparts had been before them, with the result that mass emigration would continue to be the scourge of each generation. The community's own means were small and they could offer little by way of employment for women, but by offering an education they could better equip them for employment abroad, or help them improve their living conditions at home.

When Dame Bernard took over as headmistress at the school in the 1930s, she immediately began re-structuring the classrooms and the school syllabus. The Domestic Economy school at St Maurs was closed and the building east of the Abbey, which once housed the Turkish Bath, was partially demolished and rebuilt as classrooms to accommodate a day school for local girls. The day school was named Scoil Áine and for some years operated independently of the boarding school. Here the daughters of employees, local farmers, artisans and merchants were given a full secondary school education free of charge. For girls whose homes were some distance from the school, accommodation was provided at a nominal fee, at St Maurs and at the head gardeners house; they were free to return home at the weekend. The full boarders alone wore the school uniform, this resembled the nuns' habit and had a detachable white collar. In later years, when the two schools were amalgamated, the day pupils too were given a uniform, but this differed in style from that of the boarders.

With the amalgamation of the two schools the school syllabus was altered so as to provide an education more suited to the needs of the daughters of the emerging Irish Free State, while still offering all the advantages of a European finishing school. The nuns wished to be recognised as supporters of the newly developing State and of the Irish Government's educational policy. Outside teachers were brought in to teach the nuns the Irish language and, following Dame Bernard's visit to the Department of Education, Kylemore was accepted as an "A" school: this meant that all subjects were now taught through the medium of the Irish language.

In 1929 the Land Commission purchased that section of the estate leased out by tenants and part of Pollacappul, Lemnaheltia and Addergoole. The tenants then went on to purchase their holdings under the Land Purchase Acts. The nuns retained Mweelin (656 acres) and part of Lemnaheltia (75 acres),

© Kylemore Abbey

Rajkumari Rajendra Kumari of Jamnagar and Rajkumari Manher Kumari of Jamnagar
The Indian Princesses with fellow students on the steps of Kylemore in 1930s

Addergoole (296 acres) and Pollacappul (491 acres), for their own use. This left them with a little over 1,525 acres, about one hundred and fifty acres of which was arable and pasture, the rest being mountain grazing and forest. Later, in the 1940s, the nuns succeeded in buying back the 2,200 acres of Addergoole from James B. Joyce of Clifden.

The nuns also retained the fishing rights as established by Mitchell Henry. Addergoole House, which Henry had converted into staff accommodation, a laundry and dairy, continued to be used as such. Part of the second floor accommodation was given over to Dom Merten, the community chaplain. For a time the possibility of opening a Benedictine monastery at the farm was under consideration and became the subject of correspondence between Dom Merten and Abbot Marmion, but this was abandoned with the opening of Glenstal Abbey in Co Limerick in 1927. Other buildings on the farm; the gamekeeper's house, workmen's houses, the workshops etc., were put to a variety of uses over the years. There was usually a steward to manage the farm, but the nuns themselves kept a close eye on its operation, and many of the permanent employees, families such as the Nees and Aspells, whose grandfathers had first come to Kylemore under Mitchell Henry, continued to live there.

The farm left the community pretty much self-sufficient; they kept sheep, dairy cows, cattle, horses, pigs, poultry and other farmyard animals, and grew oats, potatoes, turnips and other vegetables. They killed their own sheep, pigs and poultry, planted and harvested their vegetables and cut turf for fuel. Fortunately for them, the sawmill had failed to attract a buyer at the public auction and remained in use for many years. All the farm work was initially done by horses; they purchased their first tractor in the 1950s, labour was plentiful and the nuns themselves did a great deal of work. Most of the lay sisters had farming backgrounds, and would help with harvesting, and there was always a sister in charge of the poultry.

Wedding party of William and Mary Ellen Aspell, 16 October 1946.

William was chauffeur to the nuns for many years. The couple's wedding breakfast at the Abbey was a gift from the nuns. William Walsh (father of Sr Brendan) Ellen (Hope) Lydon, Patrick Lydon, Peter Aspell, William Aspell, Mary Ellen (Nee) Aspell, Agnes Nee, Sr Brendan Walsh, May & Pat Nee (parents of the bride)

At Kylemore, as at Macmine, young postulants continued to arrive and under Prioress Dame Placid, who also acted as Novice Mistress, six nuns were professed in the first ten years, all of whom were lay sisters and came from Counties Galway and Mayo: Sr Peter King, St Jarlath O'Brien, Sr Teresa Greaney, Sr Paul Monaghan, Sr Ita O'Flaherty and Sr Brigid Walle.

However, as the number of students at the school was still low, Dame Odilon, in her capacity as Bursar, was finding that the farm and school were insufficient to support a growing community. To help finance the loans taken out in the purchase of Kylemore, and to cover the cost of more recent refurbishment, it would be necessary to seek out other sources of income. In keeping with the Benedictine tradition of hospitality the community decided that, during school holidays, the principal rooms in the Abbey would be used as a guesthouse. The nuns' enclosure was to remain quite separate and no outsider was allowed beyond the locked doors. The guests were invited to partake in the Divine Office, so that they might 'associate in the peace' and experience the benefits of liturgical prayer. Dame Margaret was appointed guest mistress and Dame Odilon, with the backing of her Abbess and the community, set about attracting guests. To reduce costs no domestic outsiders were hired, and the running and management of the guesthouse was carried out by the nuns themselves. The young nuns worked hard preparing the rooms in the short time between the breakup of school and the opening of the guesthouse: all desks had to be removed, walls washed and painted, beds put in place, and usually all in the space of one week.

Guests were also accommodated at the farm, the head gardener's house, St Maurs and Stella Maris, formerly the coachman's house. Between all, the nuns could accommodate around sixty guests. Bearing in mind that the Divine Office at the time took up about two and a half hours in the day, and that more time had to be allocated to reading and meditation, this made for a very full day.

Word of the opening of the guesthouse was spread through religious and community friends, and the response was tremendous. The guesthouse was a success, the fishing rights attached to the estate proving an obvious boon, and over the years a steady clientele of priests, fishermen and tourists was built up. At times there were so many priests in the house that twelve or fourteen Masses would be said in the chapel in one day. Stories are still told of the judges, doctors, Harley Street surgeons, British Army Brigadier Generals, the Roman Catholic and Protestant clergy, all of whom regularly fished together in the daytime and enjoyed the splendid meals prepared by the nuns in the evening. It was also a popular destination for honeymoon couples, and for women travelling alone. The guests made their own entertainment, musicians brought their own instruments, and singers, amateur and professional alike, were called upon to perform. Friendships were formed and attachments made and, for some, love stories began which led to marriage and a life-long association with the nuns at Kylemore. All income derived from this venture was utilised to repay the very heavy loans carried by the community as a result of the purchase of Kylemore and other community expenses.

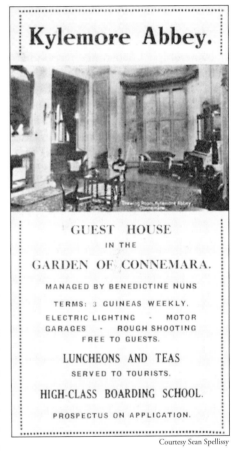

Courtesy Sean Spellissy

Guest House advertisement

Sr Brendan

Sr Bernadette

Sr Dymphna

One English guest, a Miss Silk, expressed an interest in joining the monastery and later returned as a novice in 1930. A convert to Catholicism, she was principal of a large primary school in England, and following her profession in 1933, when she was given the name Dame Josepha, she became a teacher in the junior school.

The first local girl to be professed was Elizabeth Walsh. Elizabeth's grandfather had come from Tipperary and worked for Mitchell Henry as a ploughman on the Home Farm. Her father Willie Walsh married a local girl, Ann Lydon, and the family lived at Mullaghglass House, remaining on under the Manchesters and later the nuns. After the death of her mother Elizabeth came to live at Addergoole with her aunt, May Nee. May's husband, Patrick, was employed by the nuns at Addergoole and he and his family lived over the workshops in the farm yard. From an early age Elizabeth expressed a desire to become a nun and was eventually accepted by Lady Abbess when she was fifteen years old. She was professed in 1931 and given the name Sr Brendan.

Sr Brendan was followed by two Conroy sisters from Lettergesh. The girls' father, Thomas Conroy, had worked as a coach driver at the Castle under Mitchell Henry and the Manchesters. While still young the sisters stated their intention to enter a convent; Ellen, the younger of the two, wished to join the Benedictines at Kylemore, and Kathleen had already made plans to join a missionary order in England. On entering Kylemore on 15 September 1926, Ellen, aged fifteen, was given the name Sr Bernadette. Soon afterwards she was visited by Kathleen, who was immediately struck by the plainchant; unaccompanied vocal music used in the Benedictine Order since Mediaeval times, and, on making enquiries, found herself drawn to the Benedictine way of life. Changing her plans, Kathleen, aged twenty-one, entered Kylemore two weeks later, on 29 September and was given the name Sr Dymphna. Sr Dymphna made her final profession in 1932. Sr Bernadette, because of her age, was not professed until 8 December 1933. Sadly, after a short illness, Sr Bernadette died on 26 February 1934, less than three months after her profession. Sr Dymphna worked for many years in the guesthouse and, although greatly saddened by the loss of her sister, went on to live out a very long, fulfilled and happy life, and is now, at the time of writing, the oldest member of the community.

Four more nuns were professed in the 1930s, one sister and three Dames; Sr Francis Langan from Headford, Co Galway, Dame Gertrude O'Connor from Cork, Dame Lucy Horan from Shinrone in Co. Offaly and Dame Agnes Finnegan, from Westport, Co Mayo. Dame Agnes was destined to make history in the community when she later became the youngest Abbess in Europe and the first to resign under the new rule allowed under Vatican 11.

In recognition of the community's long tradition of devotion to the Sacred Heart, in 1932, Lady Abbess Maura fulfilled her promise to erect a statue in thanksgiving for their delivery to Kylemore. The large statue of the Sacred Heart was put in place half-way up Duchruach mountain by a group of ten men; John Joyce, Tom Conroy, Tommy Kearney, Jack Coyne, Pat Nee, John Lydon, Anthony McDonald, Frank Keane, J.J. MacLoughlan and Michael Fitzsimons, the carpenter. Using a large hand barrow made by Fitzsimons, the statue was carried up a previously prepared path. The men were followed by members of the community reciting the rosary. At the designated spot the statue was blessed and cemented into place on a platform overlooking the Abbey.

© Kylemore Abbey

Statue of the Sacred Heart

With the varying demands of the school, farm and guesthouse, the community worked from early morning until last thing at night, from one end of the year to another. Work was only interrupted by long prayer sessions and periods of meditation; there was little time for recreation, although the rule did allow for it. Each season brought its own tasks, its own demands and needs to be attended. However, all of that was put aside on 23 January 1939 when the community came together with friends to celebrate Lady Abbess Maura Ostyn's Golden Jubilee.

The Most Rev. Dr Joseph Walsh, coadjutor Bishop of Tuam, celebrated Pontifical Mass and, to her great joy, a telegram was received from the Holy Father, sent by Cardinal Pacelli, who was to ascend the Papal throne a month later. Sadly, the following year, on a visit to the farm, the Lady Abbess caught a chill, which developed into double-pneumonia and eventually caused her death, on 11 November 1940, she was aged seventy-two. Lady Abbess Maura had indeed been a strong and inspirational Abbess. Under her care the community had survived the transfer from Ypres to Kylemore, had faced hardship and overcome all difficulties placed before them. There had been an increase in community numbers and, thanks to the hard work of the entire community, all debts were now almost completely cleared.

In the election that followed, Mother Prioress Mary Placid Druhan was elected 13th Abbess. Lady Abbess Placid (1941–1953), was born in Wexford in 1876 and was a pupil in the school in Ypres before entering the monastery at the age of fifteen. She was of a more retiring nature than her predecessor and did not

© Kylemore Abbey

Lady Abbess Placid Druhan (1941–1953)

Lady Abbess Placid Druhan with her Community 1942

Back Row left to right: Sr Paul Monaghan, Sr Gerard Judge, Sr Columba Egan, Sr Oliver Greally, Sr Peter King, Sr Dymphna Conroy, Sr Ita O'Flaherty, Sr Francis Langan, Sr Jarlath O'Brien, Sr Baptiste Griese, Sr Bernadette Feeney, Sr Brendan Walsh.

Middle Row: Sr Winifred Hodges, Sr Hildergard, Sr Romana King, Dame Agnes Finnegan, Sr Brigid Walle, Dame Gertrude O'Connor, Dame Margaret Mary Delourme, Sr. Gabriel Bohan, Dame Scholastica Murphy, Sr Teresa Greaney, Dame Gregory Quaid, Sr Patrick Mannion, Sr Elizabeth Dasbach, Sr Aiden Casey, Dame Josepha Silk, Sr Marta Kilgannon. Dame Lucy Horan.

Front Row (seated): Dame Magdalen Lee, Dame Bernard Stewart, Dame Teresa Howard, Rt. Rev Lady Abbess Placid Druhan, Dame Odilon Allaeys, Dame Benedict Curtis.

Front Row novices: Sr Mary, Sr Raphael Conroy, Sr Michael Moloney, Sr John O'Malley.

© Kylemore Abbey

get involved in the running of the estate to the same extent. However, under her care, and with the assistance of her council, the community continued to thrive. In the early 1940s five young novices were under Dame Teresa's instruction and were later accepted into the community; Sr Bernadette Feeney from Roscommon, Dame Gregory Quaid from Limerick, Dame Michael Moloney from Limerick, her sister, Dame Mechtilde, who would later become Abbess, and Dame John O'Malley from Mayo. They were joined by Virginia Conroy, a native of Kylemore and one of the first students to attend the day school. Having trained as a nurse in England, Virginia returned and joined the monastery in 1942; she was given the name Dame Raphael and would later take up the position of Infimarian to the community. Two more ex-pupils joined in the late 1940s; Dame Mary O'Toole, a native of Clifden, professed in 1946, and Dame Agatha Martin, from Dublin, professed in 1949. Dame Mary O'Toole become a teacher in the school and was head-mistress there for twenty-five years, and in time become Abbess. Dame Agatha was one of four Martin sisters who attended the school. She trained as a children's nurse in Temple Street Hospital before entering the monastery and becoming a teacher.

During World War II numbers at the boarding school dropped dramati-cally and were slow to rise in the following years. By contrast the day school saw an increase in its numbers as more and more local girls were seeking

© Kylemore Abbey

Abbess Placid's Golden Jubilee 1946

secondary school education. In the years that followed the end of the war the guesthouse proved extremely popular among English priests and fishermen. Anxious to escape the food scarcities back home, the regular guests jealously guarded their accommodation booking at Kylemore where the nuns continued to provide home-grown fruit and vegetables, and farm-reared fowl, lamb and beef.

Lady Abbess Placid celebrated her Golden Jubilee in 1946. The Pontifical Mass was again celebrated by the Most Rev. Dr Joseph Walsh, who had since been made Archbishop of Tuam.

Lady Abbess Placid continued to serve her community for a further seven years, until her death in 1953. The Lady Abbess was taken ill with a bad cold on Holy Thursday, which soon developed into pneumonia, and she died suddenly on Easter Monday, 6 April 1953, at the age of seventy-seven. The community suffered a further loss a month later with the death of Dame Teresa Howard, on 12 May. From the time they had left Ypres until their arrival in Wexford, Dame Teresa's family connections had proved invaluable to the community. Her uncle, John Redmond M.P., had used his influence on their behalf with government, church and the general public, to win them a secure home and financial assistance in their difficult transfer from Belgium to Ireland. Dame Teresa herself was remembered as a loving Novice Mistress, a great liturgist and chantress.

Dame Agnes Finnegan was elected Abbess in August 1953. However, because of her young age – she was thirty-six – special permission had to be

© Kylemore Abbey

Lady Abbess Agnes Finnegan
(1953–1981)

obtained from Rome before the ceremony of Abbatial Benediction could take place. History was made when the ceremony was eventually performed by Dr Walsh, on 5 October 1953, and Lady Abbess Agnes Finnegan (1953–1981), became the youngest Abbess in Europe. She was also the first Abbess to be elected from among those who had entered the community since its arrival in Ireland and, although the nuns were unaware of it at the time, she would be the last to be elected for life. A native of Westport, Lady Abbess Agnes came to Kylemore as a student in 1932, at the age of fifteen. On one trip back to school she had the distinction of travelling on the last train out of Galway for Clifden. It was 27 April 1935, the day the railway closed down after just thirty years in operation; alighting at Recess she was met by the community car which transported her to Kylemore.[12]

Chapter 15

Night of Destruction

There were forty-two nuns in the community at the time of Lady Abbess Agnes's election, twenty-six of whom were Dames. The profession of Sr Pius O'Meara from Tipperary, in 1957, brought up the number of lay sisters to seventeen. Only four of the original Ypres nuns remained, the rest had passed away and were laid to rest in the cemetery next to the Gothic Church. This was the highest number attained in the history of the community and would not be equalled in the foreseeable future.

Life under Abbess Agnes went on pretty much as before, the guesthouse was enjoying enormous popularity and Kylemore Abbey was becoming a popular destination for almost every tourist visiting Connemara. To accommodate the growing number of day visitors to the Abbey, lunches and afternoon teas were served in the two dining rooms on the first floor and a small shop was opened in the hall, selling religious objects and craft work made by the nuns. Lady Abbess could look with satisfaction on her thriving community and may perhaps have even felt a degree of confidence about the future. But soon this diligent, lively community was to be brought to a full stop when, in the early hours of Sunday 25 January 1959, a fire broke out in the sewing room in the west wing of the Abbey and the entire building, with its sixty-eight occupants, was put in danger.

It was a beautiful, calm, moonlit night, with no wind, but very cold and frosty. Inside the Abbey the community of thirty-six nuns, including four elderly nuns who had been invalids for some years, thirty students, aged between seven and seventeen, and two lay mistresses, were sleeping in their beds.[1] Lady Abbess Agnes would recall the events of the night many years later:

> I remember going to bed that night and it was very, very cold and I was thanking God that I had a bed to go to, and I was thinking of people who were suffering and living rough, that was what was going

through my mind. Anyway, I went to bed and I remember waking up, I think about two in the morning, and I heard a crackling sound, it had snowed a short time before that and then it had frozen over, and so I thought it was the frozen snow falling off the roof. And as I was thinking this the door opened and in came my next door neighbour, Dame Michael, "Oh! Lady Abbess there is a fire." she said. I jumped out of bed and put on the light, there was no light, the electricity had gone out, and I looked out the window and I saw, over in the distance towards the yard, flames, flames of fire. The two of us ran around waking everybody up. I ran up to the school dormitory, and I called the nun sleeping there and told her to get the girls up. We got them out the back way, there was a door leading onto the mountain at the back. If that door had not been there we would all have been burnt. We had just got out in time when the whole dormitory was up in flames. Dame Michael was great, she went around calling the nuns. I ran down to the Post Office at the gate, I couldn't get in to phone so I called up to the Post Master, Mr Fitzsimons. And after quite a lot of banging he answered the door and we rang the fire brigade in Clifden.[2]

Clifden in turn alerted the Galway, Westport and Castlebar brigades. The nuns rushed from their cells and began to congregate in the library, where the Chaplain, Rev. Fr Prendergast, had placed the Blessed Sacrament, rescued from the Chapel. On the first floor, the more lively Sisters made their way out through the French window of Sr Gabrial's room. Sr Bridget, an elderly Sister, was slow to move and had to be help by Dame Mechtilde. Willie Aspell, 'our faithful driver', was waiting outside and he, together with other men from the estate, helped the nuns around the back of the Abbey to safety: 'It was no easy trek in the dark on a very rough terrain of mountain, a true feat of gallantry on his part. Back up again we went for Sr Gabriel, an invalid for many years. But by this time she had been wrapped in blankets and shawl, helped by our faithful guide and myself [Dame Mechtilde], we set out once again, literally carrying our dear Sister to safe keeping in the Library of the main building'.[3]

The children escaped through the exit door at the end of the dormitory and were taken off to the farm under the care of Dame Agatha. Two lay teachers; Mary Murphy (22), from Abbeygate St in Galway and Maura Stephens (22), from Lower Salthill, Galway, whose room was close to the fire, jumped from their bedroom window on to a roof and were brought to safety by Willie Aspell. They arrived in the front hall with wet towels wrapped around their heads to protect themselves from the fumes.

The fire, which had begun in the sewing room in the rear of the west wing, was spreading upwards to the kitchen and laundry and up to the children's dormitory above, and the flames were clearly visible leaping out of the windows. The nuns attempted to rescue some archival material from the Bursar's office, but were beaten back. Whatever furniture could be reached was taken outside and left on the terrace. The fire quickly spread from room to room with the result that, by the time the first fire brigade arrived, the entire Venetian Wing, the rear of the central block and the bell tower, were already in flames. In an attempt to curtail its spread, Mr Doyle, the farm manager, cut down some beams and, at the request of the nuns, he placed medals of St. Benedict at all the enclosure doors. The Clifden fire brigade was first to arrive and was soon followed by the Galway brigade.

The Galway brigade had received the call at 2.20 a.m. and arrived at Kylemore in just one hour fifteen minutes. Thick fog and an icy surface made the Connemara roads treacherous, but a recently purchased Dennis F8 fire engine made the quick response time possible. In all, eight brigades from Clifden, Galway, Westport, Castlebar, Claremorris, Gort, Loughrea and Athenry were in attendance at various stages over the next couple of days: 'One by one the brigades roared down the avenue to the mansion. The engines were drawn up side by side along the lake and then a semi-circle of hoses was directed on the fire'. The Galway firemen later told the nuns that they could see 'the reflection in the sky at Recess and were sure they would be unable to control the fire'.[4] When they turned into the avenue, the fire captain later recalled being greeted by a 'magnificent view of the Abbey in flames reflected on the lake'. The Abbey had its own fire hydrants still in place since the time of Mitchell Henry, but these were of the old screw type and useless to modern equipment; in the end it was simpler for the firemen to pump up the water from Lough Pollacappul.[5]

Neighbours from far and near came to offer help. At daylight Dame Gregory fixed an altar on a small table in one of the school rooms, 'and you never saw such a motley congregation crowded around the Priest. Several nuns in the night habits with blankets or rugs around them . . . Children came with uniforms, others in night clothes, some with blankets. Two mistresses in dressing gowns. People in the next room and some of the firemen, but it was very devotional'.[6] Blackened faces peered out from under the blankets and coats: 'The air was filled with toxic acid. Everyone was suffering from running eyes and sore throats . . . Sr Martha set up a temporary kitchen unit in St Cecilia's where she provided hot cups of tea and toast to all who passed by'.[7]

Courtesy of Capt. P.B. Sugrue

Captain P.B. Sugrue, B.E.

The chief fire officer was Captain P.B. Sugrue, B.E., assisted by Station Officer J. Dolan and Sub-Officer J. Lillis.[8] According to Capt. Sugrue, the source of the fire was an electrical fault in the sewing room and could be traced to an old fuse board, which was later kept at the Galway fire station as an example of the danger of such obsolete equipment. A year earlier a fire had broken out in the same room, but this was quickly brought under control and caused little damage. Capt Sugrue had visited the Abbey on that occasion and advised the nuns to re-wire the entire building; this was in progress when the second fire broke out. Two of the firemen went into the heavy black smoke to find a trapdoor which brought them to the roof. Gingerly moving forward they began hosing down the roof, preventing its spread. Their action brought a halt to the fire and saved the Abbey from further destruction.

As the day dragged on the firemen worked, their hoses 'playing on the smouldering ashes, now and then flames would burst forth'. But they were lucky there was no wind. Some of the nuns and the two mistresses had lost all of their clothing. Captain Sugrue later took the mistresses home to Galway in his car, dressed only in their night attire.

Fireman fighting the outbreak at Kylemore Abbey yesterday.

KYLEMORE ABBEY SWEPT BY FIRE

Fireman on the roof.
Irish Press 26 January 1959

The children too lost everything: 'A fireman found the leg of a doll'. Dame Scholastica and Dame Josepha 'lost their teeth and glasses and all their clothes'. Dame Josepha was forced to retire to bed until something could be got for her. Three of the nuns went to Galway on Monday afternoon to purchase clothes and boots. As Sunday night drew in, the nuns were scattered to various houses on the estate and thirteen accepted accommodation at the Mercy Convent in Leenane.

Throughout the night the nuns could hear the fire engines working and wondered how much of their home would be left in the morning. But the fire had not spread further. In the sisters' dormitory only Sr Martha's cell was showing signs of water damage; miraculously the fire had stopped short at each door leading to the Enclosure. Deeply saddened, the nuns took stock of their loss: 'The tower bell melted into thin air . . . Leaded roofs were no more; stairways, dormitories, guest rooms were in shambles, iron bedsteads hung off the remaining turrets, a sorry sight, but thank God only goods and chattels were caught in the flames. No person was injured, all just suffering from shock'.[9] The granite walls had stood strong against the flames, but that section of the building which had not succumbed to the fire was almost all affected by the water and the heat, and was considered dangerous. Among the valuables lost was a 100 year old carpet made by Dame Xavier, one of the nuns at Ypres, and used on special occasion in the Choir: 'It was of Eastern design and was only used for very special feasts'.[10]

Among the historic articles saved from the blaze were the flag of Ramillies, the James II portrait, the lace made by Mary Queen of Scots, a broken altar stone from the Ypres monastery presented to the community by an Irish soldier and the portraits of the early Abbesses of Ypres: 'All the rest of the Sacristy things are saved, the choir was not touched, but everything was carried away in case of damage'.

On Sunday some radio reporters had called and Dame Scholastica had made a valiant appeal for help. Next morning all the daily newspapers carried pictures and reports, and the post office was inundated with telephone calls seeking news. Dame Odilon and Dame Scholastica were appointed to deal with all inquiries.[11] Sympathy for the nuns and their loss was tinged with the regret that Ireland might well lose one of its most beautifully located attractions. The *Irish Independent* commented: 'The Abbey, set in splendid scenic surroundings, has been a famous tourist centre for many years. It has accommodation for 40 guests . . . the convent has won fame as a girls school and as a centre of souvenir craftsmanship carried out by the nuns'.[12] The *Irish Press,* quoting Mrs Maureen Bailey, manager of the Irish Tourism Association offices in Galway, wrote: '"Practically everybody holidaying in the West visits Kylemore . . . this fire will be a loss for them, too." '[13]

Historic Kylemore Abbey Damaged By Fire

A view of Kylemore Abbey.

Irish Independent 26 January 1959

On Monday morning the nuns attended mass at the farm and afterwards went to the Abbey to see if there was anything they could salvage from the wreckage. The first visitor of the day was the Abbot of Glenstal, offering sympathy and support. He was followed by many more and all day long friends came with gifts and promises of future support: 'His Grace the

AFTERMATH OF FIRE

Furniture salvaged from Kylemore Abbey is placed in front of the building.

KYLEMORE ABBEY PUPILS RETURN TO HOMES

All the pupils of Kylemore Abbey, Connemara, which was damaged by fire early on Sunday morning, have returned to their homes in various parts of the country. Examination of the building yesterday revealed that the damage is more extensive than at first believed.

Much of the ceiling work and the french-polished panelling in the greater part of the Abbey suffered from effects of the fire-fighting and the heat.

Members of the community were busy yesterday searching the ruined section for lost belongings. People from the district called to the Abbey to offer assistance.

Mass was again celebrated yesterday in Adergoole House, near the community farm, as the condition of the oratory was still considered dangerous, although it was untouched by the flames.

Irish Independent 27 January 1959

Bishop of Down sent a big cheque with a letter of sympathy. The Abbot of Downside wired on Monday morning'.[14] His Grace the Archbishop of Tuam wrote saying he was heartbroken on hearing the news. Early Tuesday morning a lorry loaded with all kinds of goods arrived from Fr Laurence, the Prior of Roscrea. Later on the same day a van full of blankets and sheets etc., 'a gift of Archbishop McQuaid. Each day the post brought fresh gifts from all over Ireland, the Convents and Religious Houses excelled in offering help'.[15]

Feverish activity took place over the following days and weeks as Lady Abbess and her Council deliberated over what action to take. The extent of the damage had to be assessed, an architect and building contractor found, the cost of restoration to be established and the source for funding to be considered: 'Insurance Inspectors came and went. Volunteer Service from Galway came to remove rubble from the interior of the house. A Sale of Work was being organised, to be held in the Mansion House in Dublin. Former students then living in Boston began fund-raising. Builders, architects, contractors, plumbers, electricians all were calling to estimate the damage done and to consider what was now to be done. Hours were spent in round-table conferences'.[16]

In the meantime some of the nuns returned from Leenane and were given accommodation wherever room could be found. Four novices, accompanied by Dame Gregory, the Novice Mistress, were sent to Oulton Abbey in England to continue their studies. In time the day began to settle into a routine: 'Mass at 9.30 a.m. (we have to wait for daylight). A short thanksgiving then down to the farm. Breakfast and some return to the Abbey . . . Dinner at 2 p.m., Supper 6.30 p.m., Willie Aspell calls for the garden people at 7 p.m.', Lady Abbess made her way to Stella Maris a little later.[17]

For two days the nuns thought the Abbey cats had perished in the fire, until Dame Walburga found *Tiddles* looking lost and frightened: 'The two cats were very frightened during the fire and were not seen until Tuesday. When I came to the Abbey, *Tiddles* was crying by the back door. I called her and she came along the passage like a race horse and nearly knocked me down, she was pleased. Lady Abbess got the same welcome from her and said she was to go to Stella Maris, but yesterday Dame Bernard was tired of her. Sr Maura took her to the garden'. The second cat, *Pershy*, did not make an appearance until Thursday.[18]

In an effort to attain some degree of normality, Lady Abbess Agnes decided to go ahead with the profession of one of her novices, Maeve O'Beirne. Maeve was born in England of an Irish father and was a past pupil of the school. When the family moved to Ireland in 1938 she was sent as a boarder to the junior school. After her Leaving Certificate she studied first agriculture and later law. Although called to the Bar in 1953, she declined to practise and instead ran the family farm in Kilmessan, Co Meath. Returning to Kylemore as a postulant in 1957, she was given the name Sr Benedict in religion and was professed on 15 October 1959.

Lady Abbess and her council eventually settled on the restoration plans drawn up by the architect P.J. Sheahan from Limerick. The consulting engineers for the project were J.A. Kenny and Partners, the quantity surveyor, Henry C. Tierney and the contractor was John Sisk and Sons. Although work began almost immediately it was three years before the Abbey was fully restored and normal life resumed. The exterior of the central block of the newly restored Abbey was unaltered. Inside, however, the large rooms had, where possible, been partitioned and converted into smaller classrooms and the Venetian Wing was now purpose-built school dormitories. To the east a new two storey building had been added to accommodate the infirmary and nuns' sleeping quarters. All in all the nuns were pleased with the outcome: 'we returned to a glorious New Wing which was now called St. Joseph's, for it was through his intercession that we were able to finance the proceedings with the building. Gladly did we sing out *Te Deum* and our Divine Office once again. The fire was a blessing in disguise. We now have running water, hot water, heating in our cells, a real luxury, gratefully we sing our *Magnificat* every day. While it was a night to remember, we sing *Thank You Lord For Your Great Goodness To Us*'.[19]

Following the fire it was decided not to reopen the junior school and guesthouse. The shop at the entrance hall, selling crafts and religious objects, would be retained, but the serving of lunches and afternoon teas was to cease. The building was now more suited to accommodate students and so the nuns concentrated their efforts on expanding the boarding school and running an

English language Summer School. The Summer School ran through July and August, offering two courses of three weeks duration, and attracted students from all over Europe. Once again the nuns rolled into action. Again there was just a short break between the end of the school year and the arrival of the first group of Summer students, then a few days again between the departure of the first group and the arrival of the next. And on the departure of the second group the entire school had to be made ready for the beginning of the new school year in September. The Summer School proved to be a success and remained in operation for five years.

Chapter 16

Winds of Change

The 'big fire', as it became known at the Abbey, had brought many changes to community life, but nothing in the community's history quite equalled the dramatic changes brought about by the Second Vatican Council. Pope John XXIII convoked the Second Vatican Council in 1961, to initiate changes, in keeping with tradition, that would better equip the Church for the modern world. All Catholics would be affected by the deliberations and decrees of the Council, but those most affected undoubtedly were the priests and other religious.

For the monastic community, the major change was juridical. As well as the Rule of St Benedict, the nuns are obliged to follow Constitutions, approved by the Holy See: 'The Constitutions interpret the precept of the Rule in accordance with the spirit and sound tradition of monastic life'.[1] The Constitutions for Kylemore Abbey were approved by the Holy See in 1939, but these had to be adapted to incorporate all changes resulting from Vatican II.

Up until this time a woman entering an enclosed community was expected to live out her life within the monastery boundaries, with little or no contact with the outside world. She left behind her family, friends and the world in general and gave over her life to prayer, community life and work in the service of the community and others. The nuns were permitted visits from their immediate family and friends, but these would be few and far between. They were allowed out into the world to attend college, for medical reasons and on short trips to attend to community business. Some spent time in other convents, often abroad, either for health reasons, to further their education or to develop some skill needed to enhance community life. With Vatican 11 all of that was to change.

Under the changes the division of Choir Dame and lay sister, or Converse sister, was dispensed with; from then on the title Sister was given to all. The daily prayer was shortened and changed from Latin to the vernacular: devotions that had grown up during the centuries were dropped, but all liturgical prayer was kept. The vernacular, however, did not entirely supersede Latin at Kylemore, Latin Vespers are still sung each Sunday evening and plainchant remains the dominant music in the nuns' worship.

The monastic habit was modified, but not abandoned: the very wide sleeves were narrowed and the headgear was simplified. Elections for the position of Abbess were to be held every six years, and not on the death of the Abbess, as was the practice up until then. At Kylemore Lady Abbess Agnes asked that her title be changed to Mother Abbess. The Council's hope for Church Unity was warmly adopted by Kylemore and each year the community hosts a Church Unity Day for clergy of all denominations. The event is recognised as one of the most important ecumenical events in the Archdiocese of Tuam.

By far the most popular change to come under Vatican 11 was the one which allowed the nuns regular trips home to visit aging parents and to holiday with family and friends. However, for many that first trip home had come too late, forbidden under the strict rules of enclosure to attend the funerals of their parents, the irony of being allowed home to an empty house was not lost on them.

To assist her in this transition, Mother Abbess Agnes attended week-long seminars in England, accompanied by Sr Benedict O'Beirne. There she joined Abbesses from Benedictine houses in Britain to discuss and debate how best to move forward in the spirit of Vatican 11. A strongly rooted community such as Kylemore was not shaken or shattered by the winds of change. Adaptations were calmly accepted, without fuss, and with no loss of the essential monastic vocation. However, it was some years before the many changes demanded by the Council were fully implemented and it was 1981 before new Constitutions, drawn up by the community, were approved. During this time the community continued to attract novices: Sr Peter Gallagher, professed in 1965, Sr Clare Morley, professed in 1967, Sr Magdalena FitzGibbon, professed in 1970, Sr Josephine O'Malley, professed in 1976, Sr Dorothy Ryan, professed in 1979, Sr Karol O'Connell, professed in 1982, Sr Marie Bernard Crossan, professed in 1983, Sr Rosario Ni Fhlaherta, professed in 1984 and Sr M Aidan Ryan, professed in 1988. The community also welcomed into their midst Sr Bernard Hayes, Sr Margaret Mary Powell and Dame Mary Groves, all of whom were members of the Benedictine community at Oulton Abbey in Staffordshire, England.

Despite the closing down of the guesthouse, visitors continued to flock to the doors of the Abbey. Drawn by the beauty of its location and by the peaceful ambiance of its surroundings, they came seeking entry to the Abbey and grounds, and to purchase a souvenir in the craft shop. To expand the range of crafts on offer Mother Abbess Agnes, with the assistance of her Bursar, Sr John, succeeded in acquiring a small business loan from Bord Tráchtála (Board of Trade) and a small pottery was set up close to the Abbey. Shortly thereafter it became obvious that the building was unsuitable and the decision was made to convert the old coach house into a pottery, shop and tea room.

Members of Bord Tráchtála and Bord Fáilte (Irish Tourist Board) came to Kylemore and, recognizing the potential for further development, allocated grants to assist the nuns in their efforts. With the rise of tourist numbers in the area, Bord Fáilte was anxious to offer Kylemore Abbey as a tourist destination. Their encouragement and advice was greatly appreciated by the nuns and fully acted upon. Sr Agatha travelled to Youghal Pottery to train as a potter and, with the closure of the Summer School, more nuns were employed in the shop and tea rooms.

© Kylemore Abbey

Sr Agatha Martin with Kylemore pottery

Far reaching changes were also underway at the school and farm. With the introduction of free student transport by the government in the 1960s accommodation was no longer required for local girls and the number of day pupils rose rapidly. The boarding school continued to attract students

Students in the 1940s

from Europe, the United States of America, Australia and Mexico, as well as those from Ireland. To cater for the increase in numbers the teaching staff was increased to sixteen lay teachers and five nuns. The curriculum continued to be that laid down by the Department of Education, with extra subjects added to suit the demands of the day, such as computer studies, music, speech and drama, languages and sports.

In the meantime the nuns began scaling down the farm. Throughout the 1950s the rising cost of labour lead to a slow but steady curtailment of

© Kylemore Abbey

Students in the 1950s

© Kylemore Abbey

agricultural activity. In the 1960s the sheep flock was sold, cattle and a small number of cows were kept, and all the arable land was converted to grassland. When the Christian Brothers Industrial School at Letterfrack was closed down in 1973 the Office of Public Works, who were interested in making a National Park in Connemara, purchased the land. The OPW then approached the nuns and eventually purchased one thousand acres; part of the townlands of Addergoole and Mweelin, for a sum of £44,000, which was subsequently incorporated into the National Park. The nuns continue to farm the remainder and Addergoole farmhouse has been retained for community and school use. Lack of funds in the 1960s and 1970s saved the old farm buildings from 'modern' redevelopment, with the result that the farm is a lovely example of almost two hundred years of agricultural development and practices. The farmyard alone, with its pre and post Famine buildings, is thought to be one of the finest examples of agricultural heritage to be found in Ireland.

At present, the nuns hold 290 hectares (under 1,000 acres), of which 46 hectares is set aside for grazing, the rest comprises forestry, mountain and lake. Under the supervision of Sr Benedict, they keep cattle and suckler cows, selling the calves as weanlings, and make silage rather than hay. They joined the Rural Environmental Protection Scheme in 1997, and are continuing to work within that scheme. The Scheme encourages farmers to farm in an environmentally friendly manner in keeping with traditional methods and habitat conservation. The farm still provides eggs, butter, jams, Christmas cakes and puddings for the Abbey and shop.

© Kylemore Abbey

Sr Benedict O'Beirne

Having successfully guided the community through this period of change and development, Mother Agnes, after twenty-eight years as Abbess, took advantage of the provision allowed under Vatican II, and resigned voluntarily in 1981, the first Abbess of the community to do so.

In the twenty years that followed Mother Agnes's resignation the community elected three Abbesses, each of whom played her part in successfully guiding the community through times of change and challenge.

© Kylemore Abbey

© Kylemore Abbey

© Kylemore Abbey

Mother Abbess Mechtilde Moloney (1981–1987)

Mother Abbess Mary O'Toole (198 –1993)

Mother Abbess Clare Morley (1993–2001)

Mother Abbess Mechtilde Moloney (1981–1987), was born in Limerick and professed in 1945. She was Prioress for twenty-eight years, was a teacher in the school and Bursar to the community. Her sister, Sr Michael, is also a member of the community.

Mother Abbess Mary O'Toole (1987–1993), was born in Clifden, Co Galway. A student at the school before entering the monastery in 1944, she was professed in 1946. She was Bursar to the community and Headmistress of the school for twenty-five years.

Mother Abbess Clare Morley (1993–2001), was born in Clarecastle, Co Clare and professed on 21 October 1965. A teacher in the school for over twenty years, she was Novice Mistress for nine years and Headmistress for two years.

In more recent times the community had to face the fact that the Abbey and many of the buildings on the estate were in serious need of repair and restoration. Thirty years on from the fire, the Abbey was showing signs of deterioration, there was dry rot in the walls and the roof was leaking in several places. At the time the community consisted of twenty-six nuns, fifteen of whom were over sixty-five. For Sr Magdalena, the recently appointed Bursar, a quick glance at the books was sufficient to give a clear indication that five teaching salaries and a fledgling tourism industry was insufficient to sustain an aging community and to maintain Kylemore, if it was to remain their home:

In times of rainstorm sections of the Abbey roof began to collapse and any monies that we made really went into that – restoration, restoration – it become a reoccurring word, an everyday word at Kylemore. We just had to address it as it happened . . . .the school had to be repaired, next the farm house was repaired and then we went around the entire place doing a little bit here, a little bit there, plugging the holes, more or less . . . we opened up a patch of the wall in the main hall and found dry rot behind the panels; we had to go up three stories to have the rot removed. There were mushrooms like faces looking out at us, it was absolutely horrendous, very frightening, some of us even had nightmares afterwards. And I wonder if it is fully under control even yet. One can only hope.[2]

Sr Magdalena made it her personal mission to conserve the Abbey so that the Benedictine tradition could live on in its ideal setting. Like her predecessor, Dame Odilon, she decided to allow the estate itself be a source of revenue for the community, and in so doing enable the public to partake of that peace and tranquillity which is so much a part of the Abbey and so essential an ingredient in the community's way of life.

In the decade leading up to the Millennium Sr Magdalena, with the support and backing of her Abbess and community, took on project after

Sr Josephine, Sr Peter, Sr Magdalena, Sr Dorothy, Mother Agnes, Mother Abbess Mary and Dom Paul McDonnell O.S.B.

© Kylemore Abbey

project to restore the Abbey and the key heritage features on the estate. First to be tackled was the school, next the dry rot in the Abbey building itself and at the same time the grounds were cleared and the old walks revealed. The shop and tea-rooms were enlarged to cater for the steady increase in visitor numbers, and by 1993 the main hall and some of the reception rooms were restored and open to the public.

© Kylemore Abbey

President Mary Robinson and the Community at the reopening of the Gothic Church 28 April 1995

When work on the Abbey was completed the nuns turned their attention to the Gothic Church, which was in an extraordinary state of disrepair and had been closed for almost twenty years. The deterioration of the building had led to major problems with dampness and its future lay in doubt. The certain loss of such an architectural gem became of great concern to the community and to their visitors, as Sr Magdalena would later explain: 'People would come and say, "will you ever restore and re-open it", and they would frequently give a contribution, by way of encouragement, and so there was always a small fund in a special bank account for the restoration of the church. Well, would we or wouldn't we, was the question. If it were not restored, it would be irretrievably lost and that would be so sad, particularly because it was a church, and we felt we could not let it happen'. Ireland would have lost a significant piece of its architectural heritage. But to restore the building to its former splendour would require heavy borrowing, the employment of outside expertise and great patience on the part of the community: 'It was a tremendous task, but it meant an awful lot to us and we could not let it deteriorate any further. So we took on the actual challenge of restoration. And thankfully God gave us the necessary strength and courage to meet the challenge'.[3]

Following consultation with her financial advisors it was estimated that the works would cost in excess of £500,000. Sr Magdalena drew up a business plan and set to work attracting financial support from friends of the community, benefactors, past pupils, the National Heritage Council and European Regional Development Funds. The restoration work began in 1991, under the direction of Timothy Foley, of Buchan Kane & Foley Architects, and was completed in 1995.

On 28 April 1995, the nuns were proud to welcome President Mary Robinson to the Abbey for the official reopening of the Church, which was blessed by Michael Neary D.D., Archbishops of Tuam. In preparation for the opening the east avenue, which had been abandoned for many years, was cleared and landscaped.

In keeping with the spirit of conservation the community also undertook a tree planting project to regenerate the wonderful woodland. This led, naturally enough, to thoughts of restoring the Victorian Walled Garden. The restoration of the garden was to prove an even more daunting task and again large funds were needed. Since the departure of Mitchell Henry the garden had gone into decline, with the result that by the time the

Dr James McDaid, Minister for Tourism, Sport & Recreation, with Head Gardener Ann Golden and members of the restoration team, at the reopening of the Walled Garden 13 October 2000

© Kylemore Abbey

nuns arrived some of the glasshouses had already been dismantled. The nuns did not require the vast array of flowers offered by the garden, neither did they need the exotic fruits from the glasshouse and they certainly could not afford their upkeep. They employed a Head Gardener until the 1940s and kept up the vegetable garden, a small flower garden and some of the fruit trees. But as the years went by, and labour grew expensive, and the number of young novices began to fall, the garden was becoming more and more difficult to retain. Sr Benedict, with the help of two local gardeners, Mike Thornton and John Joyce, brought the entire garden back under cultivation for a brief period in the 1960s. However, in time it proved more cost effective to buy in vegetables and fruit, and so gradually sections of the garden were abandoned and left to nature.

Restoration work began in 1995 and is still ongoing. The first phase was expected to cost £1.6 million. The nuns contribution was in excess of £800,000, which was raised through bank loans and fundraising, and the final figure was reached with financial assistance from the European Regional Development Fund, under the Great Gardens of Ireland Restoration Programme which is administered by Board Fáilte, with the assistance of FÁS Community Employment Scheme and the Heritage Council of Ireland. The garden was officially opened by Dr James McDaid T.D., Minister for Tourism, Sport and Recreation, on 13 October 2000. The projected cost of the second phase, the restoration of the glasshouses, is estimated at £2 million.

Since the opening up of the Abbey, Gothic Church and Victorian Walled Garden the community has become one of the biggest employers in north-west Connemara, with up to one hundred and thirty employed there at the height of the tourist season. Many members of staff are direct descendants of Mitchell Henry's tenants and former students of Kylemore school.

**Kylemore Staff
May 2002**

Back Row Left to Right: Ollie Gray, Petrina Coyne, Michelle Conroy, Ann Guy, Kathy Snow and Bridget Nee. Front Row: Pauline Lydon, Siobhan O'Neill, Isabelle Pittorie, Marianne McDermott and Mary Coyne.

© Kylemore Abbey

Back Row Left to Right: Mary Ruddy,
Margaret-Anne O'Neill, Kathleen Faherty
and Margaret Curley.
Front Row: Tracey Nolan and Christine
Folan.

© Kylemore Abbey

Paddy Joe Joyce, Declan Guy, Padraic
Faherty & Joe Mannion.

© Kylemore Abbey

© Kylemore Abbey

Back Row Left to Right: Louise Boyland, Barbara Aspell and Bridget Madden. Front Row: Donal Coyne, John Noel Mullen and Mary Stanton.

At a time when other communities are closing their schools and selling off their property, Kylemore Abbey is one of the few remaining girls' boarding schools left in the country. In the year 2002 there are one hundred and sixty-two pupils attending the school, eighty of whom are boarders. Included in the 6th year class photograph for 2002 is Rajkumari Yogini Kumari of Sirohi, standing in the spot occupied by her grandmother, Rajkumari Rajendra Kumari of Jamnagar, in the 1930s school photograph. Princess Yogini was completing her second year at Kylemore and was due to sit her leaving certificate examination before returning home to India in June.

© Kylemore Abbey

Final year students 2002

217

The school continues to attain high standards in scholarship and music, and now, for the first time in its history, it has a lay Principal. The community still maintains an active presence within the school, on the Board of Management, as members of the teaching staff, as supervisors and counsellors.

The Kylemore community at the time of writing stands at eighteen; six members, including two former Abbesses, having passed away in the previous three years. It remains the only Benedictine community for nuns in Ireland and, like other religious orders, is experiencing a serious decline in vocations. Sr Benedict, the community archivist is, however, optimistic: 'This House has witnessed a fall in numbers in the past and has survived to tell the tale. This too shall pass. And today's dilemma will simply be a case study for the historians of the future'.

However, although few in number, the nuns at Kylemore are as firm in their mission today as at any time in the Order's three hundred and thirty year history. As a community, the nuns live a lifestyle which has been part of the tradition of the Roman Catholic church for over a thousand years. As individuals they were drawn to this life by a strong belief in the power of prayer and in the beauty of the plainchant. They chose the Benedictine Order because of its commitment to Prayer and Work – *Ora et Labora*.

Nolan in his book, *The Irish Dames Of Ypres*, writes of the importance of prayer in the world:

> Today, as always, it is impossible to measure the importance of prayer in the life of the individual and in the life of the Church. It is also impossible to measure its effects, only the individual can give testimony to that and the skeptic will always find a more practical explanation for almost every event or happening. But for those who believe, the need for prayer and contemplation and intercession is as real today as it was at anytime in the past.

Kylemore Abbey attracts a vast number of visitors each year, all of whom are welcomed in the spirit of St Benedict and invited to participate in the community liturgy and prayer. Those unable to do so may have their special intentions recorded in the main hall of the Abbey, for inclusion in the community's prayers. It is the community's intention that all who visit the Abbey can find 'a haven for personal reflection where one can contemplate the Love of God and His place in their lives':

> Our mission as Benedictine women is to live in community, sharing our liturgy and hospitality with all, in a spirit of peace in and for the world.[4]

In the autumn of 2001 the nuns elected their former Bursar, Sr Magdalena, as their new Abbess. The Abbatial Blessing took place on 8 December 2001 and was conferred by Archbishop Michael Neary, D.D., in attendance was Dom Paul McDonnell O.S.B.; community Chaplain, several abbots and abbesses, the Church of Ireland Archbishop of Dublin, Dr Walton Empey, the Bishop of Tuam, Rev. Dr Richard Henderson, local Catholic clergy, the Abbess's family and community friends. During the ceremony Mother Abbess Magdalena was presented with the staff of office, a ring and a pectoral cross. In a tradition unique to this house, she was also presented with the Ypres Crozier, a silver Abbatial crozier dating from 1721. To mark the occasion, Dom Paul wore the 17th century Ypres vestments, made from the dress of Archduchess Isabella of Spain, and lovingly protected by the nuns down through the centuries.

Taking cognizance of the past history of the community and of the house, the new Abbess is confident for the future. Kylemore will continue to welcome pilgrims to its doors and to offer them the opportunity to share in community prayer:

© Kylemore Abbey

Mother Abbess Magdalena FitzGibbon, 7th Abbess of Kylemore. 8 September 2001

© Kylemore Abbey

Rev. Joe Quinn, Adm. Tuam; Right Rev. Dr Richard Henderson, Bishop of Tuam; Mother Abbess Magdalena FitzGibbon; Most Rev. Dr Michael Neary, Archbishop of Tuam; Most Rev. Dr Walton Empey, Archbishop of Dublin and Dom Paul McDonnell O.S.B.

'We need to enable people to visit our Abbey and encourage them to pray with us. For us, enclosure is not about exclusion, it is about inclusion, the fruit of which is, sharing with all who come to our monastery, particularly with those who are lonely and the disaffected. Our stability and spirituality give us a deep and rich humanity and a peace, which is the tranquillity of order. As Tennyson says, "more things are wrought by prayer than the world dreams of". St Benedict would have us *listen* – "to leave more open, than ever before, the living door which is Christ" for the new generation.

I believe Monastic life holds a key to the secret of stability, peace and tranquillity. We, then, have a responsibility towards the healing of society, to help, through our liturgy, our prayer life and our hospitality, through our *Ora et Labora*. This is the challenge of the new millennium for us in Kylemore'.[5]

© Kylemore Abbey

Mother Mechtilde Moloney,
Mother Abbess Magdalena FitzGibbon
and Mother Clare Morley

Kylemore Community 2002

Left to Right Back Row: Sr Dorothy Ryan, Sr Benedict O'Beirne, Sr Margaret Mary Powell, Mother Mary Clare Morley, Sr Dymphna Conroy, Sr Aidan Ryan, Sr Michael Moloney

Middle Row: Mother Mechtilde Moloney, Mother Josephine O'Malley, Dame Mary Groves, Mother Abbess Magdalena FitzGibbon, Sr Bernard Hayes

Front Row: Sr Rosario Ni Fhlatherta, Sr Karol O'Connell, Sr Marie Bernard Crossan, Sr Noreen Peter Gallagher and Sr John O'Malley

(Sr Pius O'Meara absent)

© Kylemore Abbey

Epilogue

Throughout the one hundred and forty year history of the Kylemore Estate it has been recognised that Mitchell Henry somehow managed to encapsulate, within its environs, an aura of peace and tranquillity. With the arrival of the Benedictine Community this was transformed by a spiritual mission, so that for the Community, and for their many visitors, Kylemore came to provide the space, in time and location, for the contemplation of the Divine.

Henry viewed his achievements at Kylemore as a successful social experiment. For the nuns, the measure of their success will not be reckoned in this world, but in the next.

The social impact of the nuns on this northern corner of Connemara has been considerable. The nuns brought with them a tradition of prayer, education and hospitality and recent restoration works has brought both employment and enhanced tourism in the region.

The restoration work carried out by the nuns has also brought into focus the significant contribution the Kylemore Estate makes to the heritage of the county. The study of Kylemore contributes greatly to our understanding of 19th century life in County Galway. It shows the advances made in agriculture, fisheries, horticulture and engineering at that time.

With a sensitive restoration plan the nuns have given us back an architectural treasure in the Gothic Church and a place of great beauty in the Walled Garden. The true genius of Mitchell Henry's agriculture engineering still lies undisturbed at the Monastery's farmyard, where 19th century buildings and engineering works await restoration.

Kylemore is as vibrant today as at any time in its history and still retains a duel focus; for the community within, the focus is on the eternal, for the community without, with the nuns working as a leaven, the focus is on a treasured resource and inspiring heritage.

The future is a closed book to us. But the history of Kylemore and the special genius of its location would fortify one's hope and belief that those who live and work and pray there would find it an inspiring home for many more generations into the future.

Appendix I

Tenants for the townlands of Mullaghglass, Lemnaheltia, Lettergesh West, Tooreena, Shanaveag, Currywongaun, Pollacappul, Lettergesh East, as listed in property deed, dated 1854.

No	Denominations	Tenants	Rent when due
1	Mullaghgloss	widow Coyne and Conelly	May and November
2	"	Valentine Conelly	"
3	"	Thomas Conelly	"
4	"	Frank Carney	"
5	"	Toby Cribben	"
6	"	Michael Coyne	"
7	"	Michael McAneboy	"
8	"	James Donellan	"
9	"	Thomas Donellan	"
10	"	Cormick Farty	"
11	"	Michael Farty	"
12	"	Thomas Foland	"
13	"	Martin Coyne	"
14	"	Patrick Faherty	"
15	"	John Gibbons	"
16	"	John Gibbons	"
17	"	John Gibbons Harry	"
18	"	Patt Gibbons	"
19	"	Myles Gibbons	"
20	"	Peter Joyce	"
21	"	Thomas Joyce	"
22	"	Martin Joyce	"
23	"	Widow Joyce	"
24	"	Andrew Mally	"
25	"	widow Mally	"
26	"	John and Michael Reynolds	"
27	"	Valentine Conelly	"
28	"	John Lyden	"
29	Mullaghgloss Mountain	Martin Joyce and others	"
30	Lemnaheltia	Patrick O'Neil	March & September
31	Lettergesh West	Walter Joyce and others	"
32	Toorena (part of)	Walter Joyce	"
33	Toorena and Mullaghglofs part of	John Coure	"
34	Shanaveg	Edward Unsworth and Richard Andaton	-
35	Currywongan	Rodger Coyne and others	"
36	Currywongan	John and Michael Lyden	May & November
37	Pollacappul	Martin Coyne	March & September
38	Lettergesh East (part of)	Anthony Diamond and others	"
39	Ditto (other part of)	Thomas King	"
40	Ditto (other part of)	Farby Nee	"
41	Cottage and garden	Thomas Hynes	"

222

Years	Rent		Terms
	£	s	d
2	8	8	At will or from year to year
3	4	0	"
4	1	0	"
.	17	6	"
1	.	.	"
.	15	.	"
1	.	.	"
2	"	"	"
2	"	"	"
3	18	0	"
1	3	4	"
3	3	4	"
2	.	"	"
4	15	.	"
1	10	8	"
2	.	.	"
2	"	"	"
2	10	.	"
3	"	"	"
5	4	4	"
3	13	10	"
3	8	"	"
2	"	"	"
2	10	.	"
4	6	.	"
4	13	8	"
1	10	0	"
1	.	.	"
10	10	.	
22	"	"	Lease expiring 29th Sept. 1874
115	"	.	Same
30	"	"	Same
120	.	"	Same
18	"	"	Same
28	"	"	Same
8	"	"	At will or from year to year
34	"	"	Lease expiring 29th Sept. 1874
100	"	"	Lease or Agreement for a Lease expiring 29th September 1874
20	.	"	Lease expiring 29th Sept. 1874
20	"	"	Lease or Agreement for Lease expiring 29th September 1874
"	1	0	Lease or Agreement for a Lease expiring 29th Sept. 1874

Richard Griffith, *General Valuation of Ratable Properties in Ireland*, Co Galway, 1855.

PARISH OF BALLYNAKILL.

No. and Letters of Reference to Map.	Names.		Description of Tenement.	Area.	Rateable Annual Valuation.		Total Annual Valuation of Rateable Property.
	Townlands and Occupiers.	Immediate Lessors.			Land.	Buildings.	
	ADDERGOOLE. (Ord. S. 23.)						
1.	Thomas Eastwood,	Robert Graham,	Ho., offs., gate bldg., &ld.	913 0 31	34 0 0	20 0 0	54 0 0
2.	Robert Graham,	In fee,	Bog,	1695 3 30	20 0 0		20 0 0
3	Martin O'Flaherty,	Robert Graham,	Land,	45 1 35	1 0 0		1 0 0
			Water,	4 1 0			
			Total,	2658 3 25	55 0 0	20 0 0	75 0 0
	CURRYWONGAUN. (Ord. S. 10 & 23.)			A. R. P.	£ s. d.	£ s. d.	£ s. d.
1 a	St. John L. Clowes,	St. John L. Clowes,	House, offices, and land,	591 3 0	25 10 0	2 10 0	28 0 0
b	Anne Coyne,		House and garden,	0 1 7	0 5 0	0 7 0	0 12 0
2 A			Land,	4 3 27	0 10 0		
B	Roger Coyne,	Same,	House, office, and land,	13 3 16	2 10 0	0 10 0	3 15 0
C			Land,	3 1 13	0 5 0		
B			Land,	4 2 16	0 10 0		
A	Ellen Coyne,	Same,	Land,	21 2 9	3 0 0		4 0 0
B			House and office,			0 10 0	
1 c			Water,	4 2 28			
			Total,	644 3 36	32 10 0	3 17 0	36 7 0
	DAWROSMORE. (Ord. S. 10 & 23.)						
1	Edward Valalley,	Robert J. Wilberforce,	House and land,	7 2 27	0 18 0	0 7 0	1 5 0
2	Martin R. Harte,	Same,	Herd's ho., offs., & land,	340 1 6	49 5 0	0 15 0	50 0 0
a	John Heany,		House and land,		3 8 0	0 7 0	3 15 0
b	Roger Coyne,		House and land,		2 7 0	0 5 0	2 12 0
c	Mary Joyce,		House and land,		1 3 0	0 5 0	1 8 0
d	John Lydon,		House and land,		3 10 0	0 5 0	3 15 0
e	Bridget Conneely,		House, office, & land,		3 18 0	0 7 0	4 5 0
3 f	Thomas Conneely,	Same,	House and land,	123 1 38	2 0 0	0 7 0	2 7 0
g	Thomas Coyne,		House and land,		2 0 0	0 5 0	2 5 0
h	William Wallace,		House and land,		2 0 0	0 5 0	2 5 0
i	Michael Butler,		House and land,		2 0 0	0 7 0	2 7 0
j	Patrick Mongan,		House and land,		2 0 0	0 7 0	2 7 0
k	John Conroy,		House and land,		2 0 0	0 7 0	2 7 0
a	Doctor Lane,		Office and land,		3 0 0	0 5 0	3 5 0
b	Margaret Butler,		House and land,		0 15 0	0 5 0	1 0 0
c	John Kelly,		House, office, & land,		3 0 0	0 10 0	3 10 0
d	Martin Walsh,		House and land,		0 15 0	0 10 0	1 5 0
e	John Nee,		House and land,		1 0 0	0 10 0	1 10 0
f	Michael Mullen,		House and land,		0 13 0	0 5 0	0 18 0
4 g	Thomas Kelly,	Same,	House and land,	141 0 13	1 3 0	0 10 0	1 13 0
h	Margaret Fitzpatrick,		House and land,		0 15 0	0 5 0	1 0 0
i	Henry Mongan,		House and land,		0 13 0	0 5 0	0 18 0
j	Ambrose Bourke,		House and land,		1 0 0	0 5 0	1 5 0
k	Michael Cannivan,		House and land,		0 10 0	0 5 0	0 15 0
l	Margaret Kealy,		House and land,		0 10 0	0 5 0	0 15 0
m	Hugh Bourke,		House and land,		0 10 0	0 5 0	0 15 0
			Total,	612 2 4	90 13 0	8 14 0	99 7 0
	Three Islands belonging to Tenants of Dawrosmore (of no agricultural value).			0 0 28	—	—	—

PARISH OF BALLYNAKILL.

No. and Letters of Reference to Map.	Names.		Description of Tenement.	Area.	Rateable Annual Valuation.		Total Annual Valuation of Rateable Property.
	Townlands and Occupiers.	Immediate Lessors.			Land.	Buildings.	
				A. R. P.	£ s. d.	£ s. d.	£ s. d.
LEMNAHELTIA (Ord. S. 10, 11, & 23.)							
1	St. John L. Clowes,	Robert J. Wilberforce,	Herd's house and land,	736 0 3	10 0 0	0 5 0	0 5 0
			Total,	736 0 3	10 0 0	0 5 0	0 5 0
LETTERGESH, EAST. (Ord. S 10 & 11.)							
1	St. John L. Clowes,	Robert J. Wilberforce,	Herd's ho., off., & land,	1036 2 26	70 0 0	1 10 0	71 10 0
2	Patrick Coyne,	St. John L. Clowes,	House, office, and land,	9 2 37	2 10 0	0 7 0	2 17 0
3	Michael Lyden,	Same,	House and land,	1 1 10	0 5 0	0 5 0	0 10 0
4 a	Thomas King,	Same,	House, office, and land,	730 1 18	13 0 0	1 0 0	14 0 0
b	Simon Flaherty,	Thomas King,	House,			0 8 0	0 8 0
5 a	Thaddeus Thornton,	St. John L. Clowes,	Herd's house & land, }	367 2 15	7 5 0	0 5 0	7 10 0
b	Jeremiah Xée,	Thaddeus Thornton,	House, office, & land, }		3 15 0	0 5 0	4 0 0
			Water,	35 0 2			
			Total,	2180 2 28	96 15 0	4 0 0	100 15 0
LETTERGESH, WEST. (Ord. S 10.)							
1	St. John L. Clowes,	Robert J. Wilberforce,	Herd's house and land,	1164 0 2	79 0 0	1 0 0	80 0 0
			Water,	21 3 38			
			Total,	1166 0 0	79 0 0	1 0 0	80 0 0
	One Island belonging to	*St. John L. Clowes (of no*	*agricultural value),*	0 0 13	—	—	—
MULLAGHGLASS (Ord. E 10.)							
1 A	Thomas Joyce,	St. John L. Clowes, {	House, offices, and land,	0 3 2	0 5 0	0 10 0	3 0 0
B			Land,	5 3 20	2 5 0		
2 a	Peter Joyce,	Same,	House and land,	11 3 2	3 13 0	0 7 0	4 0 0
b	John Gibbons,	Peter Joyce,	House,			0 5 0	0 5 0
3	Myles Gibbons,	St. John L. Clowes,	House, office, and land,	5 3 36	2 7 0	0 8 0	2 15 0
4	John Gibbons,	Same,	House, office, and land,	8 0 6	1 17 0	0 8 0	2 5 0
5	Margaret Joyce,	Same,	House and land,	70 1 8	2 3 0	0 7 0	2 10 0
6	Martin Joyce,	Same,	House, office, and land,	5 3 7	1 5 0	0 5 0	1 10 0
7	Michael M'Narvy,	Same,	House, office, and land,	3 3 21	1 2 0	0 5 0	1 7 0
8	John Reynolds,	Same,	House, office, and land,	9 3 10	3 3 0	0 7 0	3 10 0
9	Thomas Folan, }	Same, {	House, office, & land, }	6 1 12	1 0 0	0 5 0	1 5 0
	Michael Faherty,		Land,		1 0 0		1 0 0
10	Michael Faherty and Michael Coyne,	Same,	House and land,	4 2 33	1 5 0	0 5 0	1 10 0
11	Patrick Faherty, } Martin Coyne,	Same, {	House and land, }	10 0 0	1 10 0	0 5 0	1 15 0
			House and land,		1 10 0	0 5 0	1 15 0
12	Michael Morrin,	Same,	Land,	8 0 0	2 0 0		2 0 0
a	Mary Lydon,	Same,	House,	—	—	0 5 0	0 5 0
13	Bridget Mealy, } Andrew Mealy,	Same, {	House and land, }	6 3 7	1 5 0	0 5 0	1 10 0
			House and land,		1 5 0	0 5 0	1 10 0
14	Thomas Conneely, } Valentine Conneely,	Same, {	House, office, & land, }	5 2 8	0 18 0	0 7 0	1 5 0
			House and land,		0 17 0	0 8 0	1 5 0
15	Valentine Conneely, } Catherine Coyne,	Same, {	Land, }	4 3 35	0 15 0		0 15 0
			House and land,		0 15 0	0 5 0	1 0 0
16	James Donlan,	Same,	House, office, and land,	9 0 36	1 10 0	0 5 0	1 15 0
17	St. John L. Clowes,	Robert J. Wilberforce,	Land,	751 0 34	45 0 0		45 0 0
a	Patrick Gibbons,	St. John L. Clowes,	House,			0 5 0	0 5 0
18	Thomas Donnelly,	Same,	House and land,	4 2 0	1 10 0	0 7 0	1 17 0
			Total,	874 1 37	80 0 0	6 14 0	86 14 0

PARISH OF BALLYNAKILL.

No. and Letters of Reference to Map.	Names.		Description of Tenement.	Area.	Rateable Annual Valuation.		Total Annual Valuation of Rateable Property.
	Townlands and Occupiers.	Immediate Lessors.			Land.	Buildings.	
1	MWEELIN. (Ord. S. 23.) Rev. Joseph Duncan,	In fee,	Herd's house and land,	652 3 29	17 10 0	0 10 0	18 0 0
			Total,	652 3 29	17 10 0	0 10 0	18 0 0
	POLLACAPPUL. (Ord. S. 10 & 23.)			A. R. P.	£ s. d.	£ s. d.	£ s. d.
1 a 2	St. John L. Clowes, John Coyne,	Robert J. Wilberforce, St. John L. Clowes,	Land House Land Water	1051 1 36 5 2 15 20 0 15	23 0 0 2 0 0	0 5 0	23 0 0 2 5 0
			Total,	1077 0 36	25 0 0	0 5 0	25 5 0
1	SHANAVEAG. (Ord. S. 10.) Richard Anderson and Edward Hemsworth,	St. John L. Clowes,	Herd's ho., off., & land,	287 1 39	10 5 0	0 15 0	11 0 0
			Total,	287 1 39	10 5 0	0 15 0	11 0 0
	TOOREENA. (Ord. S. 10.)			A. R. P.	£ s. d.	£ s. d.	£ s. d.
1 2 3 4 5 6 7 8	St. John L. Clowes, Michael Morrin, Anthony Faherty, John Garvey, Patrick Coyne, Thomas Heany, Michael Sullivan, Thomas Sullivan,	Robert J. Wilberforce, St. John L. Clowes, Same, Same, Same, Same, Same, Same,	Land, House and land, House and land, House and land, House, office, and land, House and land, House, office, and land, House and land,	831 0 38 6 3 20 6 2 29 3 3 20 5 3 36 0 3 27 22 1 38 3 3 20	68 0 0 1 0 0 1 5 0 0 15 0 0 17 0 0 10 0 3 0 0 1 5 0	0 10 0 0 5 0 0 5 0 0 8 0 0 5 0 0 15 0 0 5 0	68 0 0 1 10 0 1 10 0 1 0 0 1 5 0 0 15 0 3 15 0 1 10 0
			Total,	885 3 33	76 12 0	2 13 0	79 5 0

226

Appendix I

Tenants names taken from The Freeman's Journal 10 January 1878.

MR. M. HENRY, M.P., AND HIS TENANTS

TO THE EDITOR OF THE FREEMAN.

Currywongane, Kylemore, Galway,
January 8th.

SIR—Presuming on your love of justice, we trust you will kindly publish the accompanying protest from the entire tenantry of the Kylemore estate, every one of whom have gratefully testified that Mr. Henry has done more for them than any landlord ever did.—Signed on behalf of the tenantry,

JOHN COYNE, Tenant.
THOMAS SULLIVAN, do.
STEPHEN WALLACE, do.

The following is the document referred to :—

We, the entire tenantry of the Kylemore estate of Mitchell Henry, Esq., M.P., having heard with deep regret of the base calumny against our generous and liberal landlord, Mr. Henry, MP, think it our duty to give publicity to our feelings of indignation, and to contradict the totally unfounded charge made against his character at the Clifden meeting.

We always believed Mr. Henry to be a kind and considerate landlord, and feel bound to say in justice to Mr. Henry that to our knowledge there never was a single tenant evicted off the Kylemore estate since Mr. Henry became proprietor of it.

We have ever known him to be generous and charitable, and we feel deeply grateful for all his goodness to us.   (Signed)

Martin Coyne, John Coyne, David Gavin, Peter Hallinane, Andrew Corley, Michael Thornton, Pat Murray, Stephen Duffy, Widow Diamond, Anthony Coyne, Wm W Casson, Michael Connelly, Mary Coyne, P M'Donogh, Martin Walsh, John Nee, Charles Moxham, Thomas Kelly, John Fitzpatrick, James Varley, Hugh Burke, Mary M'Donnell, John Mullin, Michael Garvey, Widow Conneelly, Peter Joyce, Valentine Conway, Pat Joyce, Stephen Wallace, Ambrose Burke, John Lyden, Pat Keely, Pat Morgan, John Joyce, Martin King, Anthony Conry, Pat Conneely, William Wallace, Tom Coyne, Tom Coneely, Tom Coyne, Thos Joce, Pat Wallace, John Lyden, Michael Butler, Tom Sullivan, sen; Tom Sullivan, jun; Michael Laffey, Stephen Wallace, Pat Heanue, Widow Moran, Martin Flaherty, Widow Coyne, Daniel Nee, Tom Donnelly, Peter Joyce, Michl. Joyce, Pat Flaherty, Pat Kane, Gregory Conneely, Pat Lyden, Michael Coyne, John Coyne, John Coyne, Michael Mulkerins, John Keane, Martin Harwood, Wm Heanue, Frank Kearney, Tom Faherty, Tom Joyce, James Donnellan, John Gibbons, Bart Faherty, Widow Gibbons, Myles Joyce, Michael Coyne, Michael Faherty, Martin Coyne, Widow Foland, Pat O'Flaherty, Pat Gibbons, Andrew Malley, Edward Conneely, Michael Joyce, John Kance Thomas Conry, John Walsh, Michael Kerrigan, Tom Kerrigan, James Kerrigan, Martin Delany, Thomas King, John Thornton, Harry Walsh, Anthony Conry, Widow Mulkerrins, Stephen Wallace, Michael Nee, M Flaherty, J Flaherty, Martin Kane, John Conry, Martin Conry, Darby Heanue, Roger Conry, John Burke, John Kearney, M Kane, Tom Freehill, P Kane, T Kane, John M'Donnell, Pat Coyne, Darby Nee, Michael Conry, John Lyden, Michael Conry, Martin Thornton, Michael Gollehar, B Coyne, Pat Coyne, Anthony King, Pat King, Owen King, Michael King, Darby Nee.—127 tenants.

227

Appendix I

Schedule of Tenants as listed in Kylemore Castle Book of Sale 1902.

In addition to the foregoing there are

Numerous Small Holdings and Several Grazings

Including entire Villages distributed over the Estate, as set out in the following

SCHEDULE :–

No. on Estate Roll.	Description.	Name of Tenant.	£	s.	d.
	Dawrosmore.				
	On Illaunnanoon, forming part of the Estate, in Barnaderg Bay, is a disused Building, formerly used in connection with the Fishing in this Bay	In hand	-	-	-
2	Two Stone and Thatched Cottages ...	Mary Coyne	1	0	0
3	Stone and Thatched Cottage	M. Conneely	4	5	0
4	Do. do. and Byre ...	Mrs. B. O'Grady ...	2	4	6
5	Do. do.	Mrs. P. Nee	1	5	6
6	Stone and Slated Bungalow House ...	Dr. McDonnell... ...	6	10	0
7	Stone and Thatched Cottage	J. Fitzpatrick ...	3	3	9
8	Land only	Do. ...	1	1	3
9	Stone and Thatched Cottage and Two Stables	Representatives of J. Vallelly	4	0	0
10	Do. do. and Byre ...	M. Burke	3	2	10
11	Do. do.	M. Corbett	2	0	0
12	Do. do. and Byre ...	J. Mullen	4	5	0
	Garden opposite Letterfrack National School...	Schoolmaster	-	-	-
	Creggauns.				
13	Stone and Thatched Cottage and Two Byres ...	S. Wallace	2	11	0
14	Do. do.	T. Conneely	2	19	6
15	Do. do. and Two Byres ...	P. Joyce	4	5	0
16	Do. do. and Byre ...	M. Conway	4	5	0
17	Do. do. Stable and Three Byres	S. Wallace	6	7	6
18	Do. do.	Mrs. Burke	4	5	0
19	Do. do. and Salmon Store House	P. Lyden	5	0	0
20	Do. do.	P. Malley	3	8	0
21	Do. do. and Byre ...	J. Mongan	5	2	0
22	Do. do. do. ...	J. Joyce	5	2	0
23	Do. do. do. ...	M. King	6	16	0
24	Do. do. and Four Byres...	Mrs. Conroy	12	0	0
25	Stone and Felted Cottage near Dawros Bridge	In hand	-	-	-
	Cross.				
26	Stone and Thatched Cottage and Byre ...	P. Conneely	4	8	0
27	Do. do. do. ...	M. Conneely	2	6	2
27A	Do. do. ...	P. Davis	2	6	1
28	Land only	M. Conneely	1	2	0
28A	Do.	In hand (estimated)	2	4	0
28B	Do.	P. Davis	1	2	0
29} 31}	Stone and Thatched Cottage, Stable and Byre	T. Joyce	{3 {3	19 19	4 4
30	Do. do.	P. Mongan	3	19	4
32	Do. do.	T. Joyce	5	9	4
	Carried forward	£125	14	5

SCHEDULE—continued.

No. on Estate Roll.	Description.	Name of Tenant.	Rent Per Annum.		
			£	s.	d.
	Currywongaun.	*Brought forward*	125	14	5
33	Stone and Thatched Cottage, Stable and Two Byres	M. Coyne	7	13	4
34	Do. do. and Two Byres ...	J. Coyne	6	10	4
35	Do. do. do.	M. Thornton ...	6	10	4
36	Do. do. and Byre ...	D. Gavin	6	10	4
37	Do. do. do. ...	P. Hanlin	4	13	4
38	Ruined Cottage	In hand ...	.	.	.
39	Stone and Thatched Cottage	Do. (estimated) ..	0	10	0
40	Stone and Slated Cottage and Piggery ...	P. Murray	0	10	0
41	Stone and Thatched Cottage ...	S. Duffy	0	10	0
	Shanaveag.				
43	Stone and Thatched Cottage and Two Byres ...	A. Coyne	10	0	0
43A	Do. do Cart Shed and Byre	P. Conry	10	0	0
	Tooreena.				
51	Stone and Thatched Cottage, Stable and Two Byres	Mrs. C. Sullivan ...	4	0	9
52	Do. do. and Two Byres ...	T. Sullivan	1	18	3
53	Do. do. and Byre	Mrs. Garvey	1	16	0
54	Stone and Corrugated Iron Cottage and do. ...	S. Wallace	3	10	9
55		In hand	.	.	.
56		Mrs. C. Sullivan ...	1	12	4
57	Land only	M. Mulkervin	3	0	0
58	Stone and Felted Cottage and Byre	J. Keane	3	0	0
59	Stone and Thatched Cottage	Mrs. Harwood	3	0	0
60	Do. do.	J. Heanne	3	0	0
	Mullaghglass.				
61	Stone and Thatched Cottage and Barn	Mrs. Kearney	3	8	0
62	Do. do. Byre, Barn, Cart Shed, etc.	T. Faherty	10	4	0
63	Do. do. and Byre ...	T. Sullivan	3	12	3
64	Do. do. do. ...	N. Joyce	3	16	6
65	Do. do. do.	M. Donelan	3	16	6
66	Land and do.	P. Donnelly	3	0	0
67	Stone and Thatched Cottage	S. Faherty	1	18	3
68	Do. do. do. ...	M. Gibbons	3	8	0
69	Land and do.	M. Joyce	2	10	0
70	Two Stone and Thatched Cottages ..	M. Coyne, jun. ...	2	2	6
71	Stone and Thatched Cottage and Byre ...	J. Coyne	2	11	0
72	Do. do. and Two Byres ...	G. Coyne	1	9	9
73	Do. do.	E. Connolly	4	9	3
74	Do. do.	P. Flaherty	2	6	9
75	Do. do. and Byre ...	P. Gibbons	3	8	0
76	Do. do. and Two Byres ...	P. Malley	4	5	0
77	Do. do. and Byre ...	E. Conneely	1	5	6
78	Do. do. do. ...	M. Faherty	5	2	0
79	Do. do. do. ...	M. Coyne	4	0	9
80	Do. do. do. ...	Mrs. J. Nee	3	16	6
81	Do. do. and Two Byres ...	P. Donnelly	5	2	0
82	Do. do. and Byre ...	Mrs. D. Nee	4	13	6
83	Land only	M. Joyce	0	17	0
	Carried forward		£285	3	2

20

229

SCHEDULE—*continued.*

No. on Estate Roll.	Description.	Name of Tenant.	Rent Per Annum.		
			£	s.	d.
	Lettergesh West.	*Brought forward*	285	3	2
84	Stone and Thatched Cottage	P. Keane	3	2	6
85	Do. do.	M. Faherty & Co. ...	1	10	0
86	Two do. do.	Representatives of P. Keane	2	13	2
87	Stone and Thatched Cottage and Byre ...	Mr. P. Lyden	2	19	6
88	Do. do. do. ...	P. Nee	3	3	9
89	Do. do.	J. Gibbons	3	3	9
90	Do. do. and Two Byres ...	J. Coyne	2	6	9
91	Do. do. do. ...	M. Joyce	2	6	9
92	Do. do. and Byre ...	Mrs. J. Keane	1	14	0
93	Two ditto do. and Two Byres ...	T. Conry	6	16	0
94	Stone and Thatched Cottage	T. Kearney	5	0	0
95	Do. do. and Byre ...	Mrs. B. Kerrigan ...	4	13	6
96	Do. do. and Two Byres ...	Mrs. T. Kerrigan ...	4	13	6
97	Do. do.	Do.	2	11	0
	Lettergesh National School, erected in 1868, comprising Stone and Slated Schoolhouse with separate divisions for boys and girls; Stone and Slated Schoolmaster's House of four rooms and Stone and Corrugated Iron Roofed School Mistress's Bungalow of two rooms	... ...	-	-	-
98	... ...	M. Sullivan (Schoolmaster)	2	11	0
99	Stone and Thatched Cottage and Byre ...	Mrs. T. King	7	0	3
100	Stone and Slated House and Two Byres ...	J. Thornton	7	0	3
101	Two Stone and Thatched Cottages	P. Walsh	2	17	4
102	Land only	A. Conry	3	10	0
102A	Do. do.	J. Coyne	3	10	0
103	Do. and Piggery	M. Coyne	3	17	6
104	Two Stone and Thatched Cottages	Mrs. Wallace	4	0	9
105	Three do. do. and Barn ...	M. Nee	4	13	6
	Lettergesh East.				
106	Stone and Thatched Cottage and Byre ...	M. Faherty	2	19	6
107	Do. do. do. ...	J. Faherty	2	11	0
108	Do. do. do. ...	Mrs. M. Keane ...	2	11	0
109	Two do. do. do. ...	Mrs. J. Conry	4	9	3
110	Stone and Thatched Cottage, do. ...	J. Coyne	4	13	6
111	Two do. do. and Three Byres...	D. Heanne	5	19	0
112	Do. do. and Two do. ...	Mrs. M. Conry ...	5	6	3
113	Stone and Thatched Cottage and Byre ...	J. Burke	1	14	0
114	Do. do. do. ..	H. Kearney	2	19	6
115	Do. do. do. ...	P. Conroy	3	5	6
115A	Do. do. do. ...	P. Wallace	3	5	0
116	Do. do.	D. Keane	2	11	0
117	Do. do.	M. Keane	4	0	9
118	Two do. do. and Byre ...	M. McDonnell	7	10	3
119	Stone and Thatched Cottage and Barn ...	P. Coyne	4	0	9
120	Do. and Byre ...	D. Heanne	4	5	0
121	Land only	Mrs. M. Conroy ...	1	18	3
122	Stone and Thatched Cottage and Byre ...	P. Keane	1	14	0
123	Do. do.	D. Heanne	2	0	0
124	Two do. do. do. ...	Mrs. M. Thornton	3	3	9
		Carried forward ...	£441	15	2

SCHEDULE—*continued.*

No. on Estate Roll.	Description.	Name of Tenant.	Rent Per Annum.		
			£	s.	d.
	Lettergesh East—*continued.*	*Brought forward*	441	15	2
125	Stone and Thatched Cottage and Byre ...	Mrs. Gallagher	1	14	0
126	Do. do. do.	Representatives of B. Coyne	1	14	0
127	Do. do. and Two Byres ...	J. Coyne	3	3	9
128	Do. do. do.	A. King	5	0	0
129	Do. do.	O. King	5	0	0
130	Do. do. and Byre ...	P. King	5	0	0
131	Two do. do. and Two Byres ...	H. King	5	0	0
	On the Shore of Lough Fee—				
132	Stone and Thatched Cottage, Two Stables and Byre	M. Nee	10	12	6
132A	Stone and Slated House, Stable and Byre ...	P. Nee	10	12	6
	Grazings.				
42	Barnanang—Stone and Slated Cottage and Byre. Monthly tenancy	T. Joyce	60	0	0
45	Lemnaheltia—Stone and Thatched Cottage and Byre. Yearly tenancy, subject to six months' notice...	M. Coyne	20	0	0
133	Part of Greenmount. Monthly tenancy ...	S. Wallace	12	0	0
134	Cruckaunbawn and Cattle Shed. Monthly tenancy	M. Joyce	8	0	0
135	Mweelin—Stone and Slated Cottage and Byre. Yearly letting	J. Nee...	30	0	0
137	Currywongaun and Addergoole—Stone and Thatched Cottage and Byre. Yearly tenancy, subject to six months' notice	Mrs. J. Coyne	6	0	0
138	Diamond Hill and Silo. Yearly tenancy, subject to right of grazing two cows and two calves	M. Joyce	10	0	0
139	Glanmore—Stone and Thatched Cottage and Byre. Yearly tenancy, subject to six months' notice	T. F. Joyce	32	0	0
140	Part of Demesne	M. Coyne	10	0	0
141	Do. do.	T. F. Joyce	7	0	0
		Total £684 11 11			

The whole of the foregoing Small Holdings, practically without exception, include Lands or Stripings of various Areas in the Lettings, and in addition Rights of Grazing on certain Upland Pastures, which are arranged in accordance with the several Townlands.

In addition, each Tenant on the Estate has a right for cutting Peat Turf allotted to his Holding, and can claim for a further Allotment when same is worked out.

Where a Tenant has a Holding embracing a Sea Coast Frontage, a right of gathering Seaweed to such extent of Frontage is included in the Holding.

Except where specifically mentioned the Tenancies, in accordance with the Irish Land Acts, are perpetual so long as the Rent is paid either by the present Occupier or his Successor on death.

Appendix I

1901 & 1911 Census for the Townlands of Lemnaheltia, Pollacappul and Addergoole

Names on census form not always legible and are spelt here as found.
Numbers allocated to houses in 1911 do not necessarily correspond with those given in 1901.
Frequently the ages of individuals given in 1911 do not correspond with those given in 1901.

Abbreviations:
RC   Roman Catholic
CofI   Church of Ireland

1901 & 1911 CENSUS FOR LEMNAHELTIA

1901 Census Lemnaheltia.

Taken 31 March 1901.

Lemnaheltia townland contained one house, inhabited by one family, five members.
Landholder on whose holding the houses are situated: Mitchell Henry.

House No 1.

1   John Coyne, head of house. RC. Cannot read. Age 63, shepherd. Widower, born Co Galway. Spoke Irish and English.

2   Peter, son. RC. Can read and write. Age 19, labourer. Single, born Co Galway.

3   Philip, son. RC. Can read and write. Age 16, labourer. Single, born Co Galway.

4   Martin, son. RC. Age 9, scholar, born Co Galway.

5   Annie, daughter. Can read and write. Age 21, housework. Single, born Co Galway.

1911 Census Lemnaheltia.

Taken 2 April 1911.

Lemnaheltia contained one house, inhabited by one family, five members.
Landholder on whose holding the houses are situated: Duke of Manchester.

House No 1.

1   Peter Coyne, head of house. RC. Can read and write. Age 32, shepherd and land holder. Married 5 years. Born Co Galway. Irish and English.

2   Belendia, wife. RC. Can read and write. Age 33. 2 children born and 2 children still living. Born Co Galway. Irish and English.

3   Patrick, son. RC. Age 4.

4   John, son. Age 2.

5   Pat Coyne. RC. Can read and write. Age 18, general servant. Born Co Galway.

1901 & 1911 CENSUS FOR POLLACAPPUL

1901 Census Pollacappul

Taken 31 March 1901

Pollacappul townland contained seven dwelling houses all occupied. Unless stated otherwise, all occupents spoke English only. Landholder on whose holding the houses are situated: Mitchell Henry.

House No 1. [Kylemore Castle]

1   Martin Feeney. RC. Can read and write. Age 55, electrician. Widower, born in Co Galway. Irish and English.

2   Catherine Ralph. C of I. Can read and write. Age 37, housemaid. Single, born Co Wexford.

3   Kate Egan. RC. Age 20, cook. Unmarried, born Co Galway.

4   Kate Egan. RC. Can read and write. Age 17, under housemaid. Unmarried, born Co Galway.

5   Mary Simpson. Presbyterian. Can read and write. Age 21, telegraphist. Unmarried, born Dublin.

6   Louisa Simpson, visitor. Presbyterian. Can read and write. Age 22, housemaid. Unmarried, born Queens County.

7   Patrick Joyce. RC. Can read and write. Age 21, pantry boy. Born Co Galway. Irish and English.

House No 2.

1 Patrick Faherty. RC. Can read and write. Age 24, labourer. Single, born Co Galway. Irish and English.

House No 3.

1 Michael Connolly. RC. Can read and write. Age 44, stoker in garden. Married, born Co. Galway. Irish and English.

House No 4.

1 James Jeffrey. Presbyterian. Can read and write. Age 29, gardener. Single, born Scotland.

2 Denis Healy. RC. Can read and write. Age 23, gardener. Single born Killarney, Co Kerry.

3 Peter Lydon. RC. Can read and write. Age 28, gardener. Single, born Co Galway.

4 Michael Conroy. RC. Can read and write. Age 14, gardener. Single born Co Galway.

House No 5.

1 John Couper, head of house. Presbyterian. Can read and write. Age 45, estate steward. Born Scotland.

2 Marjory, wife. Presbyterian. Can read and write. Age 38. Born Scotland.

3 Jessie, daughter. Can read and write. Age 15. Telegraphist. Single. born Scotland.

4 Janie, daughter. Can read and write. Age 13, scholar. Born Scotland.

5 Susie, daughter. Can read and write. Age 12, scholar. Born Scotland.

6 George, son. Can read and write. Age 10, scholar. Born Scotland.

7 Maggie, daughter. Can read and write. Age 9, scholar. Born Scotland.

8 Allen, son. Can read and write. Age 6, scholar. Born Scotland.

9 Henry, son. Age 2. Born Co Galway.

10 Alice Kearns, visitor. RC. Can read and write. Age 24, seamstress. Single born Co Galway.

House No 6.

1 David Anderson, head of house. C of I. Can read and write. Age 33, coachman. Married, born Scotland.

2 Rose, wife. C of I. Can read and write. Age 33, born London.

3 Jane, daughter. C of I. Age 6, scholar. Born Scotland.

4 Rosa, daughter. C of I. Age 5, scholar. Born Co Galway.

5 Ernest Brimson. Boarder. C of I. Can read and write. Age 20, assistant chemist. Single, born England.

House No 7.

1 William Comfort, head of house. C of I. Can read and write. Age 51, head gardener. Married, born Scotland.

2 Jessie, wife. C of I. Can read and write. Age 50, born Scotland.

3 George E Woodfield. Visitor. C of England. Can read and write. Age 29, blacksmith. Single, born England.

1911 Census Pollacappul.

Taken 2 April 1911.

Pollacappul townland contained seven houses. Five inhabited. Landholder on whose holding the houses are situated: Duke of Manchester.

House No 1.

1 William Bosomworth, head of house. C of I. Can read and write. Age 53, game keeper. Married 30 years, born England.

2 Mary, wife. C of I. Can read and write. Age 53. Married 30 years, total number of children born alive 5, total still living 4. Born Co Armagh.

3 Margaret Roseworth, daughter. C of I. Can read and write. Age 24, drapers assistant. Single, born Co Armagh.

4 Ada, daughter. C of I. Can read and write. Age 15, scholar. Single, born Co Armagh.

House No 2.

1 Martin Gibbons. RC. Can read and write. Age 24, gardener. Single, born Co Galway. Irish and English.

2 Thomas Wallace. RC. can read and write. Age 41, gardener. Single, born Co Galway. Irish and English.

House No 3. [Kylemore Castle]

1 Martin Feeney. RC. Can read and write. Age 64, electrician. Widower, born Co Galway. Irish and English.

2 Martin Coyne. RC. Can read and write. Age 20, hall boy. Single, born Co Galway. Irish and English.

3 Lizzie Daly. C of I. Can read and write. Age 32, housekeeper. Single, born Co Cork.

4 Ellen Joyce. RC. Can read and write. Age 21. house maid. Single, born Co Galway. Irish and English.

House No 4.

1 David Anderson, head of house. C of I. Can read and write. Age 41, motor driver and mechanic. Married 17 years, born Scotland.

2 Rosa, wife. C of I. Can read and write. Age 41. 3 children born alive, 2 still living. Born England.

3 Jane, daughter. C of I. Can read and write. Age 16, scholars. Single, born Scotland.

4 Rosa, daughter. C of I. Age 14, scholar. Born Co Galway.

House No 5.

1 Edward Humphreys, head of house. Church of England. Can read and write. Age 63, postmaster. Married 30 years. Born Wales.

2 Mary, wife. C of E. Age 59. Can read and write. Married, 4 children born, 4 still living. Born England.

3 Gertrude, daughter. C of E. Can read and write. Age 28, single. Born Wales.

1901 & 1911 CENSUS FOR ADDERGOOLE

1901 Census Addergoole

Taken 31 March 1901.

Addergoole townland contained ten houses all occupied. Unless stated otherwise, all occupents spoke English only.
Landholder on whose holding the houses are situated: Mitchell Henry.

House No 1.

1 Thomas Aspell. Religion: Roman Catholic. Cannot Read. age 60. labourer. Married, born in Co Wexford.

House No 2.

1 Anne Aspell. Religion: RC. Cannot read or write. Age 61, washer woman. Married, born in Co Monaghan.

2 James, son. RC. Can read and write. Age 33, no occupation given. Unmarried, born in Co Galway.

3 Anne, daughter. RC. Cannot read or write. Age 31, washer woman. Unmarried, born Co Galway.

4 John, son. RC. Can read and write. Age 29, no occupation given. Unmarried, born Co Galway.

5 Tom, son. RC. Can read and write. Age 25, painter. Married, born in Co Galway.

6 Winifred, daughter-in-law. Can read and write. Age 23, seamstress. Married, born in England.

7 Ellen, granddaughter. RC. Age 3, born Co

Galway.

8 Willie, son. RC. Can read and write. Age 20, farmer. Unmarried, born Co Galway.

9 John W. Staunton, grandson. RC. Age 4, a school boy, born in Co Galway.

House No 3

1 John Kane. RC. Can read and write. Age 28, farm steward. Unmarried, born in Galway. Spoke Irish and English.

House No 4.

1 Maggie Brady. RC. Can read and write. Age 24, laundry maid. Unmarried, born Co Cavan.

2 Mary McDonnell. RC. Can read and write. Age 21, dairymaid. Unmarried, born Co Galway.

House No 5.

1 Patrick Hastings, head of house. RC. Can read and write. Age 46, forester. Married, born Co Galway. Spoke Irish and English

2 Catherine, wife. RC. Can read and write. Age 42, born co Galway. Spoke Irish and English

3 Thomas, son. RC. Can read and write. Age 18, labourer, not married.

4 Dominick, son. RC. Can read and write. Age 16, labourer, not married.

5 John, son. RC. Can read and write. Age 14, labourer.

6 Bridget, daughter. RC. Can read and write. Age 11, scholar.

7 Nora, daughter. RC. Can read and write. Age 9, scholar.

8 Angela, daughter. Age 2.

House No 6.

1 Roger Lydon, head of family. RC. Can read and write. Age 58, heard. Widower, born Co Galway. Irish and English.

2 Roger, son. RC. Can read and write. Age 11, scholar. Born in America. Irish and English

3 Anthony King, nephew. RC. Can read and write. Age 21, post boy. Unmarried, born in Co Galway. Irish and English.

House No 7.

1 Peter Malia. RC. Can read and write. Age 45, cow man. Married, born Co Galway . English and Irish

2 John Coyne. RC. Can read and write. Age 21, yard man. Unmarried, born Co Galway. English and Irish.

House No 8.

1 Michael King. RC. Can read and write. Age 28, game keeper. Married, born Co Galway. Irish and English.

2 Jani, wife. RC. Can read and write. Age 25, born in England.

3 William, son. RC. Age 2, born Co Galway.

4 Elisie Nora, daughter. Age two months, born Co Galway.

House No 9.

1 William Walsh. RC. Can read and write. Age 70, farmer. Married, born Co Cork. Irish and English.

2 Catherine, wife. RC. Age 60, born Co Mayo. Irish and English.

3 William, son. RC. Age 24, ploughman. Married, born Co Galway. Irish and English

4 Anne, daughter-in-law. RC. Age 18, born Co Galway.

5 Mary Ann, granddaughter. Age 1, born Co Galway.

6 Bridget, granddaughter. Age 4 months.

House No 10.

1 Peter King, head of house. RC. Can read and write. Age 25, under keeper. Unmarried, born Co Galway. Irish and English.

2 John Lyden. RC. Can read and write. Poultry boy. Born in Co Galway

1911 Census Addergoole.

Taken 2 April 1911.

Addergoole contained nine houses, houses No 7 & 9 unoccupied.
Landholder on whose holding the houses are situated: Duke of Manchester.
Numbers allocated to houses do not necessarily correspond with those given in 1901 Census.
Unless stated otherwise, all occupents spoke English only.

House No 1.

1 Patrick Hastings, head of house. RC. Can read only. Age 60, forester. Married for 33 years, born Co Mayo. Irish and English.
2 Catherine, wife. RC. Can read and write. Age 59. Married, total children born alive 10. Children still living 7. Born Co Mayo. Irish and English.
3. Dominick, son. RC. Can read and write. Age 26, motor driver. Single, born Co Galway.
4. Angela, daughter. RC. Can read and write. Age 12, scholar. Born Co Galway.

House No 2.

1 Charles Andrew Clark, head of house. Church of England. Can read and write. Age 29, poultry expert. Married for 8 years. Born in England.
2. G... [illegible] wife. C of E. Can read and write. Age 30. Married 8 years, 4 children born alive, 4 still living.
3 Charles William, son. C of E. Can read and write. Age 7, scholar. Born in England.
4 Harty, son. C of E. Cannot read. Age 5, scholar. Born England
5 Mabel Emmeline, daughter. C of E. Age 3. Born England.
6 Gillian Mary, daughter. C of E. Age 2. Born England.

House No 3

1 James Smith, head of house. C of E. Can read and write. Age 25, poultry manager. Single. Place of birth not given.

House No 4

1 Michael Nee, head of family. RC. Can read and write. Age 47. Married. Born Co Galway. Irish and English.

House No 5
1 Joseph Dunn. Church of Ireland. Can read and write. Age 27, game keeper. Single. Born Co Armagh.
2. Joseph Waller. C of I. Can read and write. Age 26, game keeper. Single. Born Scotland.
3 Owens Kelly. RC. Can read and write. Age 14, game keeper. Single. Born Co Galway.

House No 6.
1 Thomas Nee. RC. Can read and write. Age 19, cowman. Single. Born Co Galway. Irish and English.
2. Patrick Nee. RC. Can read and write. Age 16, cowman. Single. Born Co Galway. Irish and English.
3. Michael Kane. RC. Can read and write. Age 16, cowman. Single. Born Co Galway.

House No 7
Unoccupied.

House No 8
1 Bridget Aspell. head of house. RC. Age 22. Married under one year. 1 child born and alive. Born Co Galway.
2. Nora, daughter. RC. Age 9 months. Born Co Galway.
3. Anne Aspell, sister-in-law. RC. Can read. Age 38. Single. Born Co Galway.
4. John William Staunton, nephew. RC. Cannot read. Age 15, general labourer. Single. Born Co Galway.

House No 9.
Unoccupied.

Appendix II

ABBESSES OF YPRES

NAME	WHEN & WHERE PROFESSED	TERM AS ABBESS
Rt. Rev. Dame M. Marina Beaumont	1637 at Ghent	1669 - 1682
Rt. Rev. Dame M. Flavia Cary	1634 at Ghent	1682 - 1686
Rt. Rev. Dame M. Joseph Butler	1657 at Boulogne	1686 - 1723
Rt. Rev. Dame M. Xaveria Arthur	1700 at Ypres	1723 - 1743
Rt. Rev. Dame M. Magdalen Mandeville	1726 at Ypres	1743 - 1760
Rt. Rev. Dame M. Bernard Dalton	1737 at Ypres	1760 - 1783
Rt. Rev. Dame M. Scholastica Lynch	1772 at Ypres	1783 - 1799
Rt. Rev. Dame M. Brigid Bernard Lynch	1782 at Ypres	1799 - 1830
Rt. Rev. Dame M. Benedict Byrne	1795 at Ypres	1830 - 1840
Rt. Rev. Dame M. Elizabeth Jarrett	1820 at Ypres	1840 - 1888
Rt. Rev. Dame M. Scholastica Bergé	1852 at Ypres	1888 - 1890

ABBESSES OF KYLEMORE

NAME	WHEN & WHERE PROFESSED	TERM AS ABBESS
Rt. Rev. Dame Irma M. Maura Ostyn	1890 at Ypres	1916 - 1940
Rt. Rev. Dame M. Placid Druhan	1900 at Ypres	1941 - 1953
Rt. Rev. Dame Agnes Finnegan	1938 at Kylemore	1953 - 1981
Rt. Rev. M. Mechtilde Moloney	1945 at Kylemore	1981 - 1987
Rt. Rev. Mary O'Toole	1946 at Kylemore	1987 - 1993
Rt. Rev. M. Clare Morley	1965 at Kylemore	1993 - 2001
Rt. Rev. M. Magdalena FitzGibbon	1970 at Kylemore	2001 - -

Appendix II

BENEDICTINE COMMUNITY WHO ARRIVED IN IRELAND IN 1916

Abbess Mary Scholastica Bergé. 11th Abbess of Ypres.
Born 1830, Tournai, Belgium. Professed in 1852. A teacher in the school at Ypres before entering.

Mother Prioress Mary Maura Ostyn.
Born in Belgium in 1870. Professed in 1890.

Dame Mary Placid Druhan
Born 1876, Wexford. Professed in 1900. A pupil at Ypres before entering.

Dame Mary Gertrude Burgert.
Born 1849, Germany. Professed in 1888. Novice Mistress for many years.

Dame Mary Kate Aloysius Rossier.
Born 1866, Kilmore, Co Wexford. Professed in 1896. A cousin of Dame Placid Druhan.

Dame Mary Walburga Swallow.
Born 1883, Newcastle on Tyne. Professed 1902. Acted as Infirmarian to the Community for many years.

Dame M Teresa Howard.
Born 1885, Ireland. Professed 1905. A pupil at Ypres before entering. Dame Teresa was a niece of John Redmond M.P., leader of the Irish Parliamentary Party in the House of Commons. For many years Mistress of Novices and a teacher in the school.

Dame M Bernard Stewart.
Born 1889, Derry. Professed 1912. A pupil in Ypres before entering. Head Mistress of Kylemore School.

Sister Rosalie Madeleine Putte.
Born 1841, Baal, Luxembourg. Profession a lay sister in 1873.

Sister M. Helen Alphonse Murkoster.
Born 1850, Westphalia, Germany. Professed a lay sister in 1884.

Sister Mary Baptiste Griese.
Born 1854, Germany. Professed a lay sister in 1884.

Sister Catherine Margaret M Shroter.
Born 1861, Germany. Professed a lay sister in 1891.

Sister M Romana King.
Born 1872. Professed a lay sister in 1891.

Sister Emma Mary Winifred Hodges.
Born 1872, Dublin. Professed a lay sister in 1893.

Sister M Gabriel Bohan.
Born 1880, Lancashire, England. Professed a lay sister in 1900.

Dame Patrick.
Born in Ireland.

Dame Columban Plomer.
Born in England.

Novice M Odilon Allaeys.
Born 1891, Belgium.

Appendix II

PROFESSED RELIGIOUS OF KYLEMORE ABBEY

NAME	BORN	WHEN AND WHERE PROFESSED	DIED
Dame M Benedict Curtis	1887, Wexford	1917 Macmine	26 August 1954
Sr M Martha Kilgannon	1898 Galway	1918 "	28 March 1985
Dame Elizabeth M Magdalen Lee	1874, England	1919 "	14 March 1952
Sr M Columba Egan	1897, Co Mayo	1919 "	21 October 1989
Dame Margaret Mary Delourme	1920 Roubaix, France	1918 "	3 January 1963
Dame M. Scholastica Murphy	1888, Kerry	1920 "	2 October 1980
Sr M Aiden Casey	1900, Boston, USA	1920 "	29 Nov. 1980
Sr M Gerard Judge	1900, Co Galway	1921 Kylemore	22 March 1981
Sr Mary Patrick Mannion	1890, Co Galway	1921 "	20 July 1971
Sr M. Oliver Greally	1901, Co Galway	1925 "	6 May 1970
Sr M. Peter King	1881, Co Galway	1923 "	6 October 1949
Sr Paul Monaghan	1890, Co Donegal	1923 "	17 January 1973
Sr M Jarlath O'Brien	1906, Co Galway	1926 "	29 March 1999
Sr Mary Teresa Greaney	1897, Co Mayo	1927 "	27 May 1969
Sr M Ita O'Flaherty	1905, Co Galway	1925 "	17 April 1997
Sr M Brigid Walle	1896, Co Mayo	1928 "	19 Feb. 1967
Sr M Brendan Walsh	1907, Co Galway	1931 "	26 Feb. 1996
Dame M Josepha Silk	1884, England	1933 "	10 March 1974
Sr M Bernadette Conroy	1911, Co Galway	1934 "	26th Feb. 1934
Sr M Francis Langan	1906, Co Galway	1935 "	19 April 1998
Dame M Gertrude O'Connor	1886, Co Cork	1937 "	27 January 1972
Dame M.Agnes Finnegan (Abbess)	1917, Co Mayo	1938 "	10 April 2000
Sr M Bernadette Feeney	1908, Co Leitrim	1940 "	4 May 1996
Dame (later Sr) M Lucy Horan	1895, Co Tipperary	1938 "	6 January 1981
Sr M Gregory Quaid	1917, Limerick	1940 "	1 October 2000
Dame (larer Sr) M Raphael Conroy	1912, Co Galway	1944 "	12 August 2000
Dame Mary O'Toole (Abbess)	Clifden, Co Galway	1946 "	15 June 2001
Dame (later Sr) M. Agatha Martin	1925, Dublin	1949 "	9 April 1999
Sr Mary Elizabeth Dasbach	1868, Germany	Menin, Belgium	14 January 1948

Community at April 2002

NAME	BORN	WHEN AND WHERE PROFESSED
Mother Abbess M Magdalena FitzGibbon	Fermoy, Co Cork	1970 Kylemore
Mother Prioress Josephine O'Malley	Macroom, Co. Cork	1976 "
Sr Benedict O'Beirne, Archivist	England	1959 "
Sr Dymphna Conroy	Lettergesh, Co Galway	1932 "
Sr Michael Moloney	Co Limerick	1943 "
Sr John O'Malley	Newport, Co Mayo	1944 "
Mother M.Mechtilde Moloney (former Abbess)	Co Limerick	1945 "
Sr Pius O'Meara	Co Tipperary	1957 "
Sr Noreen Peter Gallagher	Dublin	1965 "
Mother Mary Clare Morley (former Abbess)	Clarecastle, Co Clare.	1967 "
Sr Karol O'Connell	Midleton, Co Cork	1982 "
Sr Marie Bernard Crossan	Co Down	1983 "
Sr Aidan Ryan	Co Down	1988 "
Sr Dorothy Ryan	Galvey, Co Limerick	1979 "
Sr Rosario Ni Fhlatherta	Aran Islands, Co Galway	1984 "
Sr Bernard Hayes	Yorkshire, England	1945 Oulton
Sr Margaret Mary Powell	Portsmouth, England	1953 Oulton
Dame Mary Groves	England	1956 Oulton

References

Abbreviations

N.L.I.   National Library of Ireland
CSORP   Chief Secretary's Office, Registered Papers

Preface

1 Harriet Martineau, *Letters from Ireland,* (London 1852), p112

Chapter 1

1 *Dictionary of National Biography,* Second Supplement, 1910-1911, p248; Burkes, *The Landed Gentry*, 1894, p937

2 International Genealogical Index, England, Westminster

3 *Dictionary of National Biography*, p248

4 A. Velpeau, *A Treatise on the Diseases Of The Breast and Mammary Region,* translated from the French by Mitchell Henry, (London 1856)

5 Mitchell Henry, *The Address Delivered At The Opening Of The Classes Of The Middlesex Hospital Medical College, Session 1859-60,* (London 1859)

6 *Evening Chronicle,* 8 December 1910; T Swindells, *Manchester Streets & Manchester Men,* (Manchester 1907), pp16-18; Sir Thomas Baker, *Memorials of A Dissenting Chapel, Its Foundation and Worthies,* (Manchester 1884), pp122-3; Old Manchester Firms, 16 July 1932, Old Clippings, MCL, Box 327 Textiles; *The North American, Philadelphia*, 18 February 1912

7 Baker, *op.cit.*, p100

8 Michael J. Turner, *Reform & Respectability: The Making of A Middle-Class Liberalism in Early 19th century Manchester,* (Manchester 1995)

9 Old Manchester Firms, 16 July 1932, Old Clippings, Manchester Central Library, Box 327 Textiles

10 Various Writers, *Fortunes Made In Business: A Series of Original Sketches, Biographical and Anecdotic,* Vol 111, (London 1887), p206

11 *Ibid.,* p207

12 *The Henry Group Of Companies*, Company Publication, (Manchester 1955) p8

13 Baker, *op.cit,* p123

14 *Manchester Guardian,* 24 November 1910

15 W. Duncombe Pink & Rev Alfred B. Beaven, MA, *Lancashire Parliamentary Representatives 1258-1885,* (London 1889), p98

16 *Middleton Guardian,* 23 November 1889

17 Les Sutton, *Mainly About Ardwick,* Vol 1, (Manchester 1980)

18 IGI, A0931, England, Lancashire

19 *Encyclopaedia of American Literature*, Steven R Serafin Editor, (New York 1999)

20 Various Writers, *op.cit.*, p214

21 *The Builder*, 24 October 1868, p776

22 *The Times*, 27 June 1870, p7

23 Valuation Office, Cancelled Books, Pollacappul, Electoral Division Renvyle, Co Galway, Book 4, p53

24 Noel P. Wilkins, *Ponds, Passes and Parcs: Aquaculture in Victorian Ireland,* (Dublin 1989), pp247-8

25 *Ibid., passim*

26 *Ibid.,* pp247-8

27 D11,092, Manuscripts Dept., National Library of Ireland

28 Registry of Deeds, 1865.32.111

29 Ms 13,725, Henry Papers, Manuscripts Dept., N.L.I

30 *Ibid.*

31 Hansard's Parliamentary Debates, Vol ccxxx 1876, p352

32 *Freeman's Journal,* 11 January 1878, p7

33 *Galway Express,* 23 July 1870

34 *Freeman's Journal,* 11 January 1878, p7

35 Charles G. Roberts, Reclamation of Bog and Moorland in Galway, in *Journal of the Royal Agricultural Society of England, Second Series,* (London 1878) p206

36 *Ibid.*, p207

37 *Ibid.*, p218

38 *Freeman's Journal,* 11 January 1878, p7

39 Patterson, Kempster & Shorthall Collection, *Damp Press Volumes Of Bills Of Quantities & Measurements*, Book 5, p426

40 *Kylemore Castle Book of Sale,* 1902

41 *Galway Express*, 23 July 1870; *Freeman's Journal*, 11 January 1878, p7

42 Charles G. Roberts, *op.cit.*, p229

43 *Ibid.*, p232

44 Dr Terence Brodie to Poor Law Commissioners, 3 May 1867, CSORP, National Archives

45 Patterson, Kempster & Shorthall Collection

46 *Galway Express*, 16 July 1870

Chapter 2

1 Paul Duffy, Engineering, in *From Queens College To National University: Essays On The Academic History of QCC/UCC/NUI, Galway,* (Dublin 1999), pp125-141; Paul Duffy, Random Notes On The Corrib, *Inland Waterways News, Vol. 23 No 3* (1996), p15; Maurice Semple, *Reflections on Lough Corrib,* (Galway 1974); Paul Duffy, pers. comm. with author; *The Building News*, 2 February 1900, p 158; Kathleen Villiers-Tuthill, *Beyond The Twelve Bens: A History of Clifden and District 1860-1923,* (Galway 1986), p90

2 Patterson, Kempster & Shorthall Collection

3 Hansard's Parliamentary Debates, Vol ccxciii 1884, p1336

4 *Galway Express*, 16 July 1870

5 Alexander Innes Shand, *Letters from The West Of Ireland 1884,* (London 1885), pp120-6

6 *Kylemore Castle Book of Sale,* 1902

7 *Ibid.*

8 *Ibid.*

9 *Galway Express* 10 July 1886

10 *Kylemore Castle Book of Sale,* 1902

11 *Ibid.*

12 *Ibid.*

13 *Ibid.*

14 *Ibid.*

15 *Ibid.*

16 *Galway Express*, 10 July 1886

17 *Ibid.*

18 *Kylemore Castle Book of Sale,* 1902

19 *Ibid.*

20 *Ibid.*

21 *Ibid.*

22 *Ibid.*,

23 Louis Mitchell-Henry, Henry Family History, a private paper

24 *Galway Express*, 10 July 1886

25 J.C. Howell Ltd, *Electric Lighting For Country Houses* (London 1896), pp19-0

26 *Ibid.*

27 *Kylemore Castle Book of Sale, 1894*

28 Charles G. Roberts, *op.cit.,* p216

29 *Kylemore Castle Book of Sale,* 1902

30 *The Irish Builder,* Notes on Early Gardening in Ireland, 15 May 1872, p139

31 Charles G. Roberts, *op.cit.,* p553

32 *The Irish Builder, op.cit.*

33 *Kylemore Castle Book of Sale,* 1894 & 1902; *Galway Express*, 16 July 1870; *The Irish Builder, op.cit.*

34 Shand, *op.cit.,* p126

35 *Kylemore Castle Book of Sale,* 1902

36 *Ibid.*

37 *Kylemore Castle Book of Sale,* 1894 & 1902; *Galway Express*, 16 July 1870

38 Census of Ireland 1901

39 *The Irish Builder, op.cit.*

40 *Galway Express*, 16 July 1870

41 *The Irish Builder, op.cit.*

42 *Galway Express*, 11 October 1884, p4

43 *Kylemore Castle Book of Sale,* 1902

44 *Galway Express*, 11 October 1884, p4

45 John Joyce, interview with Eithne Kane, 1999, Kylemore Archives

46 Charles G. Roberts, *op.cit.,* p217

47 S.U.Roberts, Description of Means Adopted For Unwatering Works Of River Drainage, *Trans. Inst. C.E.I.*, Vol 3, 1849, pp1-8; Duffy, Engineering, *From Queens College To National University,* pp125-141

48 Charles G. Roberts, *op.cit.,* p217; Charles Hodgson C.E., had a peat briquetting machine, constructed by Gwyne & Son, erected in the Maam Valley in 1854. After some initial success the venture failed due to repeated fracture of machine parts. By 1860 Hodgson had perfected a machine capable of producing 100 tons of briquettes a week, this was in operation at Derrynea near Portarlington. (Duffy pers. comm. with author)

49 Charles G Roberts, *op.cit.,* p216

50 *Kylemore Book of Sale,* 1902

51 Charles G. Roberts, *op.cit.,* p217

52 *Kylemore Book of Sale,* 1902

53 *Ibid.*

Chapter 3

1 Charles Eason, *An Almanac and Hand-Book for Ireland For The Year 1877,* (Dublin 1877), pp101-3

2 Charles G. Roberts, *op.cit.,* p211

3 James Hack Tuke, *Irish Distress and Its Remedies. The Land Question. A Visit to Donegal and Connaught In The Spring Of 1880,* (London 1880), pp70-4

4 Charles G. Roberts, *op.cit.,* p222-228

5 *Ibid.,* p210

6 *Ibid.,* p210; pp218-219

7 *Ibid.,* p231

8 *Ibid.,* p229

9 *Ibid.,* pp206-232

10 Eason, *op.cit.*

11 Charles G. Roberts, *op.cit.,* p229

12 Eason, *op.cit.*

13 *Galway Express* 23 July 1870

14 See Kathleen Villiers-Tuthill, *Patient Endurance: The Great Famine in Connemara,* (Dublin 1997), pp138-2

15 Tuke, *op.cit.*

16 *Galway Vindicator,* 27 April 1881, p3

17 Charles G Roberts, *op.cit.,* p210

18 see Wilkins, *op.cit.*

19 British Parliamentary Papers 1898 [325], Henry letter to the Commissioners of Irish Fisheries, p24

20 *Kylemore Castle Book of Sale, 1902*

21 *Ibid.*

22 *Galway Express,* 11 October 1884 p4

23 *Kylemore Castle Book Of Sale,* 1902

24 *Galway Express,* 23 July 1870

25 *Ibid.,* 5 March 1870

Chapter 4

1 *The Manchester Review,* V7 1954-56 (vol 7), pp431-6

2 Mitchell Henry to George Wilson, 4 July 1864, Wilson Papers, Local Studies Unit, Manchester Central Library

3 Mitchell Henry to George Wilson, 20 July 1864, Wilson Papers, *op.cit.*

4 fl865/lh, Local Studies Unit, Manchester Central Library

5 Mitchell Henry to George Wilson, 28 June 1865, Wilson Papers, *op.cit.*

6 Duncombe Pink & Beaven, *op.cit.,* pp300-1

7 Ibid.

8 *Manchester Guardian,* 7 November 1868

9 To The Electors Of The City Of Manchester, Manchester Election 1868 Papers, Local Studies Unit, Manchester Central Library

10 Mitchell Henry On The Irish Church, Manchester Election 1868 Papers, *op.cit.*

11 *Ibid.*

12 Duncombe Pink & Beaven, *op.cit.,* pp300-1

13 L. Stephen & S. Lee, Editors, *The Dictionary of National Biography,* Supplement. Vol.22, (Oxford University Press 1968), pp273-91

14 *Manchester Guardian,* 31 October 1868

15 W F Cleary, Mr Mitchell Henry & Ireland, Manchester Election 1868 Papers, *op.cit.*

16 *Middleton Guardian,* 23 November 1889, Q942.72m5, Local Studies Unit, Manchester Central Library

17 *Manchester Guardian,* 17 November 1868

18 *Middleton Guardian, op.cit.*

19 *Manchester Guardian*, 18 November 1868, p4

20 *Ibid.,* 17 November 1868; 18 November 1868; 19 November 1868

Chapter 5

1 *Galway Vindicator*, 7 March 1874, p3

2 *Galway Express*, 18 February 1871, p2

3 David Thornley, *Isaac Butt and Home Rule*, (London 1964), p37; p117

4 *Galway Express*, 18 February 1871, p2

5 *Ibid.,* p4

6 *Ibid.,* 11 February 1871, p3

7 Hansard's Parliamentary Debates, Vol ccxii 1872, pp1763-83, I Butt

8 *Galway Express*, 25 February 1871, p3

9 Hansard's Parliamentary Debates, Vol ccxxxvii 1878, pp394-6, M Henry

10 *Ibid.*

11 *Ibid.,* Vol ccxv 1873, pp2060-2, M Henry

12 *Ibid.,* Vol ccxvii 1873, pp207-9, M Henry

13 *Ibid.,* Vol ccx 1872, p1213, M Henry

14 *Ibid.,* Vol ccxv 1873, pp2060-2, M Henry

15 *Ibid.,* Vol ccxii 1872, p1764, I Butt

16 *Ibid.,* Vol ccxii 1872, p1626, The Attorney General for Ireland, Mr Dowse

17 *Ibid.,* Vol ccxii 1872, p290, Colonel Wilson-Patten

18 *Ibid.,* Vol ccxii 1872, pp1783-1799, M Henry

19 *Ibid.,* Vol ccxiv 1873, p898, Chief Secretary for Ireland, The Marquess of Hartington

20 *Galway Express*, 17 August 1872, p3

21 Hansard's Parliamentary Debates, Vol ccix 1872, p1475, M Henry

22 *Galway Vindicator*, 7 February 1874, p3

23 *Galway Express*, 31 January 1874, p2

24 *Galway Vindicator*, 31 January 1874 p3

25 *Ibid.,* 25 February 1874

26 *Ibid.,* 14 February 1874, p3; *Galway Express*, 14 February 1874, p3

27 *Ibid.,* 7 February 1874, p3

28 *Galway Express*, 14 February 1874, p3

29 *Galway Vindicator,* 18 February 1874, p3

30 *Galway Express*, 21 February 1874, p4

31 Thornley, *op.cit.,* p187

32 Hansard's Parliamentary Debates, Vol ccxxviii 1876, pp1358-68, M Henry

33 Thornley, *op.cit.,* p213

34 *Ibid.,* p227

35 Hansard's Parliamentary Debates, Vol ccxviii 1874, pp150-4, M Henry

36 *Ibid.,* Vol ccxx 1874, pp902-14, M Henry

37 Mitchell Henry, *The Financial and Economical Condition of Ireland*, (Dublin 1875)

38 Hansard's Parliamentary Debates, Vol ccxxviii 1876, pp1357-68, M Henry

39 Rev. W. A. Leighton, B.A., *The Lichen-Flora of Great Britain, Ireland, and the Channel Islands*, 3rd Edition, Shrewsbury (1879); Prof. M.F. Mitchell, Irish Lichenology 1858-1880: Selected letters of Isaac Carroll, Theobald Jones, Charles Larbalestier and William Nylander, in *Occasional Papers 10, National Botanic Gardens*, (Dublin 1996), pp33-0

40 *Galway Express*, 12 December 1874, p3

41 Mitchell Henry to Butt, Butt Ms 8704 (1), Isaac Butt Papers, Manuscripts Dept. N.L.I.

42 *Ibid.,* Ms 8704 (2)

43 see Villiers-Tuthill, *Patient Endurance: The Great Famine in Connemara*

44 Mitchell Henry to Butt, Butt Ms 8704 (2), *op.cit.*

45 James F Fuller, *Omniana: the Autobiography of an Irish Octogenarian*, (London 1916), p183n

46 *Kylemore Castle Book of Sale, 1894 & 1902*; Patterson, Kempster & Shorthall Collection, Books 7, 8, 9 & 10

47 *Galway Express* 10 August 1878, p3

Chapter 6

1 *Ibid.,* 7 November 1885, p4

2 Hansard's Parliamentary Debates, Vol ccxxiv 1875, p59, M Henry

3 *Ibid.,* Vol ccxxiv 1875, pp65-6, M Henry

4 *Ibid.,* Vol ccxxiv 1875, pp65-6, M Henry

5 *Ibid.,* Vol ccxxxiii 1877, p1600, M Henry

6 *Ibid.,*Vol ccxxvi 1875, p683, M Henry

7 *Ibid.,* Vol ccxxxi 1876, p300, M Henry

8 Mitchell Henry to Isaac Butt, Butt Ms 8704 (1), *op.cit.*

9 Hansard's Parliamentary Debates, Vol ccxxiv 1875, p59, M Henry

10 *Ibid.,* Vol ccxxxvi 1877, pp40-4, M Henry

11 *The Nation*, 25 August 1877, p3

12 Thornley, *op.cit.,* p337

13 *The Freeman's Journal*, 11 September 1877, p2

14 Thornley, *op.cit.,* p340

15 *The Nation*, 5 January 1878, p9

16 Galway Express, 5 January 1878, p3

17 *Ibid.,* pp3 & 4

18 *Freeman's Journal,*5 January 1878, p5

19 *The Nation*, 5 January 1878, p9

20 *Freeman's Journal*, 5 January 1878, p6

21 *Ibid.*

22 *Ibid.,* 9 January 1878, p2

23 *Ibid.,*7 January 1878, p2

24 *Ibid.*

25 *Ibid.,*8 January 1878, p2

26 *Ibid.,* 10 January 1878, p3

27 *Ibid.,*11 January 1878, p7

28 Hansard's Parliamentary Debates, Vol ccxxxvii 1878, pp120-6, M Henry

29 Thornley, *op.cit.,* p346

30 Mitchell Henry to W J O'Neill Daunt, 23 April 1878, Ms 11446, Michael MacDonagh Papers, N.L.I.

31 T.M. Healy, *Letters And Leaders Of My Day,* (London 1928), p68

Chapter 7

1 *Galway Vindicator,* 10 September 1879, p3

2 *Ibid.,* 13 September 1879, p4

3 *Connaught Telegraph*, 27 September 1879

4 *Galway Vindicator,* 24 September, p4

5 *Ibid.,* 8 November 1879

6 *Galway Express*, 3 January 1880

7 *Connaught Telegraph*, 3 January 1880

8 *Galway Vindicator,* 4 February 1880

9 *Ibid.,*1 November 1879, p3

10 *Ibid.,*5 November 1879, p3

11 *Ibid.,* p4

12 *Ibid.,* 12 November 1879

13 *Ibid.*

14 *Ibid.,* 26 November 1879, p3

15 Hansard's Parliamentary Debates, Vol ccl 1880, pp270-90, M Henry

16 *Ibid.,* pp747-8, M Henry

17 see Villiers-Tuthill, *Beyond The Twelve Bens*, pp45-0

18 *Galway Express,* 27 March 1880, p3

19 *Ibid.,* 13 March 1880, p2

20 *Ibid.,*3 April 1880, p4

21 *Galway Vindicator,*18 November 1880

22 Hansard's Parliamentary Debates, Vol cclxviii 1882, pp354-9, M Henry

23 *Ibid.*

24 *The Times*, 6 May 1889, p5

25 Tuke, *op.cit.,* p73

26 Hansard's Parliamentary Debates, Vol cclv 1880, pp1886-90, M Henry; *Galway Express,* 28 August 1880, p3

27 *Galway Express,* 6 November 1880, p4

28 *Ibid.,* 6 November 1880, p4; *Galway Vindicator,* 28 August 1880, p3; Hansard' s Parliamentary Debates, Vol ccliv 1880, pp1120-27, M Henry; Vol cclv 1880, pp1886-0, M Henry

29 *Galway Express*, 22 January 1881, p4

30 *Galway Vindicator,* 5 January 1881

31 *Ibid.*

32 *Galway Express,* 15 January 1881, p3

33 *Ibid.*; Hansard's Parliamentary Debated, Vol cclvii 1881, pp451-62, M Henry

34 Hansard's Parliamentary Debated, Vol cclvii 1881, pp451-62, M Henry

35 *Galway Express,* 15 January 1881, p3

36 *Ibid.,* 22 January 1881, p4

37 *Freeman's Journal,* 10 January 1881, p7

38 *Galway Vindicator,* 19 January 1881

39 *Ibid.,* 19 January 1881

40 Hansard's Parliamentary Debates, Vol cclvii 1881, 1834-38, M Henry

41 *Ibid.,*Vol cclviii 1881, pp27-9, M Henry

42 *Ibid.,*Vol cclix 1881, pp348-52, M Henry

43 *The Times,* 13 April 1881, p12

44 *Ibid.,* 30 March 1894, p14

45 *Ibid.,* 13 April 1881, p12

46 *Ibid.,* 14 April 1881, p9

47 *Ibid.,* 15 April 1881, p9

48 Hansard's Parliamentary Debates, Vol cclx 1881, p1124, M Henry

49 *The Times,* 13 April 1881, p12

50 Hansard's Parliamentary Debates, Vol cclxi 1881, pp1667-1695, M Henry

51 *Ibid.,* Vol cclxi 1881, pp342-351, M Henry

52 see Villiers-Tuthill, *Beyond The Twelve Bens,* pp66-79

53 Hansard's Parliamentary Debates, Vol cclxxi 1882, p949, M Henry

54 see Villiers-Tuthill, *Beyond The Twelve Bens,* pp62-5

Chapter 8

1 Hansard's Parliamentary Debates, Vol cclxvi 1882, pp1387-89, M Henry

2 *Ibid.,* Vol cclxvii 1882, p968, M Henry

3 *Ibid.,* Vol cclxx 1882, p652, M Henry

4 *Galway Express,* 6 May 1882, p3;

5 *Reports and Papers Relating To The Proceedings Of The Committee Of "Mr Tuke's Fund" For Assisting Emigration From Ireland. During The Years 1882, 1883 and 1884* (London 1964); See Gerard Moran, 'James Hack Tuke and Assisted Emigration from Galway and Mayo in the 1880's' in *The emigrant experience: Papers presented at the second annual Mary Murray*

Weekend seminar (Galway 1991); See also Villiers-Tuthill, *Beyond The Twelve Bens,* pp79-6

6 Hansard's Parliamentary Debates, Vol cclxxii 1882, pp1244-7, M Henry

7 *Galway Vindicator,* 27 April 1881, p3

8 Hansard's Parliamentary Debated, Vol cclxxii 1882, pp1244-47, M Henry

9 *Galway Express,* 8 April 1882, p4; *Galway Vindicator,* 5 April 1882

10 *Ibid.,*20 May 1882, p4

11 Hansard's Parliamentary Debates, Vol ccxciii 1884, pp306-7, M Henry

12 *Galway Express,* 10 February 1883, p4

13 *Ibid.,* 3 November 1883, p4

14 *Ibid.,* 21 February 1885, p4

15 *Ibid.,* 28 February 1885, p4

16 *Ibid.,* 9 May 1885, p3

17 *Ibid.,* 12 September 1885

18 *Ibid.,* 12 September 1885

19 *Ibid.,* 31 October 1885, p4

20 *Ibid.*

21 *Ibid.,* 14 November 1885, p4

22 *Ibid.,* 7 November 1885, p4

23 *Ibid.*

24 *Ibid.,* 5 December 1885, p4

25 *Ibid.,* 12 December 1885, p4

26 *Ibid.,* 28 November 1885, p3

27 *Ibid.,* 16 January 1886, p4

28 R.F. Forster, *Modern Ireland 1600-1972,* (London 1989), p423

29 E.J. Feuchtwanger, *Gladstone,* (London 1975), p239

30 *Galway Express,* 1 May 1886, p4

31 *Ibid.,* 1 May 1886, p3

32 *The Times,* 6 June 1892, p3

33 *Galway Vindicator,* 10 July 1886, p3

34 *The Times* 30 March 1894, p14

35 *Ibid.,* 11 July 1887, p6

36 *Ibid.,* 6 May 1889. p5

37 *Ibid.,* 6 May 1889, p5; *The Time*s 30 March 1894, p14

38 *Ibid.,* 30 March 1894, p14; see Villiers-Tuthill, *Beyond The Twelve Bens,* pp93-4

Chapter 9

1 Louis Mitchell-Henry, *op.cit.*

2 Joseph Foster, *Alumni Oroniense: The Members of the University of Oxford, 1715-1886,* (Oxford 1888), p646

3 J.A. Venn, *Alumni Cantabrigiensi: A Biographical List Of All Known Students,Graduates and Holders of Office At The University Of Campridge,* Part 11, 1752 to 1900, (Cambridge 1947), p331

4 *Galway Express,* 14 January 1888, p3

5 Louis Mitchell-Henry, *op.cit.*

6 Burkes *Landed Gentry* 1894, p937

7 Venn, *op.cit.,* p331

8 *Galway Express,* 19 February 1887 p3

9 Ellen M. Blake, *My Connemara Childhood,* (Galway 1999), pp22-25

10 Ellen M. Blake, Unpublished Blake Family Papers.

11 Louis Mitchell-Henry, *op.cit.*

12 Similar to clay-pigeon shooting but live birds were used. It was made illegal in England in the 1920s.

13 *The Times,* 23 September 1891, p5

14 A & S Henry continued to thrive for many years and traded up until 1972 when it went into liquidation and was eventually taken over by Great Universal Stores plc.,

15 *Thom's Official Directory of the United kingdom of Great Britain & Ireland for the year 1890,* p1081

16 *The Times,* 3 September 1892, p4

17 Paul Duffy unpublished manuscript

18 *A History of Kylemore Abbey and its community,* Benedictine Community Publication; *Galway Express,* 24 September 1892, p3

19 Henry Family Records

20 *The Times,* 12 May 1894

21 *Kylemore Book of Sale,* 1894

22 private correspondence with Philip Temple, Royal Commission on the Historical Monuments of England

23 *Galway Express,* 27 July 1901

24 *The Times,* 21 July 1900, p4

25 Benedictine Community Publication, *op.cit.,* p4

26 *The Times,* 30 March 1894, p14

27 see Villiers-Tuthill, *Beyond The Twelve Bens*

28 *Galway Express,* Supplement, 1 August 1903

29 *Ibid.,*26 September 1903

30 *Ibid.,*18 November 1905

31 Louis Mitchell-Henry, *op.cit.*

32 *Ibid.,*

Chapter 10

1 *Galway Express,* 24 October 1903, p3

2 *Who's Who,* 1903, Part 11

3 *The Times,* 29 November 1900, p4

4 *Ibid.,* 19 September 1900, p9

5 *Ibid.,* 29 November 1900, p4

6 *Cincinnati Enquirer,* 19 April 1956

7 *Ibid.,* 17 December 1900, p4

8 The Duke of Manchester, *My Candid Recollection,* (London) 1932, p209

9 *Cincinnati Enquirer,* 21 December 1914

10 Duke of Manchester, *op.cit.,* pp73-4

11 *Ibid.,* p89

12 *Galway Express,* 20 February 1904, p3

13 *Ibid.,* 30 April 1904, p3

14 Census of Ireland 1901 and 1911

15 Duke of Manchester, *op.cit.,* pp201-3

16 *Ibid.,* pp203-4

17 *Cincinnati Enquirer,* 21 December 1914

18 Fifth Annual Report, 1911-12, *The Woman's National Health Association* annual reports. 1908-1912; Mary Clancy, On The "Western Outpost": Local Government and Women's Suffrage in County Galway, 1898-1918 from *Galway History & Society: Interdisciplinary Essays on the History of an Irish County,* Editor: Gerard Moran, (Galway 1996), pp557-87

19 Duke of Manchester, *op.cit.*, pp70-1

20 *Ibid.*

21 Hamilton Court, State of Ohio Probate Court, No 3030

Chapter 11

1 Kylemore Abbey Manuscript

2 Dom Patrick Nolan, O.S.B., *The Irish Dames Of Ypres.* (Dublin 1908), p338

3 *Ibid.,* p53

4 *Ibid.,* p150

5 *Ibid.,* p151

6 *Ibid.*

7 *Ibid.*

8 *Ibid.,* pp162-5

9 *Ibid.,* p162

10 *Ibid.,* p151

11 Henry V. Gill, S.J., D.S.O., M.C., The Fate of the Irish Flag at Ypres, in *Studies: An Irish Quarterly Review of Letters, Philosophy and Science.* Vol VIII, No 29, 1919, (Dublin 1919), pp119-128

12 G.A. Hayes-McCoy, *A History of Irish Flags from earliest times,* (Dublin 1979), pp68-0

13 Nolan, *op.cit.,* p224

14 *Ibid.,* p270

15 *Ibid.,* p278

16 *Ibid.,* pp287-8

17 *Ibid.,* p288

18 *Ibid.,* p293

19 *Ibid.,* p308

20 E. W. Beck, F.S.A. Scot. The Irish Abbey at Ypres, in *Irish Ecclesiastical Record.* 3rd Series. Vol xii, 1891, p812

21 Nolan, *op.cit.,* pp313-4

22 Beck, *op.cit.,* p813

23 Kylemore Abbey Manuscript

24 Nolan, *op.cit.,* p253

25 Kylemore Abbey Manuscript

26 Nolan, *op.cit.,* p332

27 Kylemore Abbey Manuscript

Chapter 12

1 Dame M.Columban Plomer, O.S.B., (Member of the Community), *The Irish Nuns at Ypres: An episode of the war,* (London 1916), p25-6

2 *Ibid.,* p5

3 *Ibid.,* p12

4 *Ibid.,*pxvi

5 *Ibid.,* p18

6 *Ibid.,* p23

7 *Ibid.,* p25

8 *Ibid.,* p29

9 *Ibid.,* p37

10 *Ibid.,* p31

11 *Ibid.,* p33

12 Kylemore Abbey Manuscript

13 Plomer, *op.cit.,* p40n

14 Kylemore Abbey Manuscript

15 Plomer, *op.cit.,* p40-1

16 *Ibid.,* p49

17 *Ibid.,* p76

18 *Ibid.,* p60

19 *Ibid.,* pp60-2

20 *Ibid.,* p5

21 *Ibid.,* p74

22 *Ibid.,* p77

23 *Ibid.,* pp92-95

24 *Ibid.,* p125

25 *Ibid.,* p153

26 *Ibid.,* p159

27 *Ibid.,* p161

28 *Ibid.,* p172

29 *Ibid.,* p183

30 *Ibid.,* p190

31 *Ibid.,* p191

32 *Ibid.,* pp192-3

33 *Ibid.,* pp195-6

34 *Ibid.,* p197

35 *The Freeman's Journal,* 30 December 1914, p5

36 Gill, *op.cit.*, pp119-28

37 *Freeman's Journal*, 6 November 1915, p7

38 Plomer, op.cit., pxxiii

Chapter 13

1 Dan Walsh, *100 Wexford Country Houses*, (Wexford 1996), pp66-67; Dan Walsh, *Bree: The Story of a Co. Wexford Parish*, (Wexford 1980), pp79-2

2 Kylemore Abbey Manuscript

3 *Wexford People*, 15 November 1916, p5

4 Dame Elizabeth M Magdalen Lee, *By Strange Paths: An Autobiography by a Benedictine of Kylemore Abbey*, (Galway 2002)

Chapter 14

1 Wilkins, *op.cit.*, pp195-0

2 *Wexford People*, 11 December 1920, p2

3 *Connacht Tribune*, 23 October 1920

4 *Ibid.*, 16 October 1920

5 Sr Benedict O'Beirne in Dame Elizabeth M Magdalen Lee, *op.cit.*, p71

6 *Connacht Tribune*, 20 December 1924, p5

7 *Ibid.*, 23 October 1920

8 *Ibid.*, 20 December 1924, p5

9 *Ibid.*

10 *Ibid.*, 20 June 1925, p6

11 *Connacht Tribune*, 28 November 1931

12 see Villiers-Tuthill, *Beyond The Twelve Bens: A history of Clifden and District 1860-1923*, pp89-14

Chapter 15

1 *Irish Independent*, 26 January 1959

2 Mother Agnus, in conversation with author, July 2000

3 Mother Mechtilde, in conversation with author, July 2000.

4 Dame Wallurga Swallow to Dame Mary O'Toole, 28 January 1959, Kylemore Abbey Archives

5 Capt. P.B. Sugrue, B.E., in conversation with author

6 Dame Wallurga Swallow to Dame Mary O'Toole, 28 January 1959

7 Mother Mechtilde, in conversation with author

8 *Irish Press*, 26 January 1959

9 Mother Mechtilde, in conversation with author

10 *Ibid.*

11 Dame Wallurga Swallow to Dame Mary O'Toole, 28 January 1959

12 *Irish Independent*, 26 January 1959

13 *Irish Press,* 27 January 1959

14 Dame Wallurga Swallow to Dame Mary O'Toole, 28 January 1959

15 Mother Mechtilde, in conversation with author

16 *Ibid.*

17 Dame Wallurga Swallow to Dame Mary O'Toole, 28 January 1959

18 *Ibid.*

19 Eye Witness Account by Mother Mechtilde, Kylemore Abbey Archives

Chapter 16

1 Kylemore Abbey Manuscript

2 Sr Magdalena, in conversation with author, Summer 2000

3 *Ibid.*

4 Kylemore Abbey Mission Statement

5 Mother Abbess Magdalena FitzGibbon, in conversation with author, January 2002

Select Bibliography

Primary Sources

Private Collections

Henry Family Papers.

Blake Family Papers.

Kylemore Abbey Manuscript.

Kylemore Castle Book of Sale 1902.

Kylemore Castle Book of Sale 1894.

National Library of Ireland, Manuscripts Department

Henry Papers.

Isaac Butt Papers.

Michael MacDonagh Papers.

National Archives

Chief Secretary's Office, Registered Papers.

Landed Estates Court Rentals: July – November 1858, Vol 53.

Census of Ireland for the years 1901 and 1911.

Registry of Deeds

Deeds relating to Kylemore Estate.

Valuation Office

Cancelled Books.

Architectural Archives

Patterson, Kempster & Shorthall Collection, Damp Press Volumes Of Bills Of Quantities & Measurements.

Manchester Central Library, Manchester Archives and Local Studies

Old Clippings, Box 327 Textiles.

Wilson Papers.

Manchester Election 1868 Papers.

Science & Art Tracts.

Autographic Collection.

Letters relating to Public Schools Association.

R.M.I. Assistant Secretary's Letter Book.

International Genealogical Index, England, Lancashire 1841, 1851 & 1861; Westminster 1881.

The Henry Group Of Companies, A & S Henry Company Publication, Manchester 1955.

The Manchester Review, V7 1954–56, vol 7.

Printed Contemporary Records

National Library of Ireland

Angler's Guide to the Irish Free State, Compiled by the Department of Lands & Fisheries, Second Edition, Dublin 1930.

Angler's Guide, Compiled by the Department of Agriculture, Fisheries Branch. Fourth Edition, Dublin 1948.

British Parliamentary Papers, *letters to the commissioners of Irish Fisheries, 1898 [325]*; *Minutes of evidence taken before the Royal Commission on Agriculture*, 1880 [15].

Dictionary of National Biography, Second Supplement, 1910–1911.

Griffith, Richard, *General Valuation of Ratable Properties in Ireland*, Co Galway, 1855.

Hansard's Parliamentary Debates, 1871 – 1886.

The Parliamentary Gazetteer of Ireland, London 1845.

Thom's Official Directory of the United Kingdom of Great Britain & Ireland for the year 1890.

Secondary Sources

Archer, Thomas, F.R.H.S., *William E Gladstone and His Contemporaries: Fifty years of social and political progress*, London.

Baker, Sir Thomas, *Memorials of A Dissenting Chapel, Its Foundation and Worthies*, Manchester 1884.

Beck, E. W., F.S.A. Scot. The Irish Abbey at Ypres, in *Irish Ecclesiastical Record*, 3rd Series, Vol xii, 1891.

Benedictine Community Kylemore Abbey, *A History of Kylemore Abbey and its community*.

Blake, Ellen M., *My Connemara Childhood,* Galway 1999.

Brockbank, William, The Early History of the Manchester Medical School, in *The Manchester Medical Gazette*, Vol 47, No 3, May 1968.

Burkes, *The Landed Gentry*, 1894.

Cavenagh, Lieut.-Colonel W.O., The Irish Benedictine Nunnery at Ypres, Belgium, in *Royal Society of Antiquaries of Ireland*, Series 5, Vol xviii, 1908.

Clancy, Mary, On The "Western Outpost": Local Government and Women's Suffrage in County Galway, 1898-1918, in *Galway History & Society: Interdisciplinary Essays on the History of an Irish County*, Gerard Moran, (ed), Galway 1996.

Davis, Thomas, *The Poems of Thomas Davis.*

Duncombe Pink, W., & Rev. Alfred B. Beaven, MA, *Lancashire Parliamentary Representatives 1258-1885*, London 1889.

Duffy, Paul , Engineering, in *From Queens College To National University: Essays On The Academic History of QCC/UCC/NUI,Galway*, Dublin 1999.

Duffy, Paul, Random Notes On The Corrib, in *Inland Waterways News, Vol. 23 No 3*, 1996.

Eason, Charles, *An Almanac and Hand-Book for Ireland For The Year 1877*, Dublin 1877.

Feuchtwanger, E.J., *Gladstone*, London 1975.

Forster, R.F., *Modern Ireland 1600-1972*, London 1988.

Foster, Joseph, *Alumni Oroniense: The Members of the University of Oxford, 1715-1886*, Oxford 1888.

Fox-Davies, Arthur Charles, *Armorial Families: A Directory of Gentlemen of Coat-Armour*, Seventh Edition, London 1929.

Fuller, James F., *Omniana: the Autobiography of an Irish Octogenarian*, London 1916.

Garland, J.L., The Kylemore Flag, in *The Irish Sword*, Vol 11, No 6, 1955.

Griffith, Sir Richard John, *General Valuation of Ireland,* Dublin 1880.

Gill, Henry V., S.J., D.S.O., M.C., The Fate of the Irish Flag at Ypres, in *Studies: An Irish Quarterly Review of Letters, Philosophy and Science*, Vol VIII, No 29, 1919, Dublin 1919.

Hayes-McCoy, G.A., *A History of Irish Flags from earliest times*, Dublin 1979.

Hall, Mr & Mrs. S.C., *Ireland: Its Scenery, Character &c*, Vol 111, London 1843.

Healy, T.M., *Letters And Leaders Of My Day*, London 1928.

Healy, T.M., Editor, *A Record of Coercion: Votes of Irish Members, for the enlightenment of Irish Electors*, Dublin 1881.

Henry, Mitchell, *The Address Delivered At The Opening Of The Classes Of The Middlesex Hospital Medical College, Session 1859-60*, London 1859.

Henry, Mitchell, *The Financial and Economical Condition of Ireland*, Dublin 1875.

Howell, J.C., Ltd, *Electric Lighting For Country Houses,* London 1896.

Jenkins, Roy, *Gladstone*, London 1995.

Lane, Padraig G., The Management of Estates by Financial Corporations in Ireland after the Famine, *Studia Hibernica*, No XIV 1974.

Lane, Padraig G., The Impact of the Encumbered Estates Court upon the Landlords of Galway and Mayo, in *Journal of the Galway Archaeological & Historical Society*, 1981-1982.

Lane, Padraig G., The General Impact of the Encumbered Estates Act of 1849 on Counties Galway and Mayo, *Journal of the Galway Archaeological & Historical Society,* Vol 33, 1972-73.

Layman, A., The Benedictines in Ireland, in *The Irish Ecclesiastical Record*, 4th Series, Vol xxviii, 1910.

Lee, Dame Elizabeth M Magdalen, *By Strange Paths: An Autobiography by a Benedictine of Kylemore Abbey*, Galway 2002.

Leighton, Rev. W. A., B.A., *The Lichen-Flora of Great Britain, Ireland, and the Channel Islands*, 3rd Edition, Shrewsbury 1879.

Lyons, F.S.L., *Ireland Since The Famine*, London 1963.

Magnus, Philip, *Gladstone: A Biography*, London 1954.

Manchester, The Duke of, *My Candid Recollection*, London 1932.

Martineau, Harriet, *Letters from Ireland,* London 1852.

Mitchell, Prof. M.F., Irish Lichenology 1858-1880: Selected letters of Isaac Carroll, Theobald Jones, Charles Larbalestier and William Nylander in *Occasional Papers 10, National Botanic Gardens*, Dublin 1996.

Moran, Gerard, (ed), *Galway History & Society: Interdisciplinary Essays on the History of an Irish County*, Geography Publications 1996.

Moran,Gerard, James Hack Tuke and Assisted Emigration from Galway and Mayo in the 1880's, in *The emigrant experience: Papers presented at the second annual Mary Murray Weekend seminar*, Galway 1991.

Nolan, Rev. Dom Patrick, O.S.B., *The Irish Dames Of Ypres*, Dublin 1908.

O'Brien, R. Barry, The Flag At Ypres, in *The Irish Ecclesiastical Record*, 4th Series, Vol xxiii, 1908.

Pevsner, Nikolaus, *The Buildings of England: South Lancashire*, London 1969.

Plomer, Dame M.Columban, O.S.B., *The Irish Nuns at Ypres: An episode of the war*, London 1916.

Peard, W., M.D., LL.B., *A Year of Liberty; on, Salmon Angling In Ireland From February 1 to November 1*, London 1867.

Roberts, Charles G., Reclamation of Bog and Moorland in Galway, in *Journal of the Royal Agricultural Society of England, Second Series,* London 1878

Roberts, S.U., Description of Means Adopted For Unwatering Works Of River Drainage, *Trans. Inst. C.E.I.*, Vol 3, 1849.

Semple, Maurice, *Reflections on Lough Corrib,* Galway 1974.

Serafin, Steven R., Editor, *Encyclopaedia of American Literature*, New York 1999.

Shand, Alexander Innes, *Letters From The West Of Ireland 1884,* London 1885.

Stephen, L., and S Lee, *The Dictionary of National Biography*, Supplement, Vol 22, Oxford 1968.

Sullivan, A.M., *New Ireland: Political Sketches & Personal Reminiscences of Thirty Years of Irish Public Life,* Glasgow 1887.

Sutton, Les, *Mainly About Ardwick,* Vol 1, Manchester 1980.

Swindells, T., *Manchester Streets & Manchester Men*, Manchester 1907.

Thornley, David, *Isaac Butt and Home Rule*, London 1964.

Tuke, James H., *Irish Distress and Its Remedies, The Land Question: A Visit to Donegal and Connaught In The Spring Of 1880*, London 1880.

Tuke Fund*, Reports and Papers Relating To The Proceedings Of The Committee Of "Mr Tuke's Fund" For Assisting Emigration From Ireland. During The Years 1882, 1883 and 1884*, London 1964.

Turner, Michael J., *Reform & Respectability: The Making of A Middle-Class Liberalism in Early 19th century Manchester*, Manchester 1995.

Various Writers, *Fortunes Made In Business: A Series of Original Sketches, Biographical and Anecdotic*, Vol 111, London 1887.

Vaughan,W.E., An assessment of the economic performance of Irish Landlords, 1851–81, in *Ireland Under The Union*, F.L.S. Lyons and R.A.J. Hawkins, (eds), Oxford 1980.

Velpeau, A., *A Treatise on the Diseases Of The Breast and Mammary Region*, translated from the French by Mitchell Henry, London 1856.

Venn, J.A., *Alumni Cantabrigiensi: A Biographical List Of All Known Students,Graduates and Holders of Office At The University Of Campridge,* Part 11, 1752 to 1900, Cambridge 1947.

Villiers-Tuthill, Kathleen, *History of Clifden 1810-1860,* Galway 1982.

Villiers-Tuthill, Kathleen, *Beyond The Twelve Bens: A History of Clifden and District 1860-1923*, Galway 1986.

Villiers-Tuthill, Kathleen, *Patient Endurance: The Great Famine in Connemara,* Dublin 1997.

Walsh, Dan, *Bree: The Story of a Co. Wexford Parish*, Wexford 1980.

Walsh, Dan, *100 Wexford Country Houses*, Wexford 1996.

Who's Who, 1903.

Wilkins, Noel P., *Ponds, Passes and Parcs: Aquaculture in Victorian Ireland,* Dublin 1989.

Woman's National Health Association annual reports. 1908-1912.

Newspapers and Periodicals
Irish

Connaught Telegraph.

Connacht Tribune.

Freeman's Journal.

Galway Express.

Galway Vindicator & Connaught Advertiser.

Irish Independent.

Irish Press.

Irish Times.

Wexford People.

The Nation.

The Irish Builder, 15 May 1872.

The Building News, 2 February 1900.

English

Evening Chronicle.

Manchester Evening News.

Manchester Guardian.

Middleton Guardian.

The Times.

The Builder, 24 October 1868.

USA

The Enquirer, Cincinnati, 1900.

Cincinnati Post, 1980.

The North American, Philadelphia, 1912.

Index